WORD PLAY 2

JUNIOR CERTIFICATE ENGLISH

TERRY DONNELLY

Gill & Macmillan

Gill & Macmillan Ltd
Hume Avenue
Park West
Dublin 12
with associated companies throughout the world
www.gillmacmillan.ie

© Terry Donnelly 2010
978 0 7171 4723 6

Artwork by Oxford Designers and Illustrators
Design and print origination in Ireland by Graham Thew Design

The paper used in this book is made from the wood pulp of managed forests.
For every tree felled, at least one tree is planted, thereby renewing natural
resources.

For permission to reproduce photographs the author and publisher gratefully acknowledge the following:
© Advertising Archives: 281, 288; © AIB: 287; © Alamy: 38CL, 102T, 153BL, 153BR, 163, 181, 213, 220, 221, 248, 270,
272, 348CR, 348TR, 349TL, 364B, 364T; © Anna Rackard: 103TR; © Bill Waterson: 301; © Bridgeman: 134, 263;
© Collins Press: 127; © Corbis: 386R, 74T, 81, 125, 131, 143B, 232CR; © Des Barry/Irish Examiner: 369TR; © Eamon
Ward: 232B; © Education Photos: 362; © Frank Millar/The Irish Times: 369L; © Gary and Glenn McCoy: 297;
© Getty: 14, 19, 26, 38CR, 38L, 44, 53, 55BR, 55CL, 55L, 55TC, 55TR, 62, 65, 71, 74B, 79, 82, 83, 85C, 85L, 85R, 99,
102B, 115, 137, 147, 153TL, 153TR, 159T, 169, 191, 226, 251, 252T, 258T, 261, 265, 267R, 268, 348TL, 352, 354, 359,
363, 390; © Imagefile: 38R, 100, 101T, 122, 187, 247, 312, 348BL, 349BL, 349BR, 349C, 349TR, 350, 367; © Irish Daily
Mail: 238; © Irish Independent: 215; © Irish Times: 230, 237; © Jim Davis: 300; © Julien Behal/The Press Association of
Ireland: 314L; © Kiss: 242; © Kobal: 166, 316, 332L, 342TL, 342TR; © Kyran O'Brien: 232T; © Lar Boland: 369BR;
© Laurent Darmon at Angela de Bona, Paris & NYC: 286; © Magnum: 143T, 232CL; © Martyn Turner: 233, 298;
© Mary Evans: 255; © Movie Store Collection: 332R, 357; © National Library Ireland: 386L; © National Newspapers
of Ireland: 292; © Niall Carson/The Press Association of Ireland: 314R; © Paul Stuart: 319; © Penguin: 7; © Photocall:
216; © Photolibrary: 92, 101B; © Press Association: 200; © Reuters: 103B, 103TL, 228, 229, 231; © Rex: 113, 173, 196,
342BL, 342BR, 343; © Sportsfile: 58, 217; © Tayto: 293; © The Coca-Cola Company: 279; © Tony Gavin/Sunday
Independent: 230; © Topfoto: 23, 51, 162C, 162L, 162R, 252B, 258B; © Volkswagen Ireland: 283; © World Vision: 295;
Courtesy of University of Sussex/National Trust: 159B; Courtesy of Wikimedia Commons: 331.

The author and publisher have made every effort to trace all copyright holders, but if any has been inadvertently
overlooked we would be pleased to make the necessary arrangement at the first opportunity.

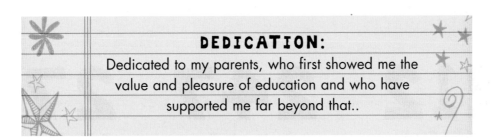

DEDICATION:

Dedicated to my parents, who first showed me the value and pleasure of education and who have supported me far beyond that..

Contents

ACKNOWLEDGMENTS:

Thanks to all the pupils, staff and teachers of the
schools I have taught in. In particular I wish to
acknowledge the enthusiasm and advice of Larry
Cotter, Seamus Kelly and Gerry Hanberry.
Thanks to the staff at Gill & Macmillan for their
patience, openness and work in making this
book possible.
Finally, thanks and love to Amber.

The author and publisher are grateful to the following for permission to reproduce copyrighted material:

Extract from the novel *17 Martin Street* by Marilyn Taylor published by The O'Brien Press Ltd, Dublin, © Copyright Marilyn Taylor; 'A Footballer' by Gabriel Fitzmaurice copyright © Gabriel Fitzmaurice, 2008. Reprinted by kind permission of Mercier Press Ltd., Cork; Extract from *A Walk in the Woods* by Bill Bryson, published by Black Swan. Reprinted by permission of The Random House Group Ltd; *All Quiet on the Western Front* by Erich Maria Remarque, published by Jonathan Cape. Reprinted by permission of The Random House Group Ltd; *An Interview with J.K. Rowling* by Lindsey Fraser from *Telling Tales*: J.K. Rowling. Literary Appreciation © Lindsay Fraser 2000. Used with permission of Egmont UK Ltd London and The Christopher Little Literary Agency; 'An Amazing Dialogue' by James Fenton reprinted by permission of United Agents on behalf of: James Fenton; Extract from *Arden City* by Timberlake Wertenbaker reprinted by permission of Faber and Faber Ltd; *August 1945* by Robert C. North from *True Tales of American Life* edited by Paul Auster. Reprinted by permission of Faber and Faber Ltd; 'Autobiography in Five Short Chapters' by Portia Nelson © 2007, from the book *There's a Hole in My Sidewalk* by Portia Nelson. Reprinted with the permission of Beyond Words Publishing, Inc., Hillsboro, Oregon. All rights reserved; 'Bad Report – Good Manners' by Spike Milligan is reprinted by permission of Spike Milligan Productions Limited; 'Base Details' by Siegfried Sassoon copyright Siegfried Sassoon by kind permission of the Estate of George Sassoon; Extract from *Bend it Like Beckham* by Narinder Dharmi, first published in the UK by Hodder Children's, an imprint of Hachette Children's Books, 338 Euston Road, London NW1 3BH; Extract from *Century Makers* by David Hillman and David Gibbs reprinted by kind permission of The Orion Publishing Group Ltd; 'Close' by Tony Curtis, first published by Arc Publications in the volume *The Well in the Rain* and reprinted with permission; 'Cold Spell' by Sandra Bunting from *Identified in Trees*, Marram Press, Galway, 2006; Extract from *Dancing at Lughnasa* by Brian Friel reprinted by permission of Faber and Faber Ltd; 'Desert Places' from *The Poetry of Robert Frost* edited by Edward Connery Lathem, published by Jonathan Cape. Reprinted by permission of The Random House Group Ltd; *Dietary Habits* from *The Health of Irish Students,* source: Department of Health and Children, reprinted with permission; 'Digging', 'When All the Others' and 'Mother of the Groom' by Seamus Heaney from *Opened Ground: Poems 1966-1996* reprinted by permission of Faber and Faber Ltd; 'Downhill Racer' by Lillian Morrison from *WAY TO GO Sports Poems* by Lillian Morrison. © 1985, 2001 by Lillian Morrison. Used by permission of Marian Reiner for the author; Extract from *The Field* by John

B. Keane copyright © John B Keane, 1991. Reprinted by kind permission of Mercier Press Ltd, Cork; Extract from *The Full Cupboard of Life* by Alexander McCall Smith is reproduced by permission of Polygon, an imprint of Birlinn Ltd (www.birlinn.co.uk); *George's Marvellous Medicine* by Roald Dahl, published by Jonathan Cape Ltd & Penguin Books Ltd. Reprinted by permission of David Higham Associates; 'Heart Sea' by Carlos Reyes from *The Stony Thursday Book*, edited by Knute Skinner; 'Hummingbird' from *A New Path to the Waterfall* by Raymond Carver, published by Collins Harvill. Reprinted by permission of the Random House Group Ltd; 'I Stepped from Plank to Plank' by Emily Dickinson reprinted by permission of the publishers and the Trustees of Amherst College from The Poems of Emily Dickinson: Variorum Edition, Ralph W. Franklin, ed., Cambridge, Mass.: The Belknap Press of Harvard University Press, © 1998 by the President and Fellows of Harvard College. © 1951, 1955, 1979, 1983 by the President and Fellows of Harvard College; 'I Would Win the Gold if These Were Olympic Sports...' by Paul Cookson. Reprinted by kind permission of Pan Macmillan, London; Extract from *The Kite Runner* by Khaled Hosseini © Khaled Hosseini, *The Kite Runner*, Bloomsbury; Extract from *Little Lady, One Man, Big Ocean - Rowing the Atlantic* by Paul Gleeson & Tori Holmes with Liam Gorman reproduced with permission from The Collins Press; 'Living' by Denise Levertov from *New Selected Poems*, Bloodaxe Books, 2003; 'Lucky Mrs Higgins' by Rita Ann Higgins from *Throw in the Vowels: New and Selected Poems* is reprinted by permission from Rita Ann Higgins and Bloodaxe Books; 'Manners' by Elizabeth Bishop from *The Complete Poems 1927-1979* by Elizabeth Bishop. © 1979,1983 by Alice Helen Methfessel. Reprinted by permission of Farrar, Straus and Giroux, LLC; Extract from *Man's Search for Meaning* by Victor Frankl, published by Rider. Reprinted by permission of The Random House Group Ltd; 'Mother to Son' by Langston Hughes from *Collected Poems of Langston Hughes*, published by Alfred A Knopf Inc. Reprinted by permission of David Higham Associates.; *Muddle Earth* by Paul Stuart. Reprinted by kind permission of Pan Macmillan, London; Excerpt from *My Boy Jack* copyright © 1997 David Haig reprinted with permission from Nick Hern Books: www.nickhernbooks.co.uk; *Out Stealing Horses* by Per Petterson, published by Harvill Secker. Reprinted by permission of The Random House Group Ltd; *Pity* by Frank O'Connor from *My Oedipus Complex and Other Stories* by Frank O'Connor (Penguin Books, 1963, 2001). Copyright Frank O'Connor, 1963, 2001. Reproduced by permission of Penguin Books Ltd; 'The People of the Other Village' from *Split Horizon: Poems by Thomas Lux.* © 1994 by Thomas Lux. Reprinted by permission of Houghton Mifflin Harcourt Publishing Company. All rights reserved; 'Poem' by Ann Wallace, published by Puffin Books.

Reprinted by permission of Penguin Books Ltd; 'The Poeteer' by Patrick Winstanley © Patrick Winstanley; 'Poetry Jump-Up' by John Agard © 1990 by John Agard reproduced by kind permission of John Agard c/o Caroline Sheldon Literary Agency Limited; 'The Question' by Allan Ahlberg from *Heard it in the Playground* by Allan Ahlberg. Viking, 1989. © Allan Ahlberg, 1989. Reproduced by permission of Penguin Books Ltd; Extract from *Red Herrings and White Elephants* by Albert Jack. Published by Metro, 3 Bramber Court, 2 Bramber Road, London, W14 9PB. Tel 020 73810666; Extract from *Sophie's World* by Jostein Gaardner, published by Weidenfeld & Nicolson, London. Reprinted by kind permission of Orion Books Ltd; 'Sharp Freckles' by Carol Ann Duffy. Reprinted by kind permission of Pan Macmillan, London; Extract from *Someone to Watch Over Me* by Frank McGuinness reprinted by permission of Faber and Faber Ltd; Excerpt by Hugo Hamilton from *The Speckled People* (© Hugo Hamilton, 2003) is reproduced by permission of PFD (www.pfd.co.uk) on behalf of Hugo Hamilton (electronic version) and by permission of HarperCollins Publishers Ltd © 2003, Hugo Hamilton (print version); *Stardust* by Neil Gaiman, published by Headline Review. Reprinted by kind permission of HarperCollins; 'Sugarfields' by Barbara Mahone published by Puffin Books. Reprinted by kind permission of Penguin Books Ltd; *Tell Me No Lies* by Malorie Blackman. Reprinted by kind permission of Pan Macmillan, London; *To Kill a Mockingbird* by Harper Lee, published by William Heinemann Ltd. Reprinted by permission of The Random House Group Ltd; 'The Trees' by Philip Larkin from *Collected Poems* is reprinted by kind permission of Faber and Faber Ltd; *The Umbrella Man* by Roald Dahl from *More Tales of the Unexpected*, Penguin Books. Reprinted by permission of David Higham Associates; Extract from *The Vampire's Assistant* by Darren Shan is reprinted by permission of HarperCollins Publishers Ltd © 2000, Darren Shan; 'Water-Burn' by Michael Longley from *Collected Poems* by Michael Longley, published by Jonathan Cape. Reprinted by permission of The Random House Group Ltd; 'Wearing Thin' by Roger McGough from *Defying Gravity* (© Roger McGough (1993)) is reproduced by permission of PFD (www.pfd.co.uk) on behalf of Roger McGough. 'When Your Face Doesn't Fit' by Roger Stephens. Reprinted by kind permission of Pan Macmillan, London. *William Shakespeare Biography* copyright Guardian News & Media Ltd 2008. Extract *Women and War* from *World War One: Women and War* by Ann Kramer, first published in the UK by Franklin Watts, an imprint of Hachette Children's Books, 338 Euston Road, London NW1 3BH.

FICTION

WELCOME! I AM MARIE LAUTREC, a novelist and expert in fiction. In this unit we will develop our understanding of what novels are and how they are created. We will focus on the techniques and features used to create fictional worlds and characters and we will also learn how to examine and discuss them.

In this chapter we will introduce and develop:

> THE WORLD OF THE TEXT;
> CHARACTER;
> FIRST PERSON NARRATIVE;
> THIRD PERSON NARRATIVE;
> RELATIONSHIPS;
> THEME.

You will also learn about the three steps to answering questions properly. In the middle of this unit you will revise basic **punctuation**, and at the end of this unit you will revise **nouns** and **pronouns** at the **Grammar Station**.

There will be questions and activities to follow each lesson, like this:

 OPENING ACT: these are questions on the text you have just read. You need to carefully read the text and the questions that follow. Make sure you understand the question. Then read the text again to find the answers.

SPOTLIGHT: this is where you are asked for your own response and analysis. When you analyse a text, you examine and reflect on the structure and features of the writing. You will be asked questions such as, what is your opinion of the text? Or you might be asked to explain writing techniques.

CENTRE STAGE: these are a variety of creative activities to stimulate your imagination and practise what you have learned. You might be asked to work with others or on your own. These exercises will help you to see how English works in action and will help you to connect the different areas of the subject.

The last section in each unit, **Curtain Call**, will give you a chance to revise what you have learned in the unit.

The World of the Text

We call a novel, drama, story or poem a text. **The world of the text** is the place where a story happens and where characters live.

The **setting** of the story is our first introduction to the world of the text. **Descriptive writing** creates pictures of the setting in our minds. **Imagery** is what we call these mental pictures.

*Here is an example of **imagery** taken from the extract that follows:*

'The houses of Wall are square and old, built of grey stone, with dark slate roofs and high chimneys.'

This description creates a picture of the town in our minds.

Now we will read the extract in full. It is the beginning of a novel called Stardust, *with the opening scene set in a town called Wall. When you are reading it, pay attention to how the world of the text is created. The text creates imagery in our minds and slowly reveals clues to the reader as to what type of world it is. What type of world do you think the writer of* Stardust *has created?*

Stardust

Neil Gaiman

There was once a young man who wished to gain his Heart's Desire.

And while that is, as beginnings go, not entirely novel (for every tale about every young man there ever was or will be could start in a similar manner) there was much about this young man and what happened to him that was unusual, although even he never knew the whole of it.

The tale started, as many tales have started, in Wall.

The town of Wall stands today as it has stood for six hundred years, on a high jut of granite amidst a small forest woodland. The houses of Wall are square and old, built of grey stone, with dark slate roofs and high chimneys; taking advantage of every inch of space on the rock, the houses lean into each other, are built one upon the next, with here and there a bush or tree growing out of the side of a building.

There is one road from Wall, a winding track rising sharply up from the forest, where it is lined with rocks and small stones. Followed far enough south, out of the forest, the track becomes a real road, paved with asphalt; followed further the road gets larger, is packed at all hours with cars and lorries rushing from city to city. Eventually the road takes you to London, but London is a whole night's drive from Wall.

The inhabitants of Wall are a taciturn breed, falling into two distinct types: the native Wall-folk, as grey and tall and stocky as the granite outcrop their town was built upon; and the others who have made Wall their home over the years and their descendants.

Below Wall on the west is the forest; to the south is a treacherously placid lake served by the streams that drop from the hills behind Wall to the north. There are fields upon

ASPHALT
a tough type of road surface

TACITURN
not talkative or open

TREACHEROUSLY
in a way that's not to be trusted

PLACID
calm

1

the hills, on which sheep graze. To the east is more woodland.

Immediately to the east of Wall is a high grey rock wall, from which the town takes its name. This wall is old, built of rough, square lumps of hewn granite, and it comes from the woods and goes back to the woods once more.

There is only one break in the wall; an opening about six feet in width, a little to the north of the village.

Through the gap in the wall can be seen a large green meadow; beyond the meadow, a stream; and beyond the stream there are trees. From time to time shapes and figures can be seen, amongst the trees, in the distance. Huge shapes and odd shapes and small, glimmering things which flash and glitter and are gone. Although it is perfectly good meadowland, none of the villagers has ever grazed animals on the meadow on the other side of the wall. Nor have they used it for growing crops.

Instead, for hundreds, perhaps for thousands of years, they have posted guards on each side of the opening on the wall, and done their best to put it out of their minds.

Even today, two townsmen stand on either side of the opening, night and day, taking eight-hour shifts. They carry hefty wooden cudgels. They flank the opening on the town side.

CUDGELS

a thick stick for hitting people

Their main function is to prevent the town's children from going through the opening, into the meadow and beyond. Occasionally they are called upon to discourage a solitary rambler, or one of the few visitors to the town, from going through the gateway.

The children they discourage simply with displays of the cudgel. Where ramblers and visitors are concerned, they are more inventive, only using physical force as a last resort if tales of new-planted grass, or a dangerous bull on the loose, are not sufficient.

INVENTIVE

good at inventing

Very rarely someone comes to Wall knowing what they are looking for, and these people they will sometimes allow through. There is a look in the eyes, and once seen it cannot be mistaken.

There have been no cases of smuggling across the wall in all the Twentieth Century, that the townsfolk know of, and they pride themselves on this.

The guard is relaxed once every nine years, on May Day, when a fair comes to the meadow.

🎭 OPENING ACT

1 Where does this story begin?

2 Describe the houses of the town of Wall in your own words.

3 Where does the only road out of Wall lead to?

4 How do the guards discourage the children from going through the gap in the wall?

5 When is the guard on the wall relaxed?

Answering Questions: The Three Steps

The following questions ask you to examine the text on a deeper level and give a personal response. Before we answer them, we will read about answering questions properly.

Step One: Opinion

When you are answering a question, you need to be like a detective looking for clues. You need to add up the clues to form your **opinion**.

When you are asked a question, you look for clues to form your **opinion**. You should give your **opinion** in a clear and simple way and use the wording of the question to help you. Here is a question from *Stardust*.

Question: Do you think the author uses good descriptive writing in this extract?

Opinion: Yes, I think the author uses good descriptive writing in this extract.

Step Two: Reason

You must always give a **reason** for your **opinion**. Like a detective explaining a case, you must explain how you came to your conclusion. Clear **reasons** will prove that your **opinion** is correct.

Question: Do you think the author uses good descriptive writing in this extract?

Opinion and Reason: Yes, I think the author uses good descriptive writing in this extract. The writer clearly describes the setting of the houses, the village and the surrounding countryside. He creates detailed imagery through his use of descriptive adjectives.

'square and old, built of grey stone, with dark slate roofs...'

Step Three: Evidence

To prove that your answer is correct, you need **evidence**. You must use quotations from the text that clearly support your reasons. See the example below.

Question: Do you think the author uses good descriptive writing in this extract?

Opinion, Reason and Evidence: Yes, I think the author uses good descriptive writing in this extract. The writer clearly describes the setting of

the houses, the village and the surrounding countryside. He creates detailed imagery through his use of descriptive adjectives. He describes the houses as 'square and old, built of grey stone, with dark slate roofs'. He describes the 'small forest woodland' and 'large green meadow' near the village.

Use the tips at the end of each question as a guide to what is needed. Now try for yourself.

 SPOTLIGHT

1 Would you like to visit the town of Wall? OPINION REASON

2 Would this opening scene encourage you to read further? OPINION REASON EVIDENCE

3 Tension is the uneasy feeling we get when we suspect something dramatic or important is going to happen. Do you think there is tension in this extract? OPINION REASON EVIDENCE

 IN YOUR OWN WORDS

DEFINITION: THE EXPLANATION THAT TELLS US THE MEANING OF A WORD IS CALLED A DEFINITION.

Now write out your own definition for the important terms you have learned so far. Use a dictionary if you need help. To help you remember new terms, it's a good idea to write them into a notes copy or to write them into the back of your class copybook. At the end of each section certain terms are highlighted, but it is helpful to write out any terms you don't know, including their definitions.

 IN YOUR OWN WORDS

THE WORLD OF THE TEXT:

IMAGERY:

TENSION:

Character

Characters are the people and creatures we read about or see in a story. Interesting characters bring stories, plays and films to life for the reader or viewer. When we care about a character or find a character interesting or amusing, we want to see what will happen to them.

Characters are created by descriptions. Good descriptive writing uses expressive **words and language** to create characters. The following examples are taken from the short extract below.

Expressive nouns: these words clearly and effectively tell us what something is.

Example: A grouch: a person who complains a lot and is often in bad humour.

Expressive adjectives: these words clearly and effectively describe nouns.
Example: Wicked: mean and morally bad.

Expressive verbs: these words clearly and effectively describe an action.
Example: Dozing: sleeping lightly.

When we can easily and clearly imagine a character or place because of descriptive writing, we say that the description is **vivid**.

The following extract is taken from a book by Roald Dahl. His books are enjoyed by children and adults around the world because of the memorable characters that he creates using vivid descriptions. Do you know of any other memorable characters from stories by Roald Dahl?

George's Marvellous Medicine

Roald Dahl

'I'm going shopping in the village,' George's mother said to George on Saturday morning. 'So be a good boy and don't get up to mischief.'

This was a silly thing to say to a small boy at any time. It immediately made him wonder what sort of mischief he might get up to.

'And don't forget to give Grandma her medicine at eleven o'clock,' the mother said. Then out she went, closing the back door behind her.

Grandma, who was dozing in her chair by the window, opened one wicked little eye and said, 'Now you heard what your mother said, George. Don't forget my medicine.'

'No, Grandma,' George said.

'And just try to behave yourself for once while she's away.'

'Yes, Grandma,' George said.

George was bored to tears. He didn't have a brother or a sister. His father was a farmer and the farm they lived on was miles away from anywhere, so there were never any children to play with. He was tired of staring at pigs and hens and cows and sheep. He was especially tired of having to live in the same house as that grizzly old grunion of a Grandma. Looking after her all by himself was hardly the most exciting way to spend a Saturday morning.

'You can make me a nice cup of tea for a start,' Grandma said to George. 'That'll keep you out of mischief for a few minutes.'

'Yes, Grandma,' George said.

George couldn't help disliking Grandma. She was a selfish grumpy old woman. She had pale brown teeth and a small puckered up mouth like a dog's bottom.

'How much sugar in your tea today, Grandma?' George asked her.

'One spoon,' she said. 'And no milk.'

Most grandmothers are lovely, kind, helpful old ladies, but not this one. She spent all day and every day sitting in her chair by the window, and she was always complaining, grousing, grouching, grumbling, griping about something or other. Never once had she smiled at George and said, 'Well how are you this morning, George?' or 'Why don't you and I have a game of Snakes and Ladders?' or 'How was school today?' She didn't seem to care about other people, only about herself. She was a miserable old grouch.

GRUNION
a type of fish

PUCKERED
pulled together in a wrinkled way

GROUSING
grumbling

GRIPING
complaining

OPENING ACT

1 What silly thing did George's mother say to him? `EVIDENCE`

2 What did George think of his grandmother? `EVIDENCE`

3 According to the narrator, what are most grandmothers like? `EVIDENCE`

 SPOTLIGHT

4 What do you think is the most vivid description in this extract? Why? OPINION
REASON EVIDENCE

5 Do you think the grandmother's character would be a good character in a film?
OPINION REASON EVIDENCE

6 What kind of character do you think George is? OPINION REASON EVIDENCE

7 Why do you think the characters created by Roald Dahl are so popular?
OPINION REASON

 CENTRE STAGE

Character Kit

Create and describe a character using your own selection of the following words. If it helps, you can describe a day in the life of the character or a fictional situation. If there are any words you don't know, look them up in a dictionary.

Nouns

Circus, moustache, trapeze, wagon, wasteland, crocodile, orchestra, saddle, sombrero, rifle, wrestler, aunt, reporter, ballet, violin, tiger, bush-tucker, billabong, sand dune, rainforest.

Adjectives

Russian, Mexican, Australian, handsome, daft, poisonous, jealous, lush, wicked, moronic, gifted, disgusting, horrendous, parched, tasty, golden, shimmering, salty, geriatric, devious.

Verbs

Growl, whistle, perform, ponder, flow, gossip, train, dance, yelp, stink, grimace, gallop, guzzle, stomp, thrash, puzzle, tangle, yodel, yell, sprint.

*You can also use expressive **adverbs**. These are words that describe verbs. You will meet nouns, adjectives, verbs and adverbs in greater detail later in the textbook.*

Adverbs

Quickly, happily, craftily, nastily, calmly, slowly, cunningly, carefully, irritatingly, hilariously, stupidly, dreamily, skilfully, cautiously, jealously, strangely, greedily, increasingly, gloomily, menacingly.

Before you begin give your character a name. Now ask yourself where your character is from and what your character does?

 IN YOUR OWN WORDS

VIVID:

First Person Narrative

WHEN I WAS A YOUNG GIRL, A LONG TIME AGO, MY MOTHER ALWAYS SAID TO ME ...

The character who tells the story is called the **narrator**. The voice they use to tell the story is called the narrative voice. An unusual narrator enables us to see the world of the text from a different or unusual perspective.

A **first person narrative** always tells the story from the narrator's own perspective, using **I**, **me** and **my**. This shows us how the story happened to the narrator.

I woke up one morning to find that **my** windows were covered in frost.

The following extract is a first person narrative told from the perspective of a woman looking back on her childhood. The world of the text is the Deep South of America in the 1930s. Atticus is the girl's father, Jem is her brother and Calpurnia is their housekeeper.

To Kill a Mockingbird

Harper Lee

LEGISLATURE

a legal organisation

Our mother died when I was two, so I never felt her absence. She was a Graham from Montgomery; Atticus met her when he was first elected to the state legislature. He was middle-aged then, she was fifteen years his junior. Jem was the product of their first year of marriage; four years later I was born, and two years later our mother died from a sudden heart attack. They said it ran in her family. I did not miss her, but I think Jem did. He remembered her clearly, and sometimes in the middle of a game he would sigh at length, then go off and play by himself behind the car-house. When he was like that, I knew better than to bother him.

When I was almost six and Jem was nearly ten, our summertime boundaries (within calling distance of Calpurnia) were Mrs Henry Lafeyette Dubose's house two doors to the north of us, and the Radley Place three doors to the south. We were never tempted to break them. The Radley Place was inhabited by an unknown entity the mere description of whom was enough to make us behave for days on end; Mrs Dubose was plain hell.

That was the summer Dill came to us.

Early one morning as we were beginning our day's play in the backyard, Jem and I heard something next door in Miss Rachel Haverford's collard patch. We went to the wire fence to see if there was a puppy – Miss Rachel's rat terrier was expecting – instead we found someone sitting looking at us. Sitting down, he wasn't much higher than the collards. We stared at him until he spoke:

'Hey.'

'Hey yourself,' Jem said pleasantly.

'I'm Charles Baker Harris,' he said. 'I can read.'

'So what?' I said.

'I just thought you'd like to know I can read. You got anything needs readin' I can do it…'

'How old are you,' asked Jem, 'four-and-a-half?'

'Goin' on seven.'

'Shoot no wonder, then,' said Jem, jerking his thumb at me. 'Scout yonder's been readin' ever since she was born, and she ain't even started to school yet. You look right puny for goin' on seven.'

'I'm little but I'm old,' he said.

Jem brushed his hair back to get a better look. 'Why don't you come over, Charles Baker Harris?' he said. 'Lord, what a name.'

''s not any funnier'n yours. Aunt Rachel says your name's Jeremy Atticus Finch.'

Jem scowled. 'I'm big enough to fit mine,' he said. 'Your name's longer'n you are. Bet it's a foot longer.'

'Folks call me Dill,' said Dill, struggling under the fence.

'Do better if you go over it instead of under it,' I said. 'Where'd you come from?'

Dill was from Meridian, Mississippi, was spending the summer with his aunt, Miss Rachel, and would be spending every summer in Maycomb from now on. His family was from Maycomb County originally, his mother worked for a photographer in Meridian, had entered his picture in a Beautiful Child contest and won five dollars. She gave the money to Dill, who went to the picture show twenty times on it.

'Don't have any picture shows here, except Jesus ones in the court-house sometimes,' said Jem. 'Ever see anything good?'

Dill had seen *Dracula*, a revelation that moved Jem to eye him with the beginning of respect. 'Tell it to us,' he said.

Dill was a curiosity. He wore blue linen shorts that buttoned to his shirt, his hair was snow white and stuck to his head like duck-fluff; he was a year my senior but I towered over him. As he told us the old tale his blue eyes would lighten and darken; his laugh was sudden and happy; he habitually pulled at a cowlick in the centre of his forehead.

When Dill reduced Dracula to dust, and Jem said the show sounded better than the book, I asked Dill where his father was: 'You ain't said anything about him.'

'I haven't got one.'

FICTION

'Is he dead?'

'No...'

'Then if he's not dead you've got one, haven't you?'

Dill blushed and Jem told me to hush, a sure sign that Dill had been studied and found acceptable. Thereafter the summer passed in routine contentment. Routine contentment was: improving our treehouse that rested between giant twin chinaberry trees in the backyard, fussing, running through our list of dramas based on the works of Oliver Optic, Victor Appleton and Edgar Rice Burroughs. In this matter we were lucky to have Dill. He played the character parts formerly thrust upon me – the ape in Tarzan, Mr Crabtree in The Rover Boys, Mr Damon in Tom Swift. Thus we came to know Dill as a pocket Merlin, whose head teemed with eccentric plans, strange longings, and quaint fancies.

But by the end of August our repertoire was vapid from countless reproductions, and it was then that Dill gave us the idea of making Boo Radley come out.

The Radley Place fascinated Dill. In spite of our warnings and explanations it drew him as the moon always draws water, but drew him no nearer than the light-pole on the corner, a safe distance from the Radley gate. There he would stand, his arm around the fat pole, staring and wondering.

The Radley Place jutted into a sharp curve beyond our house. Walking south, one faced its porch; the sidewalk turned and ran beside the lot. The house was low, was once white with a deep front porch and green shutters, but had long ago darkened to the colour of the slate-grey yard around it. Rain-rotten shingles drooped over the eaves of the veranda; oak trees kept the sun away. The remains of a picket drunkenly guarded the front yard – a 'swept' yard that was never swept – where Johnson grass and rabbit-tobacco grew in abundance.

Inside the house lived a malevolent phantom. People said he existed but Jem and I had never seen him. People said he went out at night when the moon was high, and peeped in windows. When people's azaleas froze in a cold snap, it was because he had breathed on them. Any stealthy crimes committed in Maycomb were his work.

ECCENTRIC
behaving strangely

QUAINT
old-fashioned or unusual in a charming way

REPERTOIRE
the songs or acts that people normally perform

VAPID
lacking life

SHINGLES
wooden slates

JOHNSON GRASS
a type of grass with large blades

RABBIT-TOBACCO
a type of herb

MALEVOLENT
evil

STEALTHY
secretive, sly

In this extract, many important details are introduced. These details are important to the **plot** *and help to raise expectation and tension. The* **plot** *is the twists and turns that the* **storyline** *takes as it works its way to the* **climax**, *which is the highest point of tension.*

⭐ OPENING ACT

1 How did Jem react to the death of his mother?

2 What age was the narrator, Scout, at the time the story takes place?

3 Where was Dill from? **EVIDENCE**

4 Describe Dill's appearance.

5 Who lived inside the Radley house? **EVIDENCE**

SPOTLIGHT

6 What do you think of the description of the Radley Place? `OPINION` `REASON` `EVIDENCE`

7 Identify one important character in the world of this text and explain why you think the character is important. `OPINION` `REASON` `EVIDENCE`

8 What do you learn in this extract that makes you curious to read more of the novel? `OPINION` `REASON` `EVIDENCE`

9 What character in this text would you like to learn more about? `OPINION` `REASON` `EVIDENCE`

10 Research the world of this text on the Internet, in a library or by asking an adult. If possible, try to find out three details about Mississippi State for homework.

11 Would you like to visit the world of this text? `OPINION` `REASON` `EVIDENCE`

CENTRE STAGE

Scout's Diary

Write a diary entry from the perspective of Scout on the evening that she meets Dill. It will be a first person narrative.

Before you start, discuss as a group the details that Scout could mention in her diary. Write out a list of possible details on the board.

Possible things to mention:
* everyday things like food and weather;
* her suspicions about Boo Radley;
* her first impressions of Dill.

Remember to begin the diary at the start of the day and move from there to the end of the day. Your diary will probably take five or six paragraphs and take up two or three copybook pages.

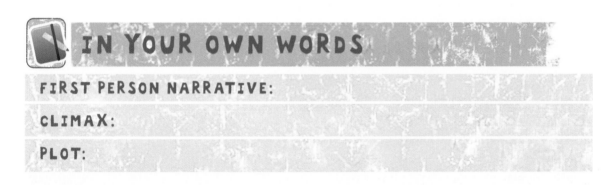

IN YOUR OWN WORDS

FIRST PERSON NARRATIVE:

CLIMAX:

PLOT:

Third Person Narrative

When she was a young girl a long time ago, her mother always said to her...

A **third person narrative** is when the narrator is telling us the story as if he/she knows everything that happens, including the thoughts inside the heads of different characters.

In a **third person narrative** the narrator doesn't personally feature in the story. Third person narratives always use the third person pronouns: *he*, *him* and *his*, *she*, *her* and *hers*.

She woke up one morning to find that *her* windows were covered in frost.

Note: third person narratives can also use **they**, **them** and **their** if there is more than one character.
For example: *She called Mike and* **they** *went to the shop together to get* **their** *lunch.*

If the central character of a novel is a character we respect and admire, then we can call that character the hero *or* heroine *of the story. It is not always immediately clear who this is. Here is an extract from the opening of a novel told in the third person. The central character in this novel is a detective called Precious Ramotswe and the novel is set in the African country of Botswana.*

The Full Cupboard of Life

Alexander McCall Smith

Precious Ramotswe was sitting at her desk at the No. 1 Ladies' Detective Agency in Gabarone. From where she sat she could gaze out of the window, out beyond the acacia trees, over the grass and the scrub bush, to the hills in their blue haze of heat. It was such a noble country, and so wide, stretching for mile upon mile to brown horizons at the very edge of Africa. It was late summer, and there had been good rains that year. This was important, as good rains meant productive fields, and productive fields meant large, ripened pumpkins of the sort that traditionally-built ladies like Mma Ramotswe so enjoyed eating. The yellow flesh of a pumpkin or a squash, boiled and then softened with a lump of butter (if one's budget stretched to that) was one of God's greatest gifts to Botswana. And it tasted so good, too, with a slice of fine Botswana beef, dripping in gravy.

Oh yes, God had given a great deal to Botswana, as she had been told all those years ago at Sunday school in Mochudi. 'Write a list of Botswana's heavenly blessings,' the teacher had said. And the young Mma Ramotswe, chewing on the end of her indelible pencil, and feeling the sun bearing down on the tin roof of the Sunday school, heat so insistent that the tin creaked in protest against its restraining bolts, had written: (1) the land; (2) the people who live on the land; (3) the animals, and specially the fat cattle. She had stopped at that, but, after a pause, had added: (4) the railway line from Lobatse to Francistown. This list, once submitted for approval, had come back with a large blue tick after each item, and the comment written in: Well done, Precious! You are a sensible girl. You have correctly shown why Botswana is a fortunate country.

*This story introduces us to the **background** of the central character. The background of a character is the personal history that influences who the person is. The **background of a plot** are the details that happened before the point where the story begins.*

 ## OPENING ACT

1 Where was Precious Ramotswe sitting? `EVIDENCE`
2 Why was it important that there were good rains that year? `EVIDENCE`
3 What was one of 'God's greatest gifts to Botswana'? `EVIDENCE`
4 What did Precious put on her list of Botswana's blessings? `EVIDENCE`
5 What approval did her work get? `EVIDENCE`

☺ SPOTLIGHT

6 Describe the world of the text in your own words.

7 What does Precious think of Botswana? `OPINION` `REASON` `EVIDENCE`

8 Find an example of good descriptive writing. `OPINION` `REASON` `EVIDENCE`

9 Do you think Precious Ramotswe is an unusual character for a detective? `OPINION` `REASON` `EVIDENCE`

10 Is there anything in this extract that might indicate that Precious Ramotswe is the heroine of this novel? `OPINION` `REASON` `EVIDENCE`

11 Write a list of Ireland's 'heavenly blessings'.

♣ CENTRE STAGE

Transformer — narrative in disguise

Transform this third person narrative into a first person narrative.

Write two paragraphs from the perspective of Precious Ramotswe.

• Use the first person pronouns *I*, *me* and *my*.

• Stay in the first person!

• Use all the different details from the text.

• Imagine and add details of your own.

• You could mention the weather, clothing, family or a friend.

IN YOUR OWN WORDS

THIRD PERSON NARRATIVE:

HERO/HEROINE:

BACKGROUND:

Punctuation Station

Capital Letters

Capital letters help us to clearly understand what is written down. They can be used to show how important something is and to indicate a noun's qualities. Capitals are also called **upper case**.

When to use **capital letters**.

1 The beginning of every sentence.

2 The beginning of direct speech.
   Example: 'Hello,' Mike said. 'You're new here.'

3 When we are using I to talk about ourselves.
   Example: 'I called you earlier.'

4 For the first letters of proper nouns:
   - people (Kate, Roland);
   - countries and cities (Fuji, Cork);
   - streets, areas and counties (Green Street, Ulster, County Kilkenny);
   - rivers, mountains and large coastal features (River Lee, Mount Rushmore, Sligo Bay);
   - months and days (June, Saturday);
   - brand names and product names (Nintendo, Honda);
   - books, plays, films, songs and poems (*Holes*, *The Godfather*, 'Wearing Thin');
   - sports teams, government bodies and organisations (Real Madrid, Department of Finance, Oxfam).

Full Stops, Commas, Question Marks and Exclamation Marks

Full stops are mostly used at the end of sentences. Commas are used to break up longer sentences. Question marks show us where a question is being asked. Exclamation marks show us surprise.

Full Stops

We use full stops for three functions.

1 At the end of a sentence.

2 When we shorten words, such as Co. instead of County, or Feb. instead of February.

3 When we are abbreviating names to initials, such as Mr T. Byrne.

Full stops are useful to break up longer sentences. Sentences that run on too long are difficult to read.

Commas

We use **commas** for three main functions.

1 To separate one part of a sentence from another, so as to aid understanding and clarity.

Example: The boy stole my bicycle, the one I got for Christmas, from the shed in my garden.

When long sentences are separated into smaller parts by commas, we call the smaller parts clauses. An example of two clauses is: **I talked to Amy about playing drums for the band,** *but she was too busy shopping in town.*

Be careful not to use too many clauses because it can get confusing. Clauses can also be joined by conjunctions, such as **and, but, yet** *and* **or***.*

2 When we are writing an address or list.

Example: I would like bananas, apples, pears and tomatoes.

3 Before and after direct speech, when necessary.

Example: 'I would love to go,' she replied, 'but I have to see if I'm allowed.'

Question Marks

Question marks indicate that a direct question is being asked.

Example: Are you sure?

A sentence that ends with a question mark or an exclamation mark doesn't need a full stop.

Exclamation marks

Exclamation marks indicate surprise, power, anger or shock.

Example: Wham! The rocket hit the side of the building in a cloud of dust.

Always follow an exclamation mark or a question mark with a capital letter.

Try to use exclamation marks sparingly in your writing. They are often overused. You only ever need one!

 OPENING ACT

Punctuate the following sentences.

1 can we go out
2 i can't believe you broke my favourite game
3 to bake the cake you need sugar flour eggs and milk
4 the ball flew into the net as it always did and the crowd roared with delight
5 has anyone seen my shoes
6 crash the horse broke out of his stable breaking the door down with his hooves
7 i called into mike as it was saturday morning but he wasn't there
8 i ran down the road which led to main street gasping for breath all the way
9 i collected the rubbish that was in my driveway there were bottles cans crisp packets and cartons
10 i was afraid of sharks which some people found funny

Relationships

When we are reading, we better understand who a character is by understanding his/her **relationships** with friends, family and enemies.

Interaction is the word for how characters react to and behave with each other. How a character interacts with others tells us a lot about who the character is.

Read the following third person extract about a childhood friendship between two characters. Pay attention to the differences between them.

Out Stealing Horses
Per Petterson

He never knocked, just came quietly up the path from the river where his little boat was tied up, and waited at the door until I became aware that he was there. It never took long. Even in the morning early when I was still asleep, I might feel a restlessness far into my dream, as if I needed to pee and struggled to wake up before it was too late, and then when I opened my eyes and knew it wasn't that, I went directly to the door and opened it, and there he was. He smiled his little smile and squinted as he always did.

'Are you coming?' he said. 'We're going out stealing horses.'

It turned out that we meant only him and me as usual, and if I had not gone with him he would have gone alone, and that would have been no fun. Besides, it was hard to steal horses alone. Impossible, in fact.

SQUINTED
drawing eyelids together to see further

'Have you been waiting long?' I said.

'I just got here.'

That's what he always said, and I never knew if it was true. I stood on the doorstep in only my underpants and looked over his shoulder. It was already light. There were wisps of mist on the river, and it was a little cold. It would soon warm up, but now I felt goose pimples spread over my thighs and stomach. Yet I stood there looking down to the river, watching it coming from round the bend a little further up, shining and soft from under the mist, and flowing past. I knew it by heart. I had dreamt about it all winter.

'Which horses?' I said.

'Barkald's horses. He keeps them in the paddock in the forest, behind the farm.'

'I know. Come inside while I get dressed.'

'I'll wait here,' he said.

He never would come inside, maybe because of my father. He never spoke to my father. Never said hello to him. Just looked down when they passed each other on the way to the shop. Then my father would stop and turn round to look at him and say:

'Wasn't that Jon?'

'Yes,' I said.

'What's wrong with him?' said my father every time, as if embarrassed, and each time I said:

'I don't know.'

And in fact I did not, and I never thought to ask. Now Jon stood on the doorstep that was only a flagstone, gazing down at the river while I fetched my clothes from the back of one of the tree-trunk chairs, and pulled them on as quickly as I could. I did not like him having to stand there waiting, even though the door was open so he could see me the whole time.

* * *

Clearly I ought to have understood there was something special about that July morning, something to do with the fog on the river and the mist over the ridge perhaps, something about the white light in the sky, something in the way Jon said what he had to say or the way he moved or stood there stock still at the door. But I was only fifteen, and the only thing I noticed was that he did not carry the gun he always had with him in case a hare should cross our path, and that was not so strange, it would only have been in the way rustling horses. We weren't going to shoot the horses, after all. As far as I could see, he was the same as he always was: calm and intense at one and the same time with his eyes squinting, concentrating on what we were going to do, with no sign of impatience. That suited me well, for it was no secret that compared with him I was a slow-coach in most of our exploits. He had years of training behind him. The only thing I was good at was riding logs down the river, I had a built-in balance, a natural talent, Jon thought, though that was not how he would have put it.

What he had taught me was to be reckless, taught me that if I let myself go, did not slow myself down by thinking so much beforehand I could achieve many things I would never have dreamt possible.

INTENSE
with fierce concentration

EXPLOITS
adventures

RECKLESS
without care or worry

FICTION

1

*Characters in a relationship often **contrast** in some way. This means there are ways in which they are different from each other. For example, one character might be aggressive while another character might be peaceful. When characters contrast, it can lead to conflict in their relationship.*

 # OPENING ACT

1 What did the narrator's friend, Jon, plan to do the morning he called to the narrator's house? `EVIDENCE`

2 How did the narrator feel in the cold? `EVIDENCE`

3 How did Jon interact with the narrator's father?

4 What did the narrator notice about Jon that morning? `EVIDENCE`

5 What was the one thing the narrator was good at? `EVIDENCE`

SPOTLIGHT

6 In a relationship, characters often learn from each other. What does the narrator learn from Jon? `OPINION` `REASON` `EVIDENCE`

7 How do the two main characters contrast in their relationship? `OPINION` `REASON` `EVIDENCE`

8 What do you think of the descriptive writing in this extract? `OPINION` `REASON` `EVIDENCE`

9 Who do you think is the leader in the relationship between the two boys? `OPINION` `REASON` `EVIDENCE`

10 The world of this text seems like a peaceful place. Would you agree with this statement? `OPINION` `REASON` `EVIDENCE`

CENTRE STAGE

Friend Wanted

Advertisements at the back of newspapers are called classifieds. Write your own classified advertisement for the perfect friend.

You might write about:
- what talents the friend should have;
- the good qualities the friend should have;
- the duties the friend will have to do;
- the type of friendship your friend can expect;
- the activities you plan on doing together.

> MILLIONAIRE WANTED. Ex-servant with full training and experience preferred. Lottery winners acceptable. Must like paying for food. Generous to a fault. Wanted to hold bike outside shop while I buy sweets. Must like playing in goalkeeper's position.

 ## IN YOUR OWN WORDS

INTERACTION:

CONTRAST:

Theme

A **theme** is a central topic or idea that is repeated and developed in a story, play or poem. To find the theme of a story, we must identify what the text is about.

For example, the story of Romeo and Juliet is about two young people trying to form a relationship against the wishes of their families. The themes are love and conflict.

Common **themes** in texts include:

- **love;**
- **nature;**
- **death;**
- **war;**
- **family;**
- **prejudice.**

The following extract is from a novel that explores the themes of war and conflict. The story is narrated from the perspective of a German soldier, Paul, who is fighting in the First World War. In this scene, Paul and some other soldiers visit a friend in a military hospital.

All Quiet on the Western Front

Erich Maria Remarque

FRONT
the area where opposing armies meet

CARBOLIC
a type of soap

TACTLESS
saying the wrong thing to someone

Before we set off to see Kemmerich we pack his things up for him – he'll be glad of them on his way home.

The clearing station is very busy. It smells of carbolic, pus and sweat, just like it always does. You get used to a lot of things when you are in the barracks, but this can still really turn your stomach. We keep on asking people until we find out where Kemmerich is; he is in a long ward, and welcomes us weakly, with a look that is part pleasure and part helpless agitation. While he was unconscious, somebody stole his watch.

Müller shakes his head, 'I always said that you shouldn't take such a good watch with you, didn't I?'

Müller is a bit bossy and tactless. Otherwise he would have kept his mouth shut, because it is obvious to everyone that Kemmerich is never going to leave this room. It

FICTION

1

makes no difference whether he gets his watch back or not – the most it would mean is that we could send it back home for him.

'How's it going, then, Franz?' asks Kropp.

Kemmerich's head drops back. 'OK, I suppose. It's just that my damned foot hurts so much.'

We glance at his bed-cover. His leg is under a wire frame, which makes the coverlet bulge upwards. I kick Müller on the shin, because he would be quite capable of telling Kemmerich what the orderly told us before we came in; Kemmerich no longer has a foot. His leg has been amputated.

He looks terrible, yellow and pallid, and his face already has those weird lines that we are so familiar with because we have seen them a hundred times before. They aren't really lines at all, just signs. There is no longer any life pulsing under his skin – it has been forced out already to the very edges of his body, and death is working its way through him, moving outwards from the centre, it is already in his eyes. There in the bed is our pal Kemmerich, who was frying horse-meat with us not long ago, and squatting with us in a shell hole – it's still him, but it isn't really him any more; him image has faded, become blurred, like a photographic plate that's had too many copies made from it. Even his voice sounds like ashes.

I remember the day when we were drafted out. His mother, a pleasant, stout woman, saw him off at the station. She was crying all the time, and her face was puffy and swollen. This embarrassed Kemmerich, because she was the least composed of all of them, practically dissolving in fat and tears. What's more, she picked me out, and kept grabbing my arm and begging me to keep an eye on Franz when we got out here. As it happens, he did have a very young face, and his bones were so soft that after just a month of carrying a pack he got flat feet. But how can you keep an eye on someone on a battlefield?

COVERLET	a bed quilt
AMPUTATED	cut off by a surgeon
PALLID	sick looking
PHOTOGRAPHIC PLATE	old photographic method where a glass plate held the negative image
DRAFTED OUT	ordered to leave for war
COMPOSED	calm

The scene and circumstances into which characters are placed is called the situation. How characters react to a situation reveals their personalities to us. The way in which a situation or plot works itself out and ends is called the **resolution**.

⬛ OPENING ACT

1 What turns the narrator's stomach? **EVIDENCE**
2 What happened to Kemmerich's watch? **EVIDENCE**
3 What adjectives does the writer use to describe how Kemmerich looks? **EVIDENCE**
4 How did Kemmerich's mother react when he was leaving for war? **EVIDENCE**
5 What happened to Kemmerich in his first month at the Front? **EVIDENCE**

📷 SPOTLIGHT

6 How did the description of Kemmerich lying in bed make you feel? **OPINION** **REASON** **EVIDENCE**
7 What do you think the resolution of this situation will be? **OPINION** **REASON** **EVIDENCE**
8 What do you think the author's attitude to war is? **OPINION** **REASON** **EVIDENCE**
9 Who do you think is the hero of this extract? **OPINION** **REASON** **EVIDENCE**
10 In war, soldiers often form close relationships. Using evidence from the extract, would you agree or disagree with this statement? **OPINION** **REASON** **EVIDENCE**

🎩 CENTRE STAGE

Letter from the Front

Write a short letter from the narrator, Paul, to Kemmerich's mother, telling her what has happened to her son.

- Decide on the details you think he might tell her about her son. You might try this as a group discussion to begin with.
- Copy details from the extract.
- Remember to be respectful and serious.
- Imagine other details. For example, you could imagine a story about an incident that happened with Kemmerich to show what a good friend he was.
- Use four paragraphs to structure your letter. Structure the paragraphs. For example:
  i) introduce yourself and describe how you know Kemmerich;
  ii) tell her what happened;
  iii) explain how he was a good friend;
  iv) tell her your hopes for the future.

IN YOUR OWN WORDS

THEME:

SCENARIO:

RESOLUTION:

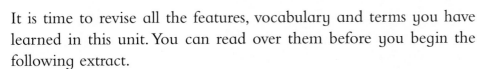

curtain call

It is time to revise all the features, vocabulary and terms you have learned in this unit. You can read over them before you begin the following extract.

When you read the extract, pay attention to the following.
- **Narrative: who is telling the story?**
- **The World of the Text: how is it created and described?**
- **Characters: who lives in the fictional world?**
- **Relationships: how do the characters interact?**
- **Themes: what is the story about?**

The following extract is set in Dublin at the start of the Second World War. The novel explores many different relationships and themes. The main character, Ben, whose mother is terminally ill, befriends a Jewish girl, Hetty, who moves in next door. He meets Hetty when he helps her to save some puppies from drowning. Ben's father, who is in the Local Defence Force, is prejudiced against Jewish people, and in this scene he reveals his prejudice. Sean is Ben's older brother.

Note: *the Second World War was known as 'The Emergency' in Ireland.*

17 Martin Street

Marilyn Taylor

In the kitchen Granny poked at the weak fire. 'It says in the papers there's no war here,' she muttered to Dad, 'only an Emergency.'

'Whatever it's called, at least we're not in it,' said Dad shortly.

'Still, flour and tea are scarce,' grumbled Granny. 'No coal or petrol. And it's a hard winter.'

'Sure, how could you feel the cold, Granny,' teased Sean, 'with all you have on?'

'That's enough, Sean,' said Dad, as, like a hen with ruffled feathers, Granny indignantly smoothed down her clothes. Ben fought back a grin, thinking of Granny's ganseys, flannel petticoats, woollen combinations and thick black stockings that hung out to dry with the rest of the washing every Monday in the sooty back yard.

Then Dad's face became stern. 'Listen here to me, now,' he said heavily. 'There's new people moved in next door, and I don't want anyone getting too pally with them.'

Sean looked up from his tea. 'Why not?'

'They're foreigners,' Dad replied sharply. 'Jews.'

'But there's lots of Jewish families in Portobello,' said Granny. 'Sure they even call it Little Jerusalem.'

'There's some living here in Martin Street – Joey and Mickser Woolfson play football with us,' put in Sean. 'Why– '

FICTION

1

'Because I say so!' Ben jumped as Dad banged his fist on the table. 'I'm telling you stay away from that house.' There was silence. He went on, 'There's too many of these foreigners here. They're different from us, and there isn't work for us all. They should go back where they came from.'

Granny, tight-lipped, handed him his sandwiches. They all knew to keep quiet when Dad was in one of his angry moods, especially without Mam on hand to smooth him over.

Fixing on his bicycle clips he grunted, 'I'm late.' Then he added, his voice softening, 'I'll just look in on Marie.' They heard him tip-toe up the stairs.

While he was drying the dishes, Ben thought over what Dad had said. The other Jewish neighbours seemed to get on well with the people in the street, and, like Sean said, everyone played together. But his dad was so certain they didn't belong here. And anyway, that girl hadn't appeared too friendly, even though he'd helped her rescue the puppies.

Dad trundled his bike through the kitchen and with relief they heard the front door slam. Through the lace-curtained parlour window Ben glimpsed him, in tin hat and green uniform, wobbling off down the road.

* * *

After his father had left, Ben climbed the stairs. From Mam's room came the familiar racking cough that the bottle from Mushatt's chemist hadn't cured. Ben tapped at the door.

Lying in the brass bed, a cream-coloured Aran shawl around her shoulders, she beckoned him in. Her long, auburn hair, once lustrous and wound into a loose knot secured with headpins, now hung lank and dull. But her level green eyes still shone; and though holding a handkerchief to her mouth, she smiled the old smile.

'How're you, Benny love?' About to reach out to him she drew back, mindful of the risk of infection. 'Did you get your tea?'

He nodded. 'Mam, there's new people next door,' and he repeated Dad's comments.

She frowned. 'Ben, those people are just a different religion.'

'But Dad said—'

'Poor Dad has a lot on his mind, but he shouldn't badmouth them. Growing up down the country he never knew any Jews.' She struggled to heave herself up in the bed. 'But Granny and your Uncle Matt and me – we grew up in Lennox Street and we were friends with all the Jewish neighbours.' She paused, and added hoarsely, 'They've always been at the wrong end of things, wherever they live.'

Extract from 17 Martin Street by Marilyn Taylor, The O'Brien Press Ltd.

AUBURN
reddish

LUSTROUS
shiny

LANK
limp

🎬 OPENING ACT

1 How does the war affect Ben's grandmother?
2 Why does Ben's father not want anyone making friends with their neighbours?
3 How did Ben's father show he was angry? EVIDENCE
4 How do we know Ben's mother is ill? EVIDENCE

5 What does Ben's mother think of Jewish people? `EVIDENCE`

6 Find two details in the extract that tell us the story is set in the past. `EVIDENCE`

🎭 SPOTLIGHT

7 What kind of relationship does Ben have with his father? `OPINION` `REASON` `EVIDENCE`

8 In what way does Ben's relationship with his father contrast with Ben's relationship with his mother? `OPINION` `REASON` `EVIDENCE`

9 Choose one of the following themes and explain how the extract explores it:
- war;
- family relationships;
- illness;
- racism. `OPINION` `REASON`

10 Why do you think people like to read stories that are set in the past? Explain your answer. `OPINION` `REASON`

11 *Time Machine:* if you were given an opportunity to visit any place or time other than your own, where and when would you choose, and why? `OPINION` `REASON` `EVIDENCE`

🎩 CENTRE STAGE

Opinion vs. Fact

An **opinion** is a statement that hasn't been proven and that is based solely on a person's views and experiences. A **fact** is a statement that can be, or is, proven to be true.

This is a walking debate, a group activity that will take a homework exercise and a full class to organise.

To prepare the debate: it might suit to do this for homework the night before the debate.

1 As a class you can choose one of the following groups:
- vegetarians;
- boys;
- girls;
- teachers.

Your teacher might suggest a different group, if it suits. You could also start by identifying different groups in your society.

FICTION

1

2 Now each student writes out five statements about each group.
Holding the debate: it might suit to begin the debate at the start of a class.

3 If possible, everyone in the class should stand in the middle of the room, holding their statements. One wall of the room is for opinions, while the opposing wall is for facts.

4 Now a student can read out a statement. Each person must decide if it is an opinion or a fact. Walk to the corresponding wall.

5 If there is a disagreement in the class it will be obvious, with students standing at each wall. You can then let one spokesperson from each group try to use a convincing argument to get students to change sides, if they wish.

6 When everyone is sure of their choice, someone can read out another statement and you can begin again by choosing the corresponding wall. You can continue like this until you have debated a number of points.

When you are finished, you can have a discussion about opinion and fact. It might help to think about or to answer the following questions.

i) Do you think you displayed prejudice during the debate? Explain.
ii) Do you think there was any prejudice in the group during the debate? Explain.
iii) Do you think it is always easy to tell the difference between opinion and fact?
iv) Can you see any problems with using opinion as fact?
v) Why do you think people sometimes give their opinions as if they are facts?

We will have a closer look at opinions and facts later in the textbook.

Grammar station

Nouns

A **noun** is the name of a **person**, **place**, **thing** or **emotion**. There are four types of noun.

1 Common Noun: common nouns are ordinary objects.
Examples: house, plate, car.

2 Proper Noun: proper nouns are particular objects or things, like people, places, days, months or certain products. Proper nouns always take a capital letter.
Examples: Brian, Galway, Monday, July, Sony.

3 Abstract Noun: abstract nouns are nouns that are often difficult to describe clearly, such as feelings, states, qualities or emotions. We can't taste, touch, see, feel or smell abstract nouns.
Examples: love, beauty, crime.

4 Collective Noun: collective nouns are groups of people, animals or objects that are collected together.
*Examples: a **staff** of teachers, a **litter** of pups, a **stack** of paper.*

Countable and Uncountable Nouns

Another way of grouping nouns is to say whether they are countable or uncountable.

Countable Nouns: these are nouns we can easily count.
Examples: goats, people, houses, computers.

Countable nouns follow the normal grammatical rules for singular and plural. We say:

*There **is** one goat (singular).*   *There **are** two goats (plural).*

When we talk about countable nouns, we say **a number of**.
*Example: there are a **number of** goats.*

With countable nouns we ask **how many?**
*Example: **How many** goats are there in the far field?*

With countable nouns we use **few, fewer, fewest**.
*Example: there are a **few** goats, **fewer** shepherds and the **fewest** number of sheep I have ever seen.*

Uncountable Nouns: these are nouns we cannot easily count.
Examples: weather, money, sugar, advice.

Common uncountable noun groups include:
Abstract nouns: wisdom, jealousy, ignorance.
Food nouns: sugar, flour, cereal.
Sport nouns: golf, rugby, soccer.
Travel nouns: accommodation, luggage, distance.
Weather nouns: snow, rain, fog.
Material nouns: oil, paper, gas.

Uncountable nouns are normally treated as singular.
We say:
*Snow **is** falling heavily.* **Not:** *snow are falling heavily.*
*Coal **is** a useful source of heat.* **Not:** *coal are a useful source of heat.*

When we talk about uncountable nouns, we say **an amount of**.
*There was **an amount of** rain last night.*

With uncountable nouns we ask **how much?**
How much *patience does a teacher need?*

With uncountable nouns we use **little, less, least**.
*With our meal we had **little** bread, **less** sugar and the **least** amount of butter yet.*

Note: *some nouns are both countable and uncountable, depending on how they are used!*
*Examples: Hair **is** best kept short.*
          *The two hairs the scientist tested **are** animal hairs.*
          *Football **is** a beautiful sport.*
          *The footballs **are** in the shed.*

🎭 OPENING ACT

1 Write out the following nouns and mark them as countable, uncountable or both:
money, advice, houses, information, tennis, trees, fireman, door, tennis ball, football, spice, glass, sand, chair, car, sea, tea, sandwich, ice, books, petrol, jealousy, toys, peace, playground, teacher, ship, knowledge, sheep, candles.

2 Write your own answers to the questions in this abstract noun questionnaire.
   i) The greatest piece of **wisdom** I was ever told was _____.
   ii) **Anger** is _____.
   iii) I think the most difficult **profession** is _____.
   iv) **Humour** is good for _____.
   v) My earliest **memory** is _____.

vi) My idea of **bravery** is _____.

vii) My **hope** for the next year is _____.

viii) The **skill** I am most proud of is _____.

ix) **Peace** in the world will only be possible when _____.

x) My **advice** to students starting first year is _____.

3 Fill in the space with the correct collective noun.

You might need to research some of these!

i) A _____ of dolphins.

ii) A _____ of sheep.

iii) A _____ of teachers.

iv) A _____ of pups.

v) A _____ of litter.

vi) A _____ of houses.

vii) A _____ of sailors.

viii) A _____ of books.

ix) A _____ of bees.

x) A _____ of soldiers.

There are many unusual collective nouns. You can have a competition to see who can find the strangest one!

Pronouns

Pronouns are sometimes used instead of nouns in a sentence. We use pronouns every day in speech and writing. There are three types of pronoun: **personal pronoun**, **possessive pronoun** and **relative pronoun**.

1 Personal Pronoun: sometimes we replace a person's name with a pronoun.

*Examples: i) **Helen** talked to me: becomes: **She** talked to me.*

*ii) I like to talk to **Helen**: becomes: I like to talk to **her**.*

Here is the list of **personal pronouns** we use to speak about ourselves or other people:

I, me, myself, you, yourself, he, him, himself, she, her, herself, it, itself, we, us, ourselves, you, yourselves, they, them, themselves.

2 Possessive Pronoun: these are pronouns that replace a noun and a possessive adjective to show ownership.

*Examples: i) That's **Hannah's bag**: becomes: That's **hers**.*

*ii) That's **my hat**: becomes: That's **mine**.*

Here is the list of **possessive pronouns** we use to show ownership:
mine, yours, his, hers, ours, yours, theirs.

3 Relative Pronoun: these are pronouns that relate to a noun in a sentence, telling us more about that noun.

*Examples: i) The cat **that** sat on the mat. (That relates the cat to the mat.)*
*ii) I am the person **who** became ill. (Who relates the I to the person.)*

Here is a list of **relative pronouns**:
who, that, which, whose, where, whom.

 ## OPENING ACT

1 Change these sentences by using a possessive pronoun where possible.
i) That's Andrew's bicycle lock.
ii) Do you have Jack's school bag?
iii) Look at Orla's new shoes.
iv) That looks like my textbook.
v) Is this your teapot?
vi) It's their moment, let them enjoy it.
vii) I think that is Mum's car.
viii) Is that her new tracksuit?
ix) That's your mess.
x) That is our family home.

2 Change each pair of sentences into one sentence by using a relative pronoun.
i) There is the cat. I fed her earlier.
ii) He is the new boy. He comes from France.
iii) I'd like to go on holidays. I'd like to go somewhere warm.
iv) Here is the pothole. The tyre was burst in it.
v) Where are my books? I need them now for class.

 ## CENTRE STAGE

Taboo

*When something is **taboo** you can't talk about it or mention it.*

How to play the game:

A student is given a **common noun** and a list of words associated with it.
For example:
Noun: teapot
Associated words: drink, tea, cup, pour, thirst, kettle.

Noun: Christmas

Associated words: Jesus, Santa Claus, reindeer, December, gifts, turkey, ham, midnight mass, twenty-fifth.

Noun: teacher

Associated words: teaching, school, classroom, student, homework, staffroom, blackboard.

Now the student must try to describe what the noun is to the class, but cannot mention the noun or the associated words. Gesturing is not allowed.

Everyone has one guess at the noun from the descriptions they are given. You can put your hand up to guess at any time, but if you get it wrong, you have no more chances!

POETRY

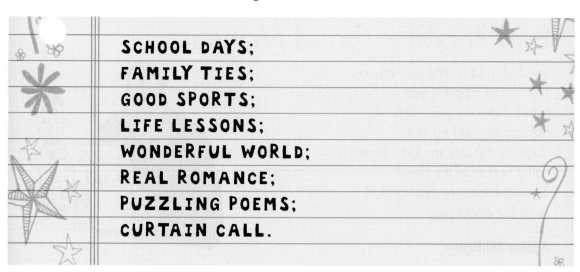

I **AM THE POET AND SCHOLAR MICHAEL MORRISON.** I specialise in Irish poetry, but I read poetry from all over the world. In this unit we will learn about the techniques and features used to create the sound and meaning of poetry. We will learn how poets use descriptive language to create the imagery that helps us imagine their world, feelings and experiences. We will see what makes poetry different from other texts and we will write some poetry of our own.

Here are the themed section headings:

> **SCHOOL DAYS;**
> **FAMILY TIES;**
> **GOOD SPORTS;**
> **LIFE LESSONS;**
> **WONDERFUL WORLD;**
> **REAL ROMANCE;**
> **PUZZLING POEMS;**
> **CURTAIN CALL.**

You can dip in and out of this unit, or you can follow the unit from beginning to end. There are eight sections in the unit and each section has its own theme.

In the **Grammar Station** we will also develop our understanding of **adjectives** and learn about their role in descriptive writing.

School Days

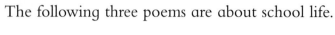

The following three poems are about school life.

Meaning

The **meaning** of a poem will not always be clear to you the first time you read it. You may need to read it a number of times and look for familiar features. This textbook is like a map that will help you to recognise these features.

When you are reading a poem, you might only understand part of a poem, such as a line or the title. Use this understanding as a signpost to guide you on your way.

Poetry is a journey that takes time, and we all have to go at our own pace.

Bad Report – Good Manners

My daddy said, 'My son, my son,
This school report is bad.'
I said, 'I did my best I did,
My dad my dad my dad.'
'Explain, my son, my son,' he said,
'Why *bottom* of the class?'
'I stood aside, my dad my dad,
To let the others pass.'

Spike Milligan

*The **subject** of the poem is who or what the poem is about on a simple level. The subject should be easy to identify. The subject matter of this poem is a father, a son and a school report.*

OPENING ACT

1 What does the father think of the son's report? EVIDENCE
2 How did the son do in the class as a whole? EVIDENCE
3 What is the son's excuse for not doing well? EVIDENCE

 # SPOTLIGHT

4 Do you think this poem is funny? OPINION REASON EVIDENCE
5 What do you think of the son's excuse? OPINION REASON
6 Why do you think the poet wrote this poem? OPINION REASON EVIDENCE

 ## IN YOUR OWN WORDS

SUBJECT:

Theme

From the first unit we remember that a **theme** is a **central topic** or idea that is **repeated** and **developed** in a piece of writing. It is what the poem is about in a deeper or more thoughtful way. We also learned that there are common themes that we come across, often in particular types of poems or stories.

Some common themes in poems about school are:

- **growth;**
- **personal development;**
- **success and failure;**
- **happiness;**
- **anger;**
- **fear;**
- **weakness;**
- **friendship;**
- **loyalty;**
- **isolation.**

Isolation is when a person is on their own and is unable or not allowed to communicate with others.

When Your Face Doesn't Fit

When your face doesn't fit
What can be done?
You can't go shopping
To buy a new one.

If you prefer work
And your class prefers play
If you dress in yellow
And they dress in grey

If your class are all bored
But you are excited
And you support City
While they cheer United

When you walk to school
Go in the school gate
And they come by car
And then lie in wait

To call out your name
And to laugh and to hit
What do you do
When your face doesn't fit?

Can you tighten a screw
And adjust it a bit?
Is that what you do
When your face doesn't fit?

Roger Stevens

POETRY

2

*One writing technique that the poet uses in this poem is the **rhetorical question**. This is when a writer asks a question with an obvious answer, a question to which an answer is not known or a question that the writer answers immediately after asking it.*

 ## OPENING ACT

1 What problem is the poet referring to when he writes 'when your face doesn't fit'?
2 Is the first solution he considers for the problem a serious solution?
3 Why do the students 'lie in wait'?
4 Identify a rhetorical question in this poem and explain why it is one. `EVIDENCE`

 ## SPOTLIGHT

5 What do you think is the most difficult question to answer in this poem? `OPINION` `REASON`
6 What do you think is the most humorous line in this poem? `OPINION` `REASON`
7 Why do you think writers use rhetorical questions? `OPINION` `REASON`
8 Do you know of any songs or films that explore the theme of growth and development? Try to find an example of each.

 ## CENTRE STAGE

Party Theme
Imagine you are organising the biggest party of the year.
Step 1: you have to think of an original theme for your party. An example of a theme could be that everyone has to come dressed as a celebrity or as characters from your favourite film.
Step 2: identify all the information that you need to present on your invitation and the order in which it should be presented.
Step 3: write out the invitation. Make sure that you clearly explain your theme. Include four rules for your party.
Step 4: use colour if you have colouring pencils. If you can, find or draw an image to brighten up your invitation.

 ## IN YOUR OWN WORDS

RHETORICAL QUESTION:

Simile

In the first unit we learned about the importance of descriptive writing. A poet, like a novelist, needs to describe the world, characters and feelings in vivid detail so people can imagine and understand what the poet has experienced and seen. Similes help to do this.

A **simile** is when you **compare** two different things in some way, using **like**, **as** or **than** to make the comparison.

Examples:

1 The sun in the distance was like a gold coin.

*In this simile the sun is being compared to a gold coin, using **like**. The sun and a gold coin are not exactly similar, but we are able to identify the qualities they share: colour and shape.*

'like a gold coin'

2 I was as lucky as a two-time lottery winner.

*In this simile the person's luck is compared to that of a lottery winner, using **as**. We know how lucky someone would be to win the lotto twice, so we know that the narrator is very lucky.*

3 The student finished her homework quicker than an elephant eating a bun.

In this simile the student's speed at doing her homework is being compared to an elephant eating a bun. We imagine an elephant eating a bun very quickly, so we know that the student finished her homework in a rush.

*The imagery of a student under pressure in school is created in the following poem through descriptive writing, including the use of a simile. We remember that **imagery** is the collection of mental pictures that words create in our minds.*

The Question

The child stands facing the teacher
(This happens every day);
A small, embarrassed creature
Who can't think what to say.

He gazes up at the ceiling,
He stares down at the floor,
With a hot and flustered feeling
And a question he can't ignore.

He stands there like the stump of a tree
With a forest of arms around.
'It's easy, Sir!' 'Ask, me!' 'Ask me!'
The answer, it seems, is found.

The child sits down with a lump in his throat
(This happens everywhere),
And brushes his eyes with the sleeve of his coat
And huddles in his chair.

Alan Ahlberg

FLUSTERED
to be under pressure and confused

HUDDLES
to curl up or pull together

*This poem has four **verses** or **stanzas**. These are the short, paragraph-like sections used to break the poem into different parts.*

OPENING ACT

1 What adjectives does the poet use to describe the student? `EVIDENCE`

2 Why does the student gaze 'up at the ceiling'?

3 How does the student feel when he is first asked the question? `EVIDENCE`

4 What simile is used in this poem? `EVIDENCE`

5 What does the poet mean by 'a forest of arms around'?

6 In the last stanza, how does the student feel when he sits down? `EVIDENCE`

SPOTLIGHT

7 Do you think the title of this poem is a good one? `OPINION` `REASON`

8 Do you think the simile used to describe the student is effective? `OPINION` `REASON` `EVIDENCE`

9 How is the answer 'found'? `OPINION` `REASON` `EVIDENCE`

10 Do you think the poet is correct when he says that 'this happens everywhere'? `OPINION` `REASON`

Here is a sample answer for **Opinion Reason Evidence**:

Question: What do you think of the descriptions of the student in this poem? `OPINION` `REASON` `EVIDENCE`

Answer: I think the student is described in vivid detail, and these descriptions help us to understand his feelings. The poet uses the simile, 'He stands there like the stump of a tree'. This image clearly shows us how the student stands out from the other pupils, who wave their arms, described as 'a forest of arms', so they can be picked to answer the question. They are like strong trees, whereas the student is only a stump of a tree.

The poet also uses expressive adjectives to describe the student. He says that the student is 'small', 'embarrassed' and 'flustered', using a range of adjectives that show us how confused and upset the student felt.

 ## CENTRE STAGE

As Useful as a Simile

Similes are an important feature of descriptive writing. They are used by poets, writers, playwrights, lyricists and comedians. You will also hear them used often in everyday speech.

Here are some simile exercises. Make sure the similes you invent are original.

A Think of a simile to describe any three of the following:
- bad weather: *The wind was as loud as …;*
- a mountain;
- a school;
- a lotto win;
- a lazy student.

B For the following similes, identify the qualities that the two things being compared might share and explain the comparisons.

1 My dog was perched on the sofa like a Persian king.
2 His joke was as popular as a clown at a funeral.
3 The headmaster has better eyesight than an eagle.
4 The wind pulled the clouds back like a curtain.
5 The curry sauce was as hot as molten lava.

IN YOUR OWN WORDS

SIMILE:

VERSE/STANZA:

Note: similes can also be comparisons using **of**. The important thing to notice is that two different things are being compared.
• The man had the face **of** a gorilla that had swallowed a bee.
• The body-builder had a chest the width **of** a bus.

Family Ties

The following four poems are all about family life. Poems about family contain themes such as love, anger, growth, forgiveness, death, loss, grief, youth and understanding.

Mood

The **mood** of a poem is the **emotion** that the poem expresses and **makes us feel inside**. The mood is created by the characters, incidents and action in the poem.

Common moods include:
• **happy;**
• **sad;**
• **angry;**
• **peaceful;**
• **calm;**
• **bitter;**
• **thoughtful;**
• **forgiving;**
• **regretful;**
• **fearful.**

What is the mood of the following poem?

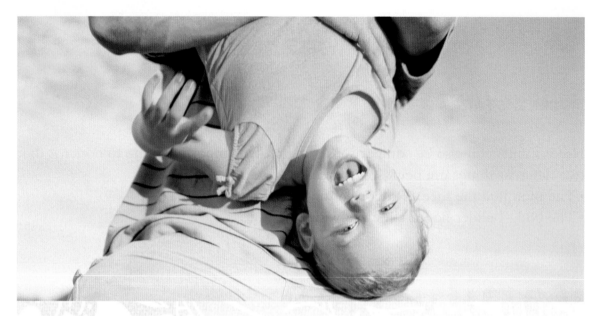

Sharp Freckles

He picks me up, his big thumbs under my armpits tickle,
    then puts me down. On his belt there is a shining silver
    buckle.
I hold his hand and see, close up, the dark hairs on his
    knuckles.

He sings to me. His voice is loud and funny and I giggle.
Now we will eat. I listen to my breakfast as it crackles.
He nods and smiles. His eyes are birds in little nests of
    wrinkles.

We kick a ball, red and white, between us. When he tackles
I'm on the ground, breathing a world of grass. It prickles.
He bends. He lifts me high above his head. Frightened, I
    wriggle.

Face to his face, I watch the sweat above each caterpillar
    eyebrow tickle.
He rubs his nose on mine, once, twice, three times, and we
    both chuckle.
He hasn't shaved today. He kisses me. He has sharp
    freckles.

Carol Ann Duffy

*A **characteristic** is a feature that we associate with a person or thing, or that helps us to identify a person or thing. For example, you could say that wearing a suit is a characteristic of businessmen, or having a parrot on one's shoulder is characteristic of being a pirate!*

OPENING ACT

1 What words in the poem suggest happiness? **EVIDENCE**
2 How does the poet describe her father's eyes? **EVIDENCE**
3 What happens when the poet's father tackles her when playing football?
4 In the last stanza, what are the characteristics of the poet's father that stand out? **EVIDENCE**
5 As a child, how does the poet manage to be face to face with her father? **EVIDENCE**

 # SPOTLIGHT

6 What is the mood of this poem? **OPINION** **REASON** **EVIDENCE**
7 How does the poet's choice of words create the mood in the poem? **OPINION** **REASON** **EVIDENCE**
8 As a child, what kind of relationship did the poet have with her father? **OPINION** **REASON** **EVIDENCE**
9 Do you think the poem accurately reflects a child's point of view? **OPINION** **REASON** **EVIDENCE**
10 What would you recognise as your main characteristics?

 # CENTRE STAGE

Mood Mime

This is a short, paired exercise for acting out mood. It is a mime, meaning you act without words. There are three different situations to act out.

1 Divide into pairs and choose one of the situations. Decide together on what is happening in the situation: it could be an argument, you could want something from each other or you could be friends.
2 Together you can decide what mood you should act in. The rest of the class can figure out what the mood of the mime is.

Here are the situations:
i) You and your brother are eating dinner together.
ii) You have entered a shop and the shop attendant walks up to you.
iii) You are a police officer stopping a car to talk to the driver.

IN YOUR OWN WORDS

MOOD:

CHARACTERISTIC:

Metaphor

A **metaphor** is when you state that one thing **is** something else because it seems or appears like that thing. The best way to understand this is through examples.

Examples:

1 That man **is** a wise old fox.
We know that the man is not actually a wise old fox, but rather he acts or appears like one.

2 His father's new jeep **is** a tank, rolling over the traffic.
The jeep is not actually a tank, but seems like a tank because it is so big.

Metaphors are often used to exaggerate the qualities of a person, activity or object. They are used in descriptive writing to create vivid imagery.

In the following poem, the poet uses a metaphor to describe death.

Close

JOURNAL
diary notebook

The last entry in my father's journal
says that he has been mending pipes
but has grown a little tired, and so
he will begin again in the morning.

He never did. Death reached
down and stole his heart away.

And yet, though I've seen
that Thief up close:
felt His breath on my face;
His eyes on my soul,

POETRY

2

I still believe that if I stop writing now,
and go out for coffee,
I can come back in an hour or two
and take up where I left off.

Tony Curtis

Note: *confused about the difference between a metaphor and a simile?*
If you say the football player is **like** a clown, it is a simile.
But if you say the football player **is** a clown, then you are using a **metaphor**.

OPENING ACT

1 What was the last entry the poet's father made in his journal? `EVIDENCE`

2 What did the poet's father plan on doing the next day? `EVIDENCE`

3 In the third stanza, what metaphor does the poet use to describe Death? `EVIDENCE`

4 How does the poet describe his father's death? `EVIDENCE`

5 What does the poet still believe at the end of the poem? `EVIDENCE`

SPOTLIGHT

6 What are the characteristics of Death in this poem? `OPINION` `REASON` `EVIDENCE`

7 How did this poem make you feel? `OPINION` `REASON` `EVIDENCE`

8 How would you describe the mood of the poem:
  • thoughtful;
  • sad;
  • angry?
  `OPINION` `REASON` `EVIDENCE`

9 Do you think the metaphor used to describe Death is a good one? `OPINION` `REASON` `EVIDENCE`

10 What message do you think the poet is telling us in the last stanza? `OPINION` `REASON` `EVIDENCE`

CENTRE STAGE

Metaphorical Makeover

In the last poem, Death was given a new image as a thief.

Give one of the following five 'characters' a makeover.
It might help to think of the qualities that each character is known for.

1 Santa: Santa could become an express delivery courier ...
2 Mother Nature …
3 Robinson Crusoe …
4 Gollum …
5 The tooth fairy …

You can present the makeover in the form of a poster, a poem, a business card or an advertisement.

L'IL RED RIDING HOOD'S
COOKERY CLASSES

"YOU'LL WOLF DOWN THESE INGREDIENTS!"

GRANDMA'S RECIPES A SPECIALITY

ALL INGREDIENTS LOCALLY SOURCED IN DARK WOODS

15 GINGERBREAD HALLS, HUNTERSVILLE. CO. WICKLOW

Narrative

A poem can be a **narrative** in a similar way to a novel or short story. A poem can contain **characters, action** and can tell a **story**. The narrator can be the poet, written in first person, or the poet can use a fictional third person narrator.

Manners

My grandfather said to me
as we sat on the wagon seat,
"Be sure to remember to always
speak to everyone you meet."

We met a stranger on foot.
My grandfather's whip tapped his hat.
"Good day, sir. Good day. A fine day."
And I said it and bowed where I sat.

Then we overtook a boy we knew
with his big pet crow on his shoulder.
"Always offer everyone a ride;
don't forget that when you get older,"

my grandfather said. So Willy
climbed up with us, but the crow
gave a "Caw!" and flew off. I was worried.
How would he know where to go?

But he flew a little way at a time
from fence post to fence post, ahead;
and when Willy whistled he answered.
"A fine bird," my grandfather said,

"and he's well brought up. See, he answers
nicely when he's spoken to.
Man or beast, that's good manners.
Be sure that you both always do."

When automobiles went by,
the dust hid the people's faces,
but we shouted, "Good day! Good day!
Fine day!" at the top of our voices.

When we came to Hustler Hill,
he said that the mare was tired,
so we all got down and walked,
as our good manners required.

Elizabeth Bishop

MARE
female horse

Repetition is often used in poetry to emphasise an event, characteristic, idea or mood. In this poem the poet repeats 'Good day' to emphasise their good manners and friendliness.

🎭 OPENING ACT

1 What advice does the poet's grandfather give in the first stanza? `EVIDENCE`
2 What did the crow do after his master hopped up on the cart? `EVIDENCE`
3 What did the poet and her grandfather do when the automobiles went by? `EVIDENCE`
4 What happened when they got to Hustler Hill? `EVIDENCE`

📷 SPOTLIGHT

5 What kind of person is the poet's grandfather? `OPINION` `REASON` `EVIDENCE`
6 What do you think of the grandfather's advice in the first stanza? `OPINION` `REASON`

7 Do you think the repetition of the words 'Good day' helps to emphasise the message of the poem? `OPINION` `REASON`

8 How are the people in the automobiles different from the poet's grandfather? `OPINION` `REASON` `EVIDENCE`

9 What kind of relationship does the poet have with her grandfather? `OPINION` `REASON`

10 'Poems can create a character just as well as a novel or short story.'
Based on this poem, would you agree or disagree with this statement? `OPINION` `REASON` `EVIDENCE`

CENTRE STAGE

Dear Editor

Write a letter to your local newspaper about one change you would like to see in modern society.

• Use your first paragraph to outline the problems you see.

• Use your second paragraph to outline your solutions.

• Use the last paragraph to outline what the positive effects of change would be.

Symbol

A **symbol** is a colour or object that **stands for** another thing. For example, white is a symbol of peace and green is a symbol of the environment. Some countries have different symbols, for example the bull symbolises Spain and the shamrock symbolises Ireland. Can you think of any other country's symbol?

When a poet uses a symbol to stand for another thing, we say the poet is using **symbolism**. In poetry, we sometimes have to figure out what symbols mean. Some symbols might seem obvious, for example a bird could symbolise freedom or the sun could symbolise happiness. Other symbols have to be figured out by reading the poem carefully.

In the next poem, try to think of everything a sugarcane field symbolises for the poet. In the early and later history of European settlement in the Americas, African slaves were used to cultivate sugarcane on sugar plantations. This poet is writing about her mother, who lived through this experience.

sugarfields

treetalk and windsong
are the language of my mother
her music does not leave me.

let me taste again the cane
the syrup of the earth
sugarfields were once my home.

I would lie down in the fields
and never get up again
(treetalk and windsong
are the language of my mother
sugarfields are my home)

the leaves go on whispering secrets
as the wind blows a tune in the grass
my mother's voice is in the fields
this music cannot leave me.

Barbara Mahone

OPENING ACT

1 What is the language of the poet's mother?
2 Where was the poet once at home?
3 Where is the poet's mother's voice to be found?
4 How do you think the 'wind blows a tune in the grass'?
5 What different words does the poet use that have to do with music?

SPOTLIGHT

6 Do you think the poet's mother was a musical woman? `OPINION` `REASON` `EVIDENCE`

7 What different things do the sugarcane fields remind the poet of? `OPINION` `REASON` `EVIDENCE`

8 What kind of relationship do you think the poet had with her mother? `OPINION` `REASON`

9 What do you think the mood of this poem is? `OPINION` `REASON` `EVIDENCE`

10 'For the poet, the sounds of nature in the sugarcane fields symbolise her mother's voice.'
   Would you agree or disagree with this statement? `OPINION` `REASON` `EVIDENCE`

CENTRE STAGE

Symbol Selection

Decide and discuss:

1 On your own: what object would you choose to symbolise yourself and why? Think of your own special characteristics.

2 As pairs:

  i) To begin, let each person write out three characteristics of your class group.

  ii) Then, in pairs, discuss and decide on an object to symbolise your class based on the class characteristics. Write out your final choice and explain it.

  You can discuss different symbols as a group afterward, and even have a vote or debate on the most suitable symbol.

3 As a group:

  i) What object would you choose to symbolise your school? Why? Write out your answer.

  ii) Take suggestions as a group and discuss them. Try to decide on the four most appropriate symbols.

4 Now create a new crest for your class or school. You can use a number of different symbols on the crest.

  A symbol for a group or team is called a mascot. It can be an animal, a person or a thing.

IN YOUR OWN WORDS

SYMBOLISM:

Good Sports

The following poems are about sport. Sporting poems explore themes such as success, failure, emotion, loyalty, fame, relationships, honesty and isolation.

Alliteration

Alliteration is the **repetition** of similar-sounding letters at the **start of words** in a sentence. Alliteration affects the sound of a poem and is used to give a poem lyrical force and rhythm.

Alliteration can also hint at the poem's meaning and can help to create mood. Here are some examples of alliteration. Listen to the sounds of the highlighted letters.

1 The roaring river rolled and raced as it ran its route down the rocks.

The r sound emphasises the fast quality of the river and gives us a feeling of the river's power and speed.

2 I folded flowers in Fiona's dress, for which I favour some success.

The f sound is soft and hints at tenderness. It suits the romantic mood of this line.

3 The kitchen cat clawed the mouse but caught the kettle with a crash.

In this example we can see how k and c make a similar sound. C can also make an s sound, for example, the sizzling sausages I savaged at the circus!

The following poem uses alliteration to emphasise speed and action.

Downhill Racer

Over the snow-covered
slopes and dips she
swoops flies skis
sighing skims bumps
and hollows rounding
the turns to race the
reeling clock zips
down down rocking
for the last speck
of speed uh-oh!
almost tumbles re-
covers now hunched
   for the long
       schuss
           in.

Did she win?
A hundredth of a second
could make the difference.
She smiles in spite of
fears removes goggles.
The mountainsides
reverberate with cheers.

Lillian Morrison

SCHUSS
a straight downhill run at high speed

REVERBERATE
echoing

Onomatopoeia is when words sound like what they mean or stand for. This includes words such as zip, bang, woof and boom. Onomatopoeic words help us to visualise what is being described, bringing the poem to life. Can you find any onomatopoeic words in the previous poem?

OPENING ACT

1 What do you think are the five most exciting verbs used in this poem? **EVIDENCE**

2 What effect does the repetition of *s* sounds create in the poem?

3 Find two examples of alliteration in the poem. **EVIDENCE**

4 How does the poet create tension when the skier nearly slips? **EVIDENCE**

5 How does the crowd react when the skier takes off her goggles? **EVIDENCE**

SPOTLIGHT

6 Find an onomatopoeic word in this poem. What effect does it have on the poem? **OPINION** **REASON** **EVIDENCE**

7 Do you think this poet has captured the excitement of downhill skiing well? **OPINION** **REASON** **EVIDENCE**

8 Why do you think the poet changes the shape of the poem at the end of the first stanza? **OPINION** **REASON**

9 What emotions do you think the skier goes through during the race and afterward? **OPINION** **REASON** **EVIDENCE**

10 'Lillian Morrison is not just a skilled poet, but she also understands her subject matter well.'

Would you agree or disagree with this statement, based on your reading of this poem? **OPINION** **REASON** **EVIDENCE**

CENTRE STAGE

Action Stations

This poem uses a lot of action verbs, such as dips, swoops and skis. These verbs give us a strong feeling of movement and excitement. Action verbs are useful for writing about sport or other exciting events. You will learn more about verbs in the next unit.

Below is a word bank of action verbs. Use these words to help you write about your favourite sport. You can write:

• a poem;

• a short piece of descriptive writing;

• a match or newspaper report.

Action verbs: attacked, raced, blasted, boomed, zipped, cruised, gasped, galloped, roared, boosted, skimmed, slipped, jumped, raced, rolled, bumped, bobbed, screamed, soared, thrashed, dived, plunged, reached, skidded, leaped, staggered, flipped, passed, thumped, slammed, whacked, walloped, sprang, thrown, hurled, crushed, collapsed, climbed, clung, flung, bounced, rebounded, smacked, clipped, stepped, zoomed, dipped, danced, hugged, soared, exploded, stretched, pumped, sailed, shot, dibbled, dunked, headed, speeded, kicked, sprinted, pounded, jogged, drummed.

IN YOUR OWN WORDS

ALLITERATION:

ONOMATOPOEIA:

Appealing to the Senses

Descriptive writing often **appeals to the senses**:

- **sight;**
- **sound;**
- **smell;**
- **taste;**
- **touch.**

When a poet appeals to the senses, we can imagine how something looks, sounds, smells, tastes and feels. This creates a more vivid image in the reader's mind.

When you are using descriptive writing, remember to appeal to the different senses as much as possible. In the following poem we can picture the narrator's world through the senses: how it looks, sounds, smells, tastes and feels.

I Would Win the Gold if These Were Olympic Sports ...

Bubble gum blowing
Goggle box watching
Late morning snoring
Homework botching

Quilt ruffling
Little brother teasing
Pizza demolishing
Big toe cheesing

Insult hurling, wobbly throwing
Infinite blue belly button fluff growing

Late night endurance computer screen gazing
Non-attentive open-jawed eyeball glazing

Ultimate volume decibel blaring
Long-distance marathon same sock wearing

Recognise all these as sports then meet...
Me! The Champ Apathetic Athlete!

Paul Cookson

BOTCHING
making a mess of

NON-ATTENTIVE
not paying attention

APATHETIC
without ambition,
uninterested

OPENING ACT

1 What action verbs can you find in this poem?
2 What do you think a 'goggle box' is?
3 How does the poet appeal to the sense of sound?
4 What does the poet mean by 'late night endurance computer screen gazing'?

SPOTLIGHT

5 What is your favourite description in this poem? Why? OPINION REASON EVIDENCE

6 Of all the 'sports' listed above, which one do you think you might be a champion at? OPINION REASON

7 Which of the following words do you think best describes this poem:
* humorous;
* cheeky;
* thoughtful?

OPINION REASON EVIDENCE

8 What effect does appealing to the senses have in this poem? OPINION REASON EVIDENCE

 ## CENTRE STAGE

Olympic Argument

Some people think that everyone in the world is a champion at one thing. The problem is the world doesn't always recognise our hidden talents! Your skill could be climbing trees, applying make-up, splashing in puddles or making smoothies.

i) Write out a list of skills you have that wouldn't be considered as normal sporting skills. Try to list at least five.
Example: expert at spitting.

ii) Take one of these skills and invent a sporting game for it. Can you think of five rules to accompany it?
Example: long-distance spitting.
Rule 1: all spit must be naturally produced ...

iii) Write a short letter to the Chairman of the Olympic Games Committee arguing for the inclusion of a new sporting event in the Olympic Games. You can use your imagination and argue that you have a group or organisation already dedicated to the sport.

Tips
* Argue for your sport's popularity with television viewers.
* Explain the rules.
* Reassure the chairman about potential problems.
* Discuss celebrity endorsements of your sport.
* Outline the benefits of the sport for young people.

 ## IN YOUR OWN WORDS

APPEALING TO THE SENSES:

Character

A **character** used in a poem can be taken from the poet's own life, from history or can be a fictional creation. A poem usually uses fewer words to describe a character than a longer text, so a poet **focuses** on one or two **characteristics** or **traits** when describing a character.

The following poem was written about a Gaelic footballer.

A Footballer

He could have played with better
But he chose his own;
Playing with his county
He'd never carry home

The trophy all aspire to
But that's not why he played:
If he played with another county
He'd feel he had betrayed

Himself, his art, his people,
So he plays out his career
Away from the glare of the headlines.
And yet sometimes you'll hear

From followers of football
The mention of his name.
It's enough that they believe in him,
His way, his truth, his game.

Gabriel Fitzmaurice

🎬 OPENING ACT

1 Who did the footballer choose to play with? `EVIDENCE`
2 What would the footballer never 'carry home'? `EVIDENCE`
3 What do you think the poet means by 'the glare of the headlines'?
4 Who believes in this footballer? `EVIDENCE`

SPOTLIGHT

5 How would you describe the character of the footballer in your own words?
OPINION REASON EVIDENCE

6 What were the footballer's reasons for playing football? OPINION REASON
EVIDENCE

7 Do you think this footballer was admired for his attitude? OPINION REASON
EVIDENCE

8 Do you think 'headlines' are important to the poet who wrote this poem?
OPINION REASON

9 Identify two themes in this poem. A list of common sporting themes can be found
at the beginning of this section. OPINION REASON EVIDENCE

CENTRE STAGE

Hero Homage

To write in **homage** is to write in praise or admiration of a person, event or thing.
Write a poem in homage of a person you admire. *Your poem doesn't have to rhyme!*

Tips

- Give your poem a title.
- Use clear and vivid descriptive language.
- Create a setting of time and place for the person.
- Describe the activity the person is known for.
- Describe an incident that shows why the person should be admired.
- Describe the character of the person.
- Describe how the person makes others feel.
- Use one simile to describe the person.

Life Lessons

The following poems explore the lessons life has to teach us. Some of the themes of these poems are learning, growth, personal development, suffering, old age and change.

Tone

The **tone** of a poem is the poet's attitude to the subject of the poem. This could be angry, happy, sad, frustrated, disappointed or amused.

The tone can be different from both the theme and the subject. For example, a poet could write about a funeral in a joking or happy tone! It might help to think of the voice the poet would use to read the poem.

In the following poem, the subject of the poem is that of the poet growing old and the themes are growth and decay. Even though the subject and themes of the poem are serious, the poet uses a humorous tone.

Wearing Thin

"You'll soon grow into it," she would say
When buying a school blazer three sizes too big.
And she was right as mothers usually are.

Syrup of figs. Virol. Cod liver oil.
Within a year I did grow into it,
By then, of course, it was threadbare.

Pulling in different directions,
My clothes and I never matched.
And in changing-rooms nothing has changed.

I can buy what I like and when
New clothes that are a perfect fit.
Full-length mirror, nervous grin,
It's me now that's threadbare, wearing thin.

Roger McGough

BLAZER
jacket

FIGS
a type of fruit

VIROL
a type of malt
drink

THREADBARE
so worn you can
see the threads

🎭 OPENING ACT

1 What was wrong with the blazer the poet's mother bought him? `EVIDENCE`

2 What was the problem with the blazer by the time the poet had grown into it? `EVIDENCE`

3 What still happens to the poet in changing rooms?

4 In the last stanza, what problem does the poet now find with buying new clothes?

📷 SPOTLIGHT

5 Have you ever had clothes that were too big for you? How did you feel about that?

6 Do you think the poet would have agreed with his mother when she first told him he'd soon grow into his blazer? `OPINION` `REASON` `EVIDENCE`

7 Why do you think the poet describes his grin with the adjective 'nervous'? `OPINION` `REASON`

8 Why do you think the poet repeats the word 'threadbare'? `OPINION` `REASON` `EVIDENCE`

9 Do you think 'Wearing Thin' is a suitable title for this poem? `OPINION` `REASON` `EVIDENCE`

🎩 CENTRE STAGE

Tone Up!

Write a poem or short newspaper article using any of these serious topic titles, but you must try to use a humorous tone!

• The End of the World.

• Lost Herd of Cows.

• Teacher in Trouble.

 **IN YOUR OWN WORDS**

TONE:

Expression

In the English language there are different varieties of spoken **expression**. The way we use the English language can change with our **background, area** and **culture**. Poets try to capture this variety of expression in written words.

*In the following poem, a male African-American poet creates the character of an African-American woman to narrate the poem. She is a **persona**, a fictional character invented to narrate the poem. Try reading the poem aloud with an emphasis on the mother's accent. What tone do you think she would use? It might help to have one student pretend to be the son and sit on a chair. The student who is pretending to be the mother can then stand in front of her 'son' and read the poem to him. Use body language!*

Mother to Son

Well, son, I'll tell you:
Life for me ain't been no crystal stair.
It's had tacks in it,
And splinters,
And boards torn up,
And places with no carpet on the floor—
Bare.
But all the time
I'se been a-climbin' on,
And reachin' landin's,

And turnin' corners,
And sometimes goin' in the dark
Where there ain't been no light.
So, boy, don't you turn back.
Don't you set down on the steps.
'Cause you finds it's kinder hard.
Don't you fall now—
For I'se still goin', honey,
I'se still climbin',
And life for me ain't been no crystal stair.

Langston Hughes

When people of a certain region or background have different words or a different manner of speaking from the standard language, it is called a **dialect**. *Dialects are formed by changes to the standard language as well as the addition of new and foreign words.*

OPENING ACT

1 What does the title tell us about the narrator of the poem?

2 What word does the narrator of the poem use to summarise how her life has been? EVIDENCE

3 What actions has the narrator of the poem done in her life? EVIDENCE

4 What does the narrator think of sitting down on the 'steps'? EVIDENCE

5 What does the narrator call her son? EVIDENCE

SPOTLIGHT

6 Do you think a stairs is a good metaphor for life? Why? OPINION REASON EVIDENCE

7 What do you think of the use of dialect in this poem? OPINION REASON

8 Do you think the poet who wrote this poem had a difficult life? *Remember, the poet is **not** the narrator of the poem!* OPINION REASON EVIDENCE

9 Do you think parents should take the role of giving advice to their children?

10 How would you read this poem? You could practise for homework and have a reading of different versions the next day.

11 Can you think of any dialects in Ireland? Give examples of words from those dialects and the meanings of those words.

CENTRE STAGE

First Note

Imagine you are the mother of the son in the poem. Write a note from the point of view of the woman to her son on his first day at secondary school. You are going to put it in his lunchbox so that he finds it during lunch break.

- Use the correct dialect.
- Give him some advice.
- Imagine some details about their family.
- Include some good wishes from another person.
- Tell him your hopes for his future.

IN YOUR OWN WORDS

EXPRESSION:

PERSONA:

DIALECT:

Imagery

We have already learned about imagery in the first unit and now we will develop our understanding of it. Poets use many **descriptive writing features** to create **imagery**. These include expressive words, action verbs, appealing to the senses, similes and metaphors.

The amount of **detail** used in descriptive writing also helps to create vivid imagery. Describing colour, sound, emotion and a variety of sensations creates a clear collection of images and pictures in our minds.

Living

The fire in leaf and grass
so green it seems
each summer the last summer.

The wind blowing, the leaves
shivering in the sun,
each day the last day.

A red salamander
so cold and so
easy to catch, dreamily

moves his delicate feet
and long tail. I hold
my hand open for him to go.

Each minute the last minute.

Denise Levertov

 ## OPENING ACT

1 What colours are used in this poem? EVIDENCE
2 What action are the leaves doing in the poem? EVIDENCE
3 What mention of time is there in the poem? EVIDENCE
4 How does the poet describe the salamander? EVIDENCE

SPOTLIGHT

5 How does the poet create the imagery of nature? `OPINION` `REASON` `EVIDENCE`

6 What do you think the 'fire' in leaf and grass is? `OPINION` `REASON`

7 Why do you think the poem is called 'Living'? `OPINION` `REASON` `EVIDENCE`

8 When does time go quickly for you? Why? `OPINION` `REASON`

9 When does time go slowly for you? Why? `OPINION` `REASON`

10 What do you think the poet is trying to tell us about life? `OPINION` `REASON` `EVIDENCE`

CENTRE STAGE

Wild Encounters

An encounter is a chance meeting with a person, animal or thing. Have you ever witnessed an animal in the wild?

Describe your experience:

• using a beginning, middle and end for your story;
• using a simile;
• appealing to different senses in your descriptions.

Message

Make hay while the sun shines

Poets sometimes write a poem to share a lesson they have learned. This can be called a point or **message**. The **central message** of a poem is the main point that the poet expresses.

An autobiography is the story of a person's life written by the person who lived it. This poet describes this short poem as an autobiography of her own life. You will learn more about biographies later, in Unit 4.

Autobiography in Five Short Chapters

I

I walk down the street.
There is a deep hole in the sidewalk
I fall in.
I am lost ... I am helpless.
It isn't my fault.
It takes me forever to find a way out.

SIDEWALK

pavement,
footpath

II

I walk down the same street.
There is a deep hole in the sidewalk.
I pretend I don't see it.
I fall in again.
I can't believe I am in the same place
but, it isn't my fault.
It still takes a long time to get out.

III

I walk down the same street.
There is a deep hole in the sidewalk.
I see it is there.
I still fall in ... it's a habit.
My eyes are open
I know where I am.
It is my fault.
I get out immediately.

IV

I walk down the same street.
There is a deep hole in the sidewalk.
I walk around it.

V

I walk down another street.

Portia Nelson

*To **summarise** is to shorten something to its main points. In this poem the poet has summarised the way she has lived her life into five short stanzas.*

 OPENING ACT

1 How does the poet feel when she first falls into the hole in the sidewalk? **EVIDENCE**

2 In the second stanza, is the poet aware of the hole in the sidewalk before she falls into it? **EVIDENCE**

3 In the third stanza, what reason does the poet give for falling into the hole? **EVIDENCE**

4 In the third stanza, who does the poet blame for her problem? **EVIDENCE**

5 What does the poet do in the fourth stanza? **EVIDENCE**

SPOTLIGHT

6 Did the poet actually fall into a hole in the sidewalk? **OPINION** **REASON**

7 Think of a way in which the poet's experience of life is similar to your own. **OPINION** **REASON**

8 Give the poem another title and explain your choice. **OPINION** **REASON**

9 In your own words, what do you think the central message of this poem is? **OPINION** **REASON** **EVIDENCE**

10 Do you think a road or street is an effective metaphor for life? **OPINION** **REASON**

CENTRE STAGE

Message in a Bottle

Imagine you are writing a message to put into a bottle. You are going to let the bottle float away in the sea.
- Write a short description of who you are and what your life is like.
- Write a piece of advice about life.
- Include your favourite line of poetry and explain why you like it.
- Write one hope for the future and include a wish for the person who finds the bottle.

Use paragraphs to separate your ideas.

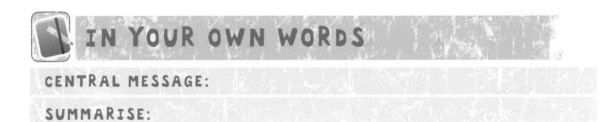

IN YOUR OWN WORDS

CENTRAL MESSAGE:

SUMMARISE:

Wonderful World

The following poems all explore themes of nature and the natural world. Imagery is very important in poetry about the natural world.

Atmosphere

The **atmosphere** of a poem is the **particular feeling** that a poem gives us through **description** and **setting**. For example, the atmosphere can be spooky, wintry or sunny. Atmosphere is created through imagery, repetition, use of detail and other descriptive writing techniques.

Note: mood and atmosphere work together in poetry. A spooky atmosphere gives a poem a fearful or frightening mood. A sunny and cheerful atmosphere gives a poem a happy mood.

What kind of atmosphere is created by the descriptions and imagery used in the next poem?

Cold Spell

Just for today
I can be a child again,
my Canadian skin rubbed rosy,
eyes bright and liquid
a deeper blue of the sky;
clouds suspended in cold breath
mirrored in a crust of frost.

Just for today,
I am allowed to skip along paths,
putting aside my age
to slide on pieces of ice
and scratch lines of love poetry
on frosted windows of cars
along the canal.

Just for today
a cold hush is broken by birds singing,
the sun shines through bare trees,
respite from endless rain.

Sandra Bunting

A **homonym** is a word that has the same spelling and sound as another word, but has a different meaning. Homonyms include bow, row, bark and spell.

Examples:
I was seasick and so had to **bow** *down at the* **bow** *of the ship.*
When I carved my name in the **bark** *of the tree, the dog started to* **bark**.
I **row** *the boat through a* **row** *of boats.*
During a sunny **spell**, *the witch learned a* **spell** *to help her* **spell**.

🎁 OPENING ACT

1 For a day, what does the poet want to be again? `EVIDENCE`
2 What does the poet want to do on this day? `EVIDENCE`
3 What breaks the 'cold hush' in the third stanza? `EVIDENCE`
4 How many senses does this poem appeal to? `EVIDENCE`
5 Who do you think is allowing the poet to skip along the paths?

🔦 SPOTLIGHT

6 How does the poet create imagery of winter in this poem? `OPINION` `REASON` `EVIDENCE`
7 Is there anything you miss that you were allowed to do as a child but not allowed to do now? Explain what it is and why you can't do it anymore.
8 What image from the poem best captures the atmosphere of a winter's day? `OPINION` `REASON` `EVIDENCE`
9 'Spell' is a homophone.
　i) What are the meanings of the word 'spell'?
　ii) Which meaning or meanings of the word 'spell' make sense in the title? `OPINION` `REASON`
10 'The wintry atmosphere of this poem gives it a mood of wonder and delight.' *Would you agree or disagree with this statement? Try to structure your answer into two paragraphs.* `OPINION` `REASON` `EVIDENCE`

CENTRE STAGE

Sensory School

Poems about the natural world often create imagery that appeals strongly to the senses. Split the class up into five equal groups. Each group represents one of the senses.

i)   For homework, every student has to find a small object or image from the natural world that strongly represents the sense of their group, and they have to bring it into school.

ii) Collect all of the objects and images together the next day, mixing them up without paying attention to what group they are from.

iii) Each object and image is held up individually, with the owner staying quiet. Everyone else has to guess what sense the object or image belongs to. When the class has agreed on the sense it belongs to, the owner can speak up and say whether the group is right or wrong.

Can you think of a simile to compare each object to?

IN YOUR OWN WORDS

ATMOSPHERE:

HOMONYM:

Rhyming Pattern

The **rhyming pattern** of a poem is the way in which a poem rhymes. The combination of **pace** and **rhyme** in a poem is called the **rhythm**. Poems that don't rhyme are called **free verse**.

*This next poem is by an American poet, Robert Frost. Notice how the first two lines of each stanza rhyme together, along with the last line. Every third line doesn't rhyme at all. The rhyming pattern of this poem is therefore **aaba**.*

Desert Places

Snow falling and night falling fast, oh, fast
In a field I looked into going past,
And the ground almost covered smooth in snow,
But a few weeds and stubble showing last.

The woods around it have it—it is theirs.
All animals are smothered in their lairs.
I am too absent-spirited to count;
The loneliness includes me unawares.

And lonely as it is that loneliness
Will be more lonely ere it will be less—
A blanker whiteness of benighted snow
With no expression, nothing to express.

They cannot scare me with their empty spaces
Between stars—on stars where no human race is.
I have it in me so much nearer home
To scare myself with my own desert places.

Robert Frost

ABSENT-SPIRITED
apart from your immediate surroundings

UNAWARES
not aware, unknowing

BENIGHTED
overtaken by night

Consonance is the repetition of similar consonant letters (letters that are not vowels) for poetic effect. Repeat the following lines aloud and listen to the musical quality of the words as the consonant sounds blend together:
And lonely as it is that loneliness
Will be more lonely ere it will be less.

By using consonance the poet gives the poem a lyrical quality.

OPENING ACT

1 Where is this poem set? **EVIDENCE**
2 Where are all the animals of the forest?
3 What quality does the snow have in the third stanza? **EVIDENCE**
4 What words in the poem help to express the poet's loneliness? **EVIDENCE**

SPOTLIGHT

5 What are the mood and the atmosphere of this poem and how are they created? OPINION REASON EVIDENCE

6 When you listen to this poem, how does it make you feel? OPINION REASON

7 Would you like to visit the world of this poem? *Try to structure your answer into two paragraphs.* OPINION REASON EVIDENCE

8 In the poem, what could a 'desert place' be a metaphor for? OPINION REASON EVIDENCE

9 Do you prefer free verse or poetry with a rhyming pattern? *Try to structure your answer into two paragraphs.* OPINION REASON

CENTRE STAGE

Poetry Aloud

To experience a poem fully, you need to hear the **sound** of the words and the **rhythm** of the poem. *Try it out!*

1 Select a few students to try different readings of 'Desert Places'. Each student can try reading it in a different tone: jolly, sad, angry, soft. Which tone works best?

2 Now let everyone look through their poetry book and choose a poem that they would like to read aloud. Decide on the tone it should be read in.

3 If you have the time, read out your poems of choice and explain why you made your choice.

4 If you can, find recordings of poets reading out their own poetry.

IN YOUR OWN WORDS

RHYMING PATTERN:

FREE VERSE:

CONSONANCE:

Personification

Personification is when a writer gives a **lifeless object** the **qualities** of a **human**. In this way a poet personifies the object.

Examples:

1 The open window **asked** the thief to come in.
The window seemed to ask the thief to come in, as it was easily entered.

2 The boat **dozed** in the midday sun.
A boat can't doze, but it appears quiet and peaceful, as if sleeping, on a sunny day.

3 The winter sun **wrapped a scarf** of cloud around its **neck**.
The sun seems to have clouds wrapped around it, like a scarf.

The following poem uses personification to create vivid imagery. It also uses many different features of descriptive writing. See how many you can spot!

The Trees

The trees are coming into leaf
Like something almost being said;
The recent buds relax and spread,
Their greenness is a kind of grief.

Is it that they are born again
And we grow old? No, they die too,
Their yearly trick of looking new
Is written down in rings of grain.

Yet still the unresting castles thresh
In fullgrown thickness every May.
Last year is dead, they seem to say,
Begin afresh, afresh, afresh.

Philip Larkin

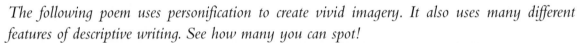

GRAIN
the pattern inside wood

THRESH
how a person separates grain from straw

The poet uses the word 'fullgrown' to describe the thickness of the leaf cover. This is a compound word, *a word made by joining two smaller words.*

OPENING ACT

1 At what time of year is the poem set? **EVIDENCE**
2 What does the poet describe the greenness of the trees as? **EVIDENCE**
3 By May, what state of growth are the trees in? **EVIDENCE**
4 What is the 'yearly trick' of the trees? **EVIDENCE**

SPOTLIGHT

5 What sense is appealed to most strongly in this poem? **EVIDENCE**
6 Find an example of personification in the poem. **OPINION** **REASON** **EVIDENCE**
7 Find another feature of descriptive writing in this poem. **OPINION** **REASON** **EVIDENCE**
8 Why do you think the poet uses repetition in the last line? **OPINION** **REASON**
9 What do you think the central message of this poem is? *Try to structure your answer into two paragraphs.* **OPINION** **REASON** **EVIDENCE**
10 What is your favourite time of year to experience the natural world? Explain why.

CENTRE STAGE

Play with Personification

1 Personify the following objects. The first step is to identify qualities of the object. Then think of similar qualities in people. The first one is done for you.
i) Rain: the rain whispered to me as I slept.   ii) River:
iii) Car: iv) Moon:
v) Mountain: vi) Tree:
2 While one person reads out their personified objects, let another person in the class try to act out the object doing the action.
3 Take one of your personified objects and illustrate it.

 IN YOUR OWN WORDS

PERSONIFICATION:

COMPOUND WORD:

Real Romance

The next poems are love poems. Many people associate poetry with romance and love, and one of the most popular purposes of poetry is to express love and affection.

Metaphorical Language

Metaphorical language is language that uses metaphors to explain or describe real objects or **abstract** things. We remember that when something is abstract, it cannot be seen, heard, tasted, smelled or touched.

Metaphorical language is often used to explain or describe abstract things, such as abilities, emotions, circumstances and qualities. Poets can use metaphorical language to develop a metaphor over many lines, stanzas or paragraphs.

Examples:

1 I was **walking on a cloud** after I got my exam results. The piece of paper was a set of **wings**, and I would use them to **soar** to university.

The student is happy with his results, not actually walking on a cloud. The metaphor is developed by describing the paper the exam results came on as a set of wings to fly to university on.

2 That boxer is a **raging bull, stampeding** through his **field** of opponents. He's too fast and powerful. You'd need to **put a ring through his nose and tie him up** if you wanted a hope of beating him.

The boxer is stronger and more ferocious than his opponents. This strength is emphasised by describing him as a bull and using the imagery of bulls to describe his opponents.

The following poem develops the metaphor created in the title throughout the poem using metaphorical language.

Heart Sea

The heart
is the largest
of the seas.

Mother of all:
it feeds
our feelings.

It has enough salt
for all our tears.

Enough salt to throw
on every open wound.

When the heart splits
all the waters of the great sea
return upriver.

Its bitter and salty waters
rise up to the throat,
even to the mouth.

They fill with tears
the eyes

of the youngest,
the most ancient.

Carlos Reyes

Sentiment is emotion and feeling, particularly stronger emotions like sorrow and love. When a poem contains a lot of emotion and feeling, we say it is sentimental.

🎭 OPENING ACT

1 What is the 'Mother of all' according to the poet?
2 How much salt does the heart have? `EVIDENCE`
3 What happens when the 'heart splits'? `EVIDENCE`
4 Whose eyes fill with tears? `EVIDENCE`

SPOTLIGHT

5 Do you think the sea is a good metaphor for the heart? Why? `OPINION` `REASON` `EVIDENCE`

6 Make a list of the ways in which you think the heart is like the sea.

7 Do you think old people can fall in love in the same way that young people can? `OPINION` `REASON`

8 How can the heart 'feed our feelings'? `OPINION` `REASON`

9 What else is the heart like? Think of another metaphor and explain it.

 ## CENTRE STAGE

A Heart-shaped Poem

Write your own poem using the metaphor you answered with in question 9.
Start by saying:
The heart is …
If you can, develop the metaphor.

IN YOUR OWN WORDS

METAPHORICAL LANGUAGE:

SENTIMENT:

UPBRINGING
EARLY ADULTHOOD
EDUCATION
RELATIONSHIPS
PROFESSION

Personal context:
- **upbringing;**
- **family life;**
- **early adulthood;**
- **maturity;**
- **relationships;**
- **health;**
- **profession.**

Context

Context is the **situation** and **circumstances** that form the **background** to a text. Knowing details about the life of a writer and the society they lived in can help to explain why the poem or story was written. It can help us to appreciate the text and to understand the meaning of it.

Social context:

- **society;**
- **education;**
- **social class;**
- **political system;**
- **opportunity;**
- **customs;**
- **traditions.**

The following poem was written by an American poet and short story writer, Raymond Carver. He wrote this poem while he was ill with cancer. The poem was written for his wife, the poet Tess Gallagher, and was published in the last book he wrote before he died, called A New Path to the Waterfall. *Does this personal context change how you feel about this poem?*

Hummingbird

Suppose I say summer,
write the word "hummingbird,"
put it in an envelope,
take it down the hill
to the box. When you open
my letter you will recall
those days and how much,
just how much, I love you.

Raymond Carver

When a text arouses emotions in the reader, such as sadness or pity, we say it is **poignant**.

Now read the following note about hummingbirds and then reread the poem.

Note: *what is a hummingbird?* Hummingbirds are small birds native to North, Central and South America. The family includes the world's smallest bird, the bee hummingbird. Hummingbirds can hover, fly sideways and can even fly backwards. This allows them to feed off the nectar in flowering plants, which they move about with lightning speed.

They are fast fliers for their size and migrate incredibly long distances every year. They spend the winter in warm climates, such as Mexico, and in spring migrate as far north as Canada and the north-west of America to stay for the summer months. Though small, these beautiful and unique birds are admired for their fierce toughness and determination.

OPENING ACT

1 What does the poet do in the first line of the poem?

2 What reason does the poet give for his actions? `EVIDENCE`

3 What two things will the poet's wife remember when she opens the letter?

SPOTLIGHT

4 What does the word 'summer' symbolise for you? `OPINION` `REASON`

5 From reading about the hummingbird, what qualities of it do you admire? `OPINION` `REASON`

6 Why do you think the poet writes the word 'hummingbird' when thinking of his wife? `OPINION` `REASON` `EVIDENCE`

7 Do you find this poem poignant? `OPINION` `REASON` `EVIDENCE`

8 How does knowing the context of the poem change your understanding of it? *Try to structure your answer into two paragraphs.* `OPINION` `REASON`

9 Do you think this poem captures the feeling of love? `OPINION` `REASON` `EVIDENCE`

CENTRE STAGE

Context Uncovered

Choose a poem from this textbook by yourself, or your teacher can nominate one poem for all the class to use. You will have to use the Internet or a library to help with research.

• Find out some biographical details about the poet.

• Find out why the poet wrote poetry or that particular poem.

• Find out if there is a story behind the poem.

• Learn about the place or the time in which the poem is set.

Write a short context to help others to understand the poem and share it with the class.

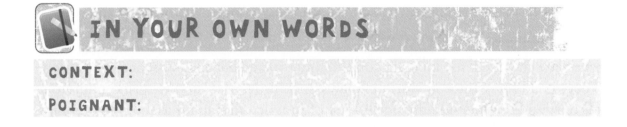

IN YOUR OWN WORDS

CONTEXT:

POIGNANT:

Assonance

Assonance is the **repetition** of similar **vowel sounds** in a sentence (**a, e, i, o** and **u**). It gives a soft, rhyming sound to a sentence. Here is a line taken from the poem below:

A**n**d n**o**dding by the fire, t**a**ke d**o**wn this b**oo**k,
A**n**d sl**o**wly r**ea**d, **a**nd dr**ea**m **o**f the s**o**ft l**oo**k

In these two lines there is a repetition and emphasis on **o** sounds, blending with **a** sounds and **e** sounds.

William Butler Yeats is a Nobel Prize-winning Irish poet. He was one of the last century's most important and popular poets. His poems are known for their lyrical quality and vivid imagery.

When You Are Old

When you are old and grey and full of sleep,
And nodding by the fire, take down this book,
And slowly read, and dream of the soft look
Your eyes had once, and of their shadows deep;

How many loved your moments of glad grace,
And loved your beauty with love false or true,
But one man loved the pilgrim soul in you,
And loved the sorrows of your changing face;

And bending down beside the glowing bars,
Murmur, a little sadly, how Love fled
And paced upon the mountains overhead
And hid his face amid a crowd of stars.

William Butler Yeats

PILGRIM
a person who makes a journey, often for spiritual reasons

MURMUR
whisper

Note: this poem contains **personification**. We know that personification describes a lifeless object or a feeling as having human qualities.

These can be **physical qualities**:
*The tree's long **arms** were stretched out over the river.*

These can be **action qualities**:
*Anger was **staring** me in the face.*

These can be **emotional qualities**:
*My car was **sad** because I had not used it for a month.*

OPENING ACT

1 When does the poet want the poem to be read? **EVIDENCE**
2 What do 'many' love in the woman? **EVIDENCE**
3 What does the poet love in the woman? **EVIDENCE**
4 What does 'love' do in the last stanza? **EVIDENCE**

SPOTLIGHT

5 Read the poem aloud. What do you think of the rhythm of the poem? **OPINION**
6 What do you think are the mood and atmosphere of this poem? **OPINION** **REASON** **EVIDENCE**
7 Find an example of personification in this poem. Do you think it is effective? **OPINION** **REASON** **EVIDENCE**
8 Do you think the poet had a personal experience that led him to write this poem? **OPINION** **REASON**
9 'The poem 'When You Are Old' is too sentimental.'
Would you agree or disagree with this statement? Try to structure your answer into two paragraphs. **OPINION** **REASON** **EVIDENCE**

CENTRE STAGE

When You Are Old

Write out ten things you hope to be or to have achieved by the time you are old.

WHEN I AM OLD ...
1. I will have walked the Great Wall of China.
2. I will have written the story of my life.
3.

Try to hold onto the list for when you are older!

IN YOUR OWN WORDS

ASSONANCE:

Puzzling Poems

The following three poems are all about writing poetry. Poems about poems can be the most puzzling part of poetry, provoking us to ponder and be perplexed!

Shape

How a poem **looks** on the page can be part of the poem's **meaning**. Aspects of how a poem looks include **colour, shape** and **position** of the words.

For exam
      ple the poe
           m could
               be about
                  a set o
                     f steps.

In the following poem the poet reflects on writing poetry and his success as a poet.

The Poeteer

I
AM
AT MY
DESK MY
PEN POISED
ANTICIPATING
A TREK THROUGH
POETIC FOOTHILLS IN
SEARCH OF LOFTY PEAKS

I
FIND
INSTEAD
MOUNTAINS
OF UNFINISHED
POEMS, MY HALF-
FORGOTTEN DREAMS

I
PUT
AWAY
MY PEN
FOREVER

Patrick Winstanley

POISED
waiting to act

FOOTHILLS
small hills below mountains

LOFTY
high-up

Concrete poetry is the name for poems that take some of their meaning from their shape.

OPENING ACT

1 Where is the poem set? `EVIDENCE`
2 What does the poet sit down to do? `EVIDENCE`
3 What does he find on his desk? `EVIDENCE`
4 What does the poet say he ends up doing? `EVIDENCE`

SPOTLIGHT

5 Why do you think the stanzas of this poem are shaped the way they are?
`OPINION` `REASON` `EVIDENCE`

6 What do you think of shaping poetry in this way? `OPINION` `REASON`

7 How does the poet use metaphorical language to describe writing poetry? *Try to structure your answer into two paragraphs.* `OPINION` `REASON` `EVIDENCE`

8 How does the poet's confidence change over the course of the three stanzas?
`OPINION` `REASON` `EVIDENCE`

9 Do you think the poet really puts away his pen forever? `OPINION` `REASON`

10 Which of the following do you think best describes the tone of this poem:
   i) sad;
   ii) humorous;
   iii) regretful?
   `OPINION` `REASON` `EVIDENCE`

CENTRE STAGE

Concrete Schoolyard

Write your own concrete poem about school. Remember, the shape has to echo or represent some aspect of the poem.

Here are some possible examples:
• a poem about maths in the shape of sums on a page;
• a poem about how you like reading in the shape of wings;
• a poem about school taking away your freedom in the shape of a cage.

IN YOUR OWN WORDS

CONCRETE POETRY:

Dialogue

Poems can contain **different voices** as well as characters. Sometimes these voices can talk to each other in a **dialogue**, similar to a story or a drama. We might not even be told who is speaking, but still hear their voices.

Here is a short poem!

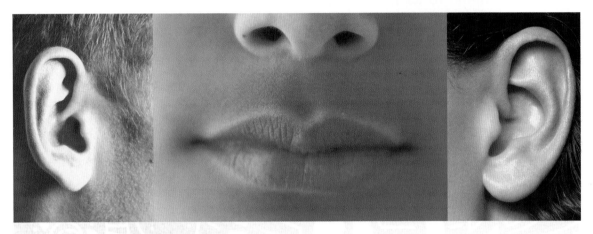

An Amazing Dialogue

'But this poem is not like that poem!'
'No, you are right, it's not.'

James Fenton

SPOTLIGHT

1 What are the voices in the poem talking about? `OPINION` `REASON`

2 Why do you think the voice says 'this poem is not like that poem'? `OPINION` `REASON` `EVIDENCE`

3 Do you think this is a proper poem? `OPINION` `REASON`

4 What do you think the tone of this poem is? `OPINION` `REASON`

5 Does this poem amuse you? `OPINION` `REASON`

CENTRE STAGE

Dialogue Devils

This might take some practice if you aren't used to improvising!

i)   Two students take the part of each voice in the dialogue above. They can decide on being two different characters, for example a teacher and a student, or the

POETRY

2

poet who wrote it and his publisher. The two actors must then read and act out the above two lines and then keep going with their dialogue by improvising the next lines. To improvise is to make it up as you go along. You can decide to have an argument or a serious discussion or a friendly chat.

ii) After a few lines your teacher says 'stop' and the students must freeze where they are. The actors remember their last lines. The next student must then move in to take the first actor's place. They take the same physical poses and repeat the last line of dialogue and keep improvising from there.

iii) Don't be afraid to let the dialogue or characters change. Remember, conflict makes for better drama!

Celebration

Poetry can also be used as a way of celebrating, just like music, dance or having a party!

Don't forget to do the Centre Stage exercise below! How you read this poem is very important.

Poetry Jump-Up

Tell me if ah seeing right
Take a look down de street

Words dancin   DANCIN
words dancin
till dey sweat
words like fishes
jumpin out a net
words wild and free
joinin de poetry revelry   SWEAT
words back to back
words belly to belly

Come on everybody
come and join de poetry band
dis is poetry carnival   FISHES
dis is poetry bacchanal
when inspiration call

REVELRY
partying

BACCHANAL
an outrageous
celebration

POETRY

2

take yu pen in yu hand
if you dont have a pen
take yu pencil in yu hand
if you dont have a pencil
what the hell
so long de feeling start to swell
just shout de poem out

Words jumpin off de page
tell me if Ah seeing right
words like birds
jumpin out a cage
take a look down de street
words shakin dey waist
words shakin dey bum
words wit black skin
words wit white skin
words wit brown skin
words wit no skin at all
words huggin up words
an saying I want to be a poem today
rhyme or no rhyme
I is a poem today
I mean to have a good time

Words feelin hot hot hot
big words feelin hot hot hot
lil words feelin hot hot hot
even sad words cant help
tappin dey toe
to de riddum of de poetry band

Dis is poetry carnival
dis is poetry bacchanal
so come on everybody
join de celebration
all yu need is plenty perspiration
an a little inspiration
plenty perspiration
an a little inspiration

John Agard

JUMPIN

REVELRY

WILD

BELLY

SHAKIN

OPENING ACT

1 Why does the poet ask the reader to tell him if he is 'seeing right'? **EVIDENCE**
2 Find a simile used in this poem. **EVIDENCE**
3 Identify one way in which repetition is used in this poem. **EVIDENCE**
4 Does the poet exclude any words from the celebration?
5 What do people need the most to join the celebration? **EVIDENCE**

 # SPOTLIGHT

6 Identify one way in which the poet personifies words in this poem. **OPINION** **REASON** **EVIDENCE**
7 What is your favourite line in this poem? **OPINION** **REASON** **EVIDENCE**
8 Do you think the dialect used in this poem is appropriate to the mood of the poem? **OPINION** **REASON** **EVIDENCE**
9 How does this poem use descriptions to create a lively and joyful mood? *Try to structure your answer into two paragraphs.* **OPINION** **REASON** **EVIDENCE**
10 Do you think a carnival is a good description for this poem? *Try to structure your answer into two paragraphs.* **OPINION** **REASON** **EVIDENCE**

CENTRE STAGE

Poetry Jump-Up!

You should try different ways of reading this poem. Here are a few suggestions, but if you can think of any other ways of reading it, share them! Some of these suggestions are complicated, so it may take a little bit of preparation.

i) Each person has one line to read. The first student reads the first line and then the next student picks up. Try reading it at least twice so that students can decide on the best way to say their line. Change volume, emphasis and tone to try out different readings.

ii) This is a fun way to read the poem in pairs. One person reads the first line softly and surprised, as if it's a question. Their partner reads the second line joyfully and loudly in answer. Then the first person reads the third line surprised, and then their partner reads the fourth line joyfully in response. Continue alternating to the end of the poem.

iii) Divide the class into two groups where they are sitting. In the first group the students have to take it in turns to read their lines individually. Each person will read at least one line. The first group will read the first line, the third line, the fifth line and so on.

The second group must read their line all together as a response to the first group. They can put as much celebration into their line as they wish!

Now when the poem is being read every first line will be read individually, and every second line will be read by a large group.

iv) You will need space to do this. If you have room, you can try dancing or acting out the poem. Divide the class into five groups. The first group are the narrators who read the poem, and they also have to act out the first stanza of two lines. The second group have to stand together and act out the second stanza. The third group have to act out the third stanza, the fourth group have to act out the fourth stanza and the fifth group have to act out the fifth stanza. While the narrators are reading out the sixth stanza, everyone has to act out their own poetry celebration. If possible, it might help to play some vibrant Caribbean or African music in the background.

v) This version might be noisy, so you should check beforehand to see if you are allowed to make some noise. If anyone has any musical instruments that they can play, they should bring them in, particularly percussion instruments or shakers. Can the musicians think of a way of matching up the words with music? You could try playing different instruments at different parts of the poem.

Can you join the acting, reading and instruments together to form one big poetry celebration?

curtain call

In this unit we've learned a lot of important terms and vocabulary that we can use to describe, understand and explore poetry. Below are lists of the most common terms to help with your poetry revision.

We've learned about important features of **descriptive writing** used in poetry:
- **expressive words and action verbs;**
- **imagery;**
- **similes;**
- **metaphors;**
- **metaphorical language;**
- **symbolism;**
- **appealing to the senses;**
- **personification.**

We've learned about different features that create and affect the meaning of the poem:

- **themes;**
- **mood and atmosphere;**
- **tone;**
- **narrative;**
- **character;**
- **dialogue;**
- **message;**
- **context;**
- **shape.**

We've learned about different features that create the sound of the poem:

- **rhyming patterns;**
- **dialect and expression;**
- **alliteration;**
- **onomatopoeia;**
- **consonance;**
- **assonance.**

We're learned about different types of poem:

- **rhyming poems;**
- **free verse;**
- **concrete poems.**

You can now read the following poems and practise answering questions.

Lucky Mrs Higgins

When our mother
won a fridge
with Becker's Tea,
she got her photograph
in the Sentinel
shaking her hands
with the man from head office.

The fridge was also
in the frame.
She wore a big wide hat
she kept on top of the wardrobe
for fridge winning days.

POETRY

②

It went nice
with the crimplene two piece
she got for Mary Theresa's wedding.

In the photo
with the fridge
and the man from head office
she didn't look anything like herself.

Rita Ann Higgins

 ## OPENING ACT

1 What happened when the poet's mother won a fridge? `EVIDENCE`
2 What did the poet's mother wear for the photograph? `EVIDENCE`
3 How did the poet feel her mother looked in the photograph? `EVIDENCE`

 ## SPOTLIGHT

4 Do you think the poet's mother was proud to win the fridge? `OPINION` `REASON` `EVIDENCE`
5 Why do you think the poet's mother put so much effort into dressing up for the photograph? `OPINION` `REASON` `EVIDENCE`
6 Why do you think the poet's mother didn't look like herself in the photograph? `OPINION` `REASON` `EVIDENCE`
7 What do you think of the use of detail in this poem? *Try to structure your answer into two paragraphs.* `OPINION` `REASON`
8 How would you describe the tone of this poem? `OPINION` `REASON` `EVIDENCE`
9 Name another poem that you have read that describes a character. Name the poem and the poet, and explain why and how the poet created the character. *Try to structure your answer into at least two paragraphs.*

Poem

Click, clack, click, clack
That's all I hear every day
I am so tired of all this
Typing
I must get away
I must get away
Is this all to life
Nothing more
Nothing real
What a bore
Click, clack, click, clack
Looking up
Through the dirty panes
I see a sunset so beautiful
It takes my breath away
I am lost in reverie
Smiling, my tired eyes
Seem refreshed and
Suddenly life takes on
A new look
Click, clack, click, clack

Anne Wallace

POETRY

2

OPENING ACT

1 Can you find an example of onomatopoeia in this poem? `EVIDENCE`
2 What senses does this poem appeal to? `EVIDENCE`
3 Can you find an example of repetition in the poem? `EVIDENCE`
4 At the start of the poem, how does the writer feel about writing poetry? `EVIDENCE`
5 How does the poet react to the sunset? `EVIDENCE`
6 By the end of the poem, how has the writer's mood changed? `EVIDENCE`

SPOTLIGHT

7 How does the poet capture the sound of the typewriter? `OPINION` `REASON` `EVIDENCE`
8 How does the poet emphasise how tired she is? *Try to structure your answer into two paragraphs.* `OPINION` `REASON` `EVIDENCE`
9 Do you think writing poetry would be a difficult profession? *Refer to the poem in your answer and try to structure your answer into two paragraphs.* `OPINION` `REASON` `EVIDENCE`
10 'Poetry can help us to appreciate ordinary but beautiful moments in our lives.' *Based on your reading of this poem or another poem on your course, would you agree or disagree with this statement? Try to structure your answer into two paragraphs.* `OPINION` `REASON` `EVIDENCE`
11 Name another poem that you have read where a person faced a challenge. *Name the poem and poet, and describe the challenge the person faced and explain the outcome of that challenge. Try to structure your answer into at least two paragraphs.*

Note: a common theme in poetry is transience. It is the quality of life being momentary and lasting only for a short time. Transience reminds us of how quickly moments pass and of how we are constantly changing.

Example:
The yellow leaves on the trees in October remind me of the transience of life.
This next poem contains transient images of nature.

Water-burn

DIVOT

a chunk of earth

We should have been galloping on horses, their hoofprints
Splashes of light, divots kicked out of the darkness,
Or hauling up lobster pots in a wake of sparks. Where
Were the otters and seals? Were the dolphins on fire?
Yes, we should have been doing more with our lives.

Michael Longley

 ## OPENING ACT

1 What does the poet say we should have been doing? `EVIDENCE`
2 Make a list of the verbs used in this poem. `EVIDENCE`
3 How long do 'sparks' last?
4 In what line is the central message of this poem revealed? `EVIDENCE`

 ## SPOTLIGHT

5 How quickly do things happen in this poem? `OPINION` `REASON` `EVIDENCE`
6 What do the verbs used in this poem suggest to you? `OPINION` `REASON` `EVIDENCE`
7 What is your favourite image from this poem? `OPINION` `REASON` `EVIDENCE`
8 If you had to give this poem another title, what would it be? `OPINION` `REASON` `EVIDENCE`
9 Do you think this poem captures the transience of life? *Try to structure your answer into two paragraphs.* `OPINION` `REASON` `EVIDENCE`
10 Name another poem that you have studied that celebrates nature. Name the poem and poet and explain how and why the poet celebrated nature. Try to structure your answer into at least two paragraphs.

 ## IN YOUR OWN WORDS

TRANSIENCE:

 ## CENTRE STAGE

Revision Template

It is important that you know a number of poems in detail for your Junior Certificate, as you will have to answer questions on them.

You can write out notes to help you remember the important details and features of the poem. You can do this for a number of poems and build up a bank of study notes.

Here is a list of possible headings for writing out notes for the poem. You might want to discuss other headings in class. Remember to provide quotations where needed.

Title of poem and poet:
Context:
Summary of poem:
Themes:
Important features and techniques:
How the poem relates to you:
Favourite line and why:
Similar poems:

Grammar Station

Adjectives

Adjectives are describing words. They are used to give readers more information about nouns.
Adjectives describe the qualities of nouns.

Examples:
1 That was some excellent advice.
2 Elvis was an angelic singer.
3 The clouds rose above the golden sunset.
4 The furious mob of supporters chased the referee.

Degree of Adjectives

Adjectives can also describe things in comparison to other things. This is called the degree of adjectives. The degrees are positive, comparative and superlative.

The positive is the first form of adjective for a thing, e.g. rich.
The man is **rich**.
The comparative is comparing two similar things to each other, e.g. rich**er**.
That man is **richer** than the other man.
The superlative is stating the thing that is the most extreme, e.g. rich**est**.
That man is the **richest**.

Positive	Comparative	Superlative
Rich	Richer	Richest
Great	Greater	Greatest
Lovely	Lovelier	Loveliest
Greedy	Greedier	Greediest
Sad	Sadder	Saddest
Happy	Happier	Happiest
Fussy	Fussier	Fussiest

How to form the degree of adjectives.

1 For most adjectives we change the ending:

Add **-er** for comparative.

Add **-est** for superlative.

Great/Great**er**/Great**est**.

2 If the adjective ends in **y**, then we drop the **y** and add **-ier** for comparative and **-iest** for superlative.

Happy/Happ**ier**/Happ**iest**.

3 For longer adjectives we add **more** for comparative and add **most** for superlative.

Determined/**More** determined/**Most** determined.

Suspicious/**More** suspicious/**Most** suspicious.

Hilarious/**More** hilarious/**Most** hilarious.

4 There are also some irregular adjectives that must be learned:

Positive	Comparative	Superlative
Good	Better	Best
Bad	Worse	Worst
Little	Less	Least
Many	More	Most
Far	Further	Furthest

OPENING ACT

1 Read the following sets of adjectives and think of a noun that you could describe using all three. The first one is done for you.

   i) Wet, cold, blue: the sea.

   ii) Grey, wet, smelly:

  iii) Blue, stinky, delicious:

  iv) Red, juicy, cold:

   v) Angry, old, intelligent:

POETRY

2

vi) Green, fresh, wet:

vii) Spicy, brown, cheap:

viii) Fluffy, stupid, white:

ix) Helpful, intelligent, hardworking:

x) Clumsy, colourful, funny:

 SPOTLIGHT

Adjective Questionnaire

Copy the following into your copybook and fill in the answers using adjectives in their positive, comparative or superlative. Try not to use the same adjective twice.

i) I think golf is a _____ sport.

ii) Dublin is the _____ city in Ireland.

iii) Dogs are the _____ animal in the animal kingdom.

iv) English homework is _____ than other subjects.

v) Swimming in the sea is _____.

vi) I am _____ than everyone else in my family.

vii) Soccer is the _____ sport in the world.

viii) Frogs legs and snails are the _____ food I've ever heard of.

ix) Irish boys are the _____boys in Europe.

x) _____ weather makes me happy.

CENTRE STAGE

Alphabet Adjective

This is a group activity. Look at the nouns listed below and think of adjectives to match. *The matching adjectives might get a little unusual!*

One student starts with an adjective beginning with *a*, then the class moves through the alphabet, with a letter for each student.

If you can't think of an adjective for your letter, then you have to skip and the next person has a go at that letter. When the class gets stuck, you have to move to a new noun.

i) Fireman.

ii) Ballerina.

iii) Goat.

iv) House.

v) Tree.

CREATIVE WRITING

I AM DR NADINE PLUME, PROFESSOR OF CREATIVE WRITING. I am here to share some tips to help you improve your creative writing skills. In Unit 1 and Unit 2 you learned about different features of writing and about the techniques writers and poets use. In this unit you will practise using these features and techniques yourself. You will practise using:

> DESCRIPTIVE WRITING;
> CHARACTER;
> PLANNING;
> PLOT;
> MODELLING.

- Descriptive writing
- Character
- Planning
- Plot
- Modelling

You can dip in and out of this unit as your essay-writing skills grow. You will also revise and learn more about **verbs** and **adverbs** at the **Grammar Station** and how you can use them to improve your writing skills.

Descriptive writing

When you are writing, you need to help your reader to imagine the world you are describing. You also need to be able to create character and atmosphere through the use of description. In this section we will focus on how important descriptive techniques work and we will learn how to use them in our own writing.

We will focus on:
- similes;
- metaphors;
- personification;
- appealing to the senses.

Similes

We know that similes are comparisons using **like**, **as** or **than**.

1 Here is a simile for stormy weather at sea:
The waves charged forward like a herd of stampeding buffaloes.

2 Here is a simile for a scary forest:
The trees in the forest stood as straight and quiet as gravestones in a cemetery.

3 Here is a simile for a character:
My friend was giddier than a monkey with fleas.

🄾 SPOTLIGHT

1 Think of your own simile for each of the following.
  i) A beach on a sunny day.
  ii) A horse galloping in a field.
  iii) A crowd at a sporting event.
  iv) The appearance of a bossy major in the army.
  v) The smell of a sandwich that has been left under a car seat for a week.
  vi) Water falling over a weir.

Similes highlight the particular qualities of an object. For example, if you said **the bus driver was like a tired bear with a toothache**, the particular qualities highlighted would be **anger** and **lack of patience**!

To write your own simile about an object or person, think about the **qualities** that stand out most.

1 A vicious dog
Qualities: sharp teeth, danger, bristling fur, low growls.
Possible simile: **the angry dog's teeth glistened like a row of razor-sharp icicles**.

2 A racehorse beginning a race
Qualities: fast and powerful, focused.
Possible simile: **the horse left the starting line like an arrow released from a bow**.

🔦 SPOTLIGHT

1 Make a separate list of the qualities that stand out for these examples. The first one is done for you
  i) A sinking ship. Qualities: frightening, panicked people, stormy water.
  ii) A rose bush. Qualities:
  iii) A deep cave. Qualities:
  iv) An abandoned village. Qualities:
  v) A lighthouse. Qualities:

2 Write a simile for each example above, focusing on one of the qualities you identified.
Example: *the sailors were* *like rats leaping from the sinking ship.*

Metaphors

We remember metaphors from the poetry unit. A **metaphor** is a way of describing something by saying it *is* another thing, without using **like, as** or **than**.

1 Here is a metaphor for life:
Life is a river that we all have to follow. You can swim against the current if you want, but it's sometimes just as good to go with the flow.

2 Here is a metaphor for a man eating rudely:
The man was a pig at the dinner table. He stuck his snout in the soup and slurped it up. Then, with a squeal of delight, he turned his greedy little eyes to the main course.

SPOTLIGHT

1 Think of a metaphor to explain one or more of the following examples. The first one is done for you.

   i) *Anger:* my temper is an angry bull. I have to keep it in a small field and watch it doesn't get free. If it ever does, please don't try to tame it, just run for cover.

   ii) *Love:*

   iii) *Stormy weather:*

   iv) *Freedom:*

   v) *A book:*

2 Now, using one or more of the following examples, try to reverse the exercise and think of something that these metaphors could explain or stand for. The first one is done for you.

   i) *A house:* a house could be a metaphor for your mind because you put different experiences and memories together in different rooms. You lock special moments away and you let old memories gather dust in the attic.

   ii) *A monkey:*

   iii) *A prison cell:*

   iv) *A key:*

   v) *A stormy sea:*

Personification

We remember that **personification** is when you give a lifeless object or an abstract thing the **qualities** of a **human**.

1 Here is a personification of the sun:

The sun was a cruel eye watching us make our way across the desert sands. It didn't blink, and we dared not hold its gaze.

2 Here is a personification of hope:

Hope came to visit me during my darkest hour in the prison cell. Hope whispered to me, *it will be okay.* I thought of sunny days by the river with family and friends and knew that someday I would experience those days again.

SPOTLIGHT

Personify one or more of the following.
  i) A crashing wave.
  ii) A tree in a scary forest.
  iii) A gentle wind blowing in the garden.
  iv) Love.

Appealing to the Senses

Vivid writing **appeals** to as many of the **senses** as possible. It can also help to create **mood** and **atmosphere**.

Read the following two descriptions.

1 I got out of bed. It was a cold winter morning.

2 I got out of bed. The cold breeze bit into my cheeks when I flung open the window. The gardens and streets were coated with a blanket of dazzling snow. The neighbourhood was alive with the shouts of children, playing in their winter woolies. Suddenly the sweet aroma of hot pancakes reached my nose. My mouth was already watering as I ran down the stairs to the warmth of the kitchen. It was the perfect start to the Christmas holidays.

It is easier to picture the world of the text from the imagery used in example 2. The mood and atmosphere of the text is festive, warm, bright and cheerful. Can you highlight where each sense is appealed to?

SPOTLIGHT

1 Describe any three of the following, using five sentences to describe each one you choose. You must appeal to at least three of the senses for each description and use one simile in each.

CREATIVE WRITING

3

i) Describe an interesting place you have been.

ii) Describe the place you hate the most.

iii) Describe a spooky place you have been.

iv) Describe what you think walking out of a subway in New York would be like.

v) Describe what you think arriving off a boat on the Aran Islands would be like.

vi) Describe what you think walking down Grafton Street in Dublin in 1950 would have been like.

2 Look at the images below and answer the questions that follow.

i) For each of the three photographs, with the exception of the sense of sight, say which sense you think is appealed to most in each image and explain why you think that.

ii) Take one of the images and imagine you are a character connected with the image. Describe what is happening in a first person narrative, using a sentence for each of the five senses.

iii) What mood and atmosphere did you create in your description?

🎩 CENTRE STAGE

Write a diary entry for one of the following characters.

1 A celebrity going to an awards ceremony.

2 A lifeboat crew member.

3 A marathon runner.

4 An actor or actress on the opening night of a play.

5 An explorer attempting to scale a mountain.

In your diary, try to describe the world of the character using:

• **similes;**

• **metaphors;**

• **personification;**

• **appealing to the senses.**

Also try to use a wide range of expressive vocabulary. Remember to create a particular mood and atmosphere!

character

Finding the right character to tell your story is as important as figuring out the action and plot that happens in the story. Every character looks at the world differently, so your story will be different depending on who your character is. Characters also react differently to situations depending on their personality.

In this section you will learn four tips that will help you to create your own character.

1 Describe the character's appearance. You can also give a hint as to what the character is like. This is a good place to use a simile or a metaphor.

John was always a bit different from the other pupils. He was like a volcano. His anger was explosive, and when not actually active, you knew it was at best dormant. You never knew when he might erupt.

2 Try a character with **a different point of view** from your own.

During World War II there was an American bomber pilot who was stationed in England. He was different from the English pilots, always smiling and less serious. He met and made friends with an English girl, the daughter of a local farmer, who delivered milk to the base. Over a few months, as the friendship grew, he fell in love with her.

3 Think of an **interesting person** you know and change a few things about them.
The old man who owned the shop was a mystery to me. He always wore blue overalls. They were almost like a uniform to him. He was jolly and chatted with everyone, even the young people. He had a wide moustache that sat like an upturned banana on his top lip.

4 Remember to **be consistent**. If your character is a calm person and something unexpected happens, the character will react calmly. If they are an angry person, they will lose their temper! A character shouldn't change without good reason.
Ann was the most sensitive person I knew. She was like one of those machines they use to detect earthquakes. Seismographs? That's it. She was always very in tune with her emotions. And she had a lot of them, too. In fact, she was like a scientific table of emotional elements.

We fell out when I fell in love with a boy she had always fancied, Mark Kennedy. She was very upset, it goes without saying. She hasn't talked to me since.

A common example of an inconsistency is when a character does something unrealistic, such as an achievement that we don't believe the character could possibly do.

 ## SPOTLIGHT

1 Identify a character in a poem, story, drama or film that interested you. Explain why the character was interesting.
2 Describe the character chosen in question 1 above using descriptive writing. Write in the third person.
3 Of the four characters used in the examples 1 to 4 above, which character interests you the most? `OPINION` `REASON` `EVIDENCE`

4 i) Think of a fictional character with a completely different point of view from your own. The character might be the opposite gender to you, have different interests or be a different age.

   ii) Write two paragraphs to describe that character. In the first paragraph describe the character's appearance, and in the second paragraph describe the character engaged in their favourite pastime.

 CENTRE STAGE

Third Person Turn Around

Here are the five characters that you had to choose from in the last section, when you wrote a diary entry.

1 A celebrity going to an awards ceremony.

2 A lifeboat crew member.

3 A marathon runner.

4 An actor or actress on the opening night of a play.

5 An explorer attempting to scale a mountain.

Choosing the same character, write a short story in the third person describing a day in the life of that character. Your story will be different from the diary because:

• it will be in the third person;

• you can describe how your character looks;

• you can describe how your character acts;

• you can show what others think of your character.

Remember to use descriptive writing!

Planning

You have learned the writing techniques used to describe setting and character and to create mood and atmosphere. Now we need to work on planning your story so that it all fits together as a story should, with a clear beginning, middle and end. We will also practise combining descriptive writing techniques with planning so that you can write your own story.

We will learn about:
- **mind-maps;**
- **point of view;**
- **using descriptive writing;**
- **paragraphs.**

Mind-maps

Before you begin a full essay, you need a plan. A useful way to begin is to start with a **mind-map**. This is a diagram that explores ideas for your story.

If you get stuck, you need to ask yourself one of the six questions:
- **Who?**
- **What?**
- **When?**
- **Where?**
- **Why?**
- **How?**

Write the name of the essay at the centre of your diagram. Then put three lines out for each heading:
- **the beginning;**
- **the middle;**
- **the end.**

Then link ideas to your headings. Look at the example below. We are going to develop this example throughout this section:

BEGINNING ———— THE LAND ———— END
BEYOND
THE SEA

BEGINNING
1. Setting by the ocean—calm sea, warm weather, leaving family to explore.
2. Journey—open sea, background and history of voyage, storm brewing.

MIDDLE
1. Lost in storm—struggle for survival, lose sail, tension builds.
2. Survive storm—make it to new land, describe land.

END
1. Meet strangers—strange language, clothes and customs.
2. Strangers are hostile—they have weapons, there is tension, makes peace with strangers, returns home.

SPOTLIGHT

Mind Your Map

Write your own mind-map for **The Land Beyond the Sea.**

Point of view

Now we have a map for an essay. We should already have a good idea of who is going to tell the story, but it is time to think about it in more detail. Can we find a different or unusual point of view?

Imagine the story **The Land Beyond the Sea** using one of these characters as a **first person narrator**:

- **an Irish monk;**
- **a Spanish explorer;**
- **a Native American;**
- **a person from a lost tribe;**
- **a Viking.**

We would get a very different story from each perspective.

SPOTLIGHT

1 From the above list, choose the narrator you would most like to use to tell the story.
2 Why did you choose your narrator?

Using Descriptive Writing

We have already learned about descriptive writing. When writing the story **The Land Beyond the Sea**, we will concentrate on descriptions for:

- **the setting;**
- **the storm;**
- **the new world;**
- **the strangers.**

SPOTLIGHT

1 Write out a simile you could use for each. Think about the mood and atmosphere you want to create.
2 Write out a list or word bank of adjectives and verbs to suggest the drama of a storm.

Paragraphs

Now we will learn how to write out a simple column plan for each paragraph. A column plan is also useful for planning diaries, letters and exam questions. There is no set rule about how many paragraphs you should use, but you should try to achieve balance.

Five Keys to Balance

1 **Introduce characters and setting at the beginning.**
2 **Develop the plot and action in the middle.**
3 **Resolve the plot at the end.**
4 **Equal time spent on beginning, middle and end.**
5 **Try to use paragraphs of similar length.**

Note: begin a new paragraph every time your story changes in a significant way. The change could be a change in action, setting, weather or time of day. You mark the end of a paragraph by leaving the rest of the line blank when you finish your sentence. You mark your new paragraph by indenting, or stepping in, your sentence.

SPOTLIGHT

1 Using the template below, write out a detailed plan for each paragraph of the story. The first column is done for you. You can continue from there or start again with your own plan.

The Land Beyond the Sea

1st Paragraph	2nd Paragraph	3rd Paragraph	4th Paragraph	5th Paragraph	6th Paragraph
Calm weather. By pier. Boat is ready. Say goodbye to family, friends. Voyage to new world.					

2 Write out one thing that a character could **see, hear, taste, smell** and **touch** in the story *The Land Beyond the Sea*.

2 Write out two examples of personification that you could use in *The Land Beyond the Sea*.

CENTRE STAGE

Put It Together

Write an essay using the title *The Land Beyond the Sea*.
Remember:
• use descriptive writing;
• use your plan;
• use a beginning, a middle and an end.

Or

1 Follow these steps to write a different essay. Draw your own mind-map for a story using one of these titles:
• Through the Desert;
• A Summer Triumph;
• Animal Kingdom;
• The City of Dreams;
• An Unexpected Discovery.

2 Write out a list of three narrators who could tell your story and choose one of them.

3 Write a column plan for your story.

4 Write your essay, and remember what's needed!

Plot

A plot is the basic storyline of your essay. In this section we will identify and learn about two basic plots. You can use them as they are or mix parts of them together.

Here are two plot types we will now learn about:
• **rags-to-riches;**
• **the heroic quest.**

Rags-to-riches

A rags-to-riches plot starts with **the central character in difficult circumstances**. The character is often **treated unfairly** by other characters. As the plot develops, the central character's **circumstances change** through a series of chance events. By the end of the story the character's **life has changed** for the better.

The circumstances of the characters who treated the central character unfairly at the beginning often change for the worse. When a character's circumstances change completely it is called a **reversal of fortune**.

 ## SPOTLIGHT

1 Do you know any examples of rags-to-riches plots from films, books, plays or TV?

2 Explain why one of the examples you found was a rags-to-riches plot.

 ## IN YOUR OWN WORDS

RAGS-TO-RICHES:

REVERSAL OF FORTUNE:

The Heroic Quest

A heroic quest is when **a character is given a quest** or challenge and sets out to achieve it. This story often begins with the character being unaware of how difficult the quest is. The character then **faces different obstacles** on the way to **achieving the heroic goal**. The **final obstacle is often the most difficult** and is the climax of the plot.

The obstacles a character faces often increase in difficulty as the story progresses. When obstacles become more difficult in this way, they are called **escalating difficulties**. Escalating difficulties create **tension** in a story, as we feel concern for the central character and are curious to know the outcome of events.

 ## SPOTLIGHT

1 Find three examples of a heroic quest from films, books, plays or TV.

2 Can you think of any goal you have struggled to achieve, meeting obstacles along the way?

3 Do you have any sporting heroes who set out on a sporting quest? Describe the beginning of their quest, the obstacles they faced and their achievements.

4 i) Can you think of a sporting match or event where there was escalating difficulties for a player or team that caused you to feel tension? Explain why it was tense.

Or

ii) Can you think of a film or story where a character faced escalating difficulties? Try to make a list of those difficulties. Which difficulty was the trickiest to overcome?

CENTRE STAGE

A Character for a Quest

1 Imagine a character and describe your character's looks, likes, dislikes and personality.

2 Identify a goal that your character has to achieve. Your character doesn't have to be aware of the goal yet! Here are some examples:
   i) fall in love;
   ii) win an important match;
   iii) make a crazy invention;
   iv) slay a dragon;
   v) solve a murder.

3 Now identify five obstacles that stand in the way of your character achieving that goal. Remember, if you want to escalate tension, make each obstacle more difficult than the one before it.

Your story can be serious or funny. For example, if your hero is a postman who has to slay a dragon:
   • realise what he has to do;
   • find someone to deliver his mail;
   • get permission from his mother;
   • travel by budget airline to the dragon's den;
   • get directions from local people.

4 Now write a story about your character.
   • Give it your own title.
   • You can use the heroic quest plot or a mixture of plots.
   • Plan your text.
   • Paragraphs.
   • Descriptive writing.
   • Stay in character.

 IN YOUR OWN WORDS

THE HEROIC QUEST:

ESCALATING DIFFICULTIES:

Modelling

Modelling is when you take a character from a story, poem or play that you have read and write your own story about them. You can also take a plot from another text and change it in some way. In this section you will read examples of modelling and practise using modelling.

New children's tales are often modelled on old ones. Adventure films are sometimes modelled on comic books. Animated films sometimes make jokes about fairytales or older films and model

part of their story on characters from these tales or films. Can you think of any examples of modelling?

The examples given below are all modelled on texts from this book. Can you recognise the original texts these extracts are modelled on?

There are some important things to remember when you are **modelling**.

1 Decide on which character you will use to narrate your story and whether to tell the story in first or third person.

Example:
You could use a **first person narrator**:
I am a gatekeeper from the town of Wall. You may not have heard of it. It is a small place, out of the way. It's not particularly exciting to live there, at least on three hundred and sixty-four days of the year. There are always exceptions, however, and they always seem to happen to me.

Or you could use a **third person narrator**:
He was nervous about visiting Kemmerich in the hospital. He didn't know what he would say to his old friend. They had shared a few good times and, just as importantly, a lot of bad times.

2 Decide on the **details** you will use.
You need to identify different aspects of the character's life and world that you will use. You can also underline details from the story, play or poem that you will use.

For example:

- setting;
- family;
- friends;
- background;
- lifestyle;

- key moments;
- weather;
- clothing;
- hopes for the future.

Example:

My grandson, Frank, looks up from the piece of wood he is carving.

'Gran, what was your grandfather like?'

I sit and look into the fire for a moment. The flames dance and whisper in the grate, weaving a spell that takes me back many years to a cold winter's day, riding a wagon into town.

'My grandfather was a gentleman of good manners. He was the first person who told me to be friendly to people if you want to do well in life. He always said, be sure to remember to always speak to everyone you meet.'

'But that's what you always say to me, Gran.'

'I know. And that's where that good advice came from.'

3 Decide on what form you will use the details in.

Here are some options:

- diary;
- narrative;
- letter.

Example:

You could take your character from a novel, but tell your story as a diary:

Dear Diary,
Today I met a new kid when I was playing in the front yard with Jem. I wasn't sure about him at first. He said his name was Charles Baker Harris, which made Jem laugh. The boy then told us that everyone called him Dill, which was a shorter name but just as funny. He said he came from Meridian, Mississippi.

Or you could take your character from a play, but tell your story as a short story:

My name is Romeo. I come from Verona in Italy. My family are the Montagues. You might have read about them in the *Verona Gazette*. They are an embarrassment to me because they are always fighting. I've been dragged into it from time to time. That's only a small part of my trouble though. The real problem began when I met and fell in love with a beautiful girl called Juliet.

Or you could take your character from a poem and then write a letter from their perspective:

Dear Cousin,

Happy Christmas. Hi, it's me, Robert. Sorry I haven't written in some time. I hope the family are well. Please say hello to Jane and little Ann. Though she is probably as tall as me now! You are probably thinking I have another reason to write. I have and I'll tell you.

I was out walking the other day in the snow and I started to feel quite depressed. I was out by the old farm. You know how it is with those deserted spaces, especially in December when the days get shorter and darker. I was feeling lonely so I decided there and then that I would write to all my relatives and invite them down to visit.

By the way, did you go and see what was down that other path in the woods near your house, the one that was overgrown?

🔦 SPOTLIGHT

1 Write down the name of a character from a story, poem or play that you would like to model a text from.
2 Decide on what form the modelling will take (diary, story, letter, speech).
3 Write out a list of details about your character that you can use in your text, taken from the other text.
4 Write a short diary, story, letter or speech based on the character and details.
Remember:
  • plan your text;
  • paragraphs;
  • descriptive writing;

- stay in character – this means your character has to be consistent, doing and saying what the reader expects of the character and can believe in.

 **CENTRE STAGE**

Curtain Call

Now you can put together all you have learned about creative writing.

- **Descriptive writing.**
- **Character.**
- **Planning.**
- **Plot.**
- **Modelling.**

Tips

- Your story doesn't have to be on a grand scale. For example, your character could be on a quest to avoid detention or a difficult exam. A character could be doing something ordinary but difficult, such as moving house or changing from first year to second year in school.
- You could tell a story from your own life using one of the plot types as a model.
- You could research and tell the story of a character from real life using one of the plot types as a model.
- You could reinvent a children's tale by using a different ending.

Choose from these titles.

1 An Average Day in School.
2 Torpedo! Torpedo!
3 The Desert Island.
4 Never Say Never.
5 Reaching the Red Carpet.
6 The Frozen North.
7 An Unexpected Holiday.
8 The Stadium Roared.
9 A Great Discovery.

Remember:

- plan;
- beginning, middle, end;
- descriptive writing.

 **IN YOUR OWN WORDS**

MODELLING:

DETAILS:

Grammar Station

Verbs and Adverbs

Verbs

Verbs are **action words** or **being words** to show what a person, creature or thing is doing. They use **tense** to tell us when the action happened.

Here are some common **verb tenses**.

Past simple tense: I watched television.
Past continuous tense: I was watching television.
Present simple tense: I watch television.
Present continuous tense: I am watching television.
Future tense: I will watch television.

Verbs can also be **regular** or **irregular**.
Examples of regular verbs: watch, climb, walk.
I watch, I watched, I will watch.
I climb, I climbed, I will climb.
I walk, I walked, I will walk.

Examples of irregular verbs: be, run, drink, think, speak.
Be: I **am**, I **was**, I will be.
Run: I run, I **ran**, I will run.
Drink: I drink, I **drank**, I will drink.
Think: I think, I **thought**, I will think.
Speak: I speak, I **spoke**, I will speak.

OPENING ACT

1 Try to think of single descriptive verbs for as many of the following actions as you can.

Example: drinking quickly and loudly: gulping.

  i) Crying loudly.
  ii) Talking a lot.
  iii) Shouting.

iv) Throwing violently.

v) Sleeping gently.

vi) Laughing quietly.

vii) Beating or hitting with power.

viii) Gulping for air.

ix) Running after someone.

x) Holding something tightly.

2 Write out the present simple, past simple and future tense of these irregular verbs in the first person.

For example: I understand, I understood, I will understand.

i) Become.

ii) Break.

iii) Catch.

iv) Choose.

v) Do.

vi) Drive.

vii) Eat.

viii) Fought.

ix) Find.

x) Go.

xi) Grow.

xii) Hear.

xiii) Keep.

xiv) Know.

xv) Lie.

xvi) Make.

xvii) Pay.

xviii) Read.

xix) Teach.

xx) Write.

If possible, listen to the answers in class and correct any that you get wrong.

Adverbs

Adverbs are words that give us more information about how an action was done. They can tell us how an action was done or when it took place. They can be used to create mood and atmosphere in descriptive writing.

Adverbs telling us **how** an action was done, e.g. *quietly, slowly, gently.*
Using these adverbs in a sentence creates a calm mood.
Adverbs telling us **when** an action was done, e.g. *shortly, immediately, soon.*
Using these adverbs in a sentence creates urgency.

Some **adverbs** are formed by adding **-ly** to adjectives.
Examples:
Adjective: *Soft* becomes **Adverb:** *Soft**ly***.
Adjective: *Clever* becomes **Adverb:** *Clever**ly***.
Adjective: *Discreet* becomes **Adverb:** *Discreet**ly***.
Not all **adverbs** end in **-ly,** e.g. *fast, hard, twice.*

Many of these are **adverbs of frequency**, e.g. *often, never, seldom.*
Degree of adverbs: the degree of adverbs is usually formed using **more** for **comparative** and **most** for **superlative**.

Examples:
Ghastly, **more** ghastly, **most** ghastly.
Cleverly, **more** cleverly, **most** cleverly.
Seldom, **more** seldom, **most** seldom.

Note: some adjectives also end in **-ly**.
Examples:
The ghast**ly**, ug**ly** man.
Was he love**ly**? Not at all!
The rule is to check if the word describes a verb. If it does, then it's an **adverb***!*

OPENING ACT

1 Use these adverbs in sentences to describe your daily life.
   i) Lately.
   ii) Happily.
   iii) Loudly.

iv) Cleverly.

v) Smoothly.

vi) Soon.

vii) Silently.

viii) Hopefully.

ix) Carefully.

x) Often.

2 What **mood** or **atmosphere** do you think is created by these adverbs?

Example:

Calmly, gently, slightly: these adverbs create a soft, soothing and gentle mood.

i) Happily, brightly, heartily.

ii) Silently, quietly, softly.

iii) Sharply, quickly, swiftly.

iv) Skilfully, smoothly, slickly.

v) Furiously, loudly, angrily.

2 Choose three of the sets of adverbs above and use each set to describe how an event happened.

*Example: The tennis player **skilfully** tapped the ball over the net. Her opponent **smoothly** changed her stride to **slickly** return it to the far corner of the court, winning the game.*

READING

I AM JACK WHITE, A PROFESSIONAL EDITOR. It is my job to read and edit the wide variety of writing that is submitted to publishers. Editing is when you read and change a text so that the grammar and punctuation are correct, the facts and figures are accurate and the writer uses the style needed and stays on the appropriate topic.

In this unit we will focus on reading non-fiction, that is, texts that tell us the story and facts of real events and characters. We will learn how to recognise the features of many different styles of non-fictional writing and identify different uses for it. You will also get a chance to practise a range of styles.

In particular we will learn about:

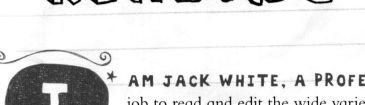

BIOGRAPHY;
AUTOBIOGRAPHY;
DIARY;
ANECDOTE;
HUMAN INTEREST;
HISTORICAL INTEREST;
TRAVEL FEATURE;
CULTURAL INTEREST.

We will also learn about **quotation marks** at the **Punctuation Station**.

Biography

A **biography** is the story of someone's life as told by another person. Biographers focus on certain aspects and moments of a person's life, leaving out any details that are seen as unimportant.

Features of biography:
- **background;**
- **achievements;**
- **personality;**
- **family;**
- **friends;**
- **profession;**
- **misfortune;**
- **social life;**
- **private life.**

Here is a short biography of William Shakespeare.

William Shakespeare

(b. 23 April 1564; d. 23 April 1616)
Playwright and poet

The most popular, most widely read and most respected writer in the English language, Shakespeare enjoys an almost mythic status internationally. He was born in Stratford-upon-Avon to Mary Arden, the daughter of a wealthy landowning family, and her husband John, a local glove-maker. It is generally assumed that Shakespeare went to King's New School, a nearby grammar school, but we know that at eighteen he married the pregnant Anne Hathaway, a woman eight years his senior, who gave birth to a daughter and then to twins soon after.

It is not until 1592 that he reappears in records, attacked in a letter written by playwright Robert Greene as 'an upstart Crow'. The closing of the London theatres during a plague epidemic from 1593 to 1594 gave the enterprising young writer an excuse to turn to poetry – it is likely that many of his 154 sonnets were composed in this brief hiatus.

MYTHIC STATUS
legendary, regarded as almost fictional

EPIDEMIC
a widespread outbreak of disease

ENTERPRISING
taking advantage of a situation

HIATUS
a break or pause in activity

READING

4

After the theatres reopened, Shakespeare joined the Lord Chamberlain's Men acting troupe, often taking part in their productions of his hugely popular plays. The troupe's success, for which Shakespeare took a share of the profits, meant that in 1597 he could afford to buy New Place, the second largest house in Stratford, and that the Lord Chamberlain's Men ploughed money into the Globe Theatre, which opened on London's South Bank in 1599.

Shakespeare spent the following decade writing constantly, receiving the new king's official patronage after Elizabeth I's death in 1603. Although his poetry was printed in 1609, Shakespeare seems not to have been concerned with the publication of his plays, so it fell to his fellow actors to compile the now-legendary First Folio editions of his collected works in 1623, which ensured his lasting fame.

Carl Wilkinson

Some biographies are written long after the subject is dead. There can often be doubts over certain aspects of biographies, such as when or how an incident actually happened. When a person expresses doubts like this, it is said that they question the **reliability** *of a biography or narrative. Sometimes many biographies can be written about the same person.*

PATRONAGE
being sponsored to produce art

FIRST FOLIO EDITIONS
famous copies of Shakespeare's collected works

▲ OPENING ACT

1 How is William Shakespeare regarded? EVIDENCE
2 Who did he marry? EVIDENCE
3 What gave Shakespeare an opportunity to write poetry? EVIDENCE
4 What did Shakespeare do in 1597? EVIDENCE
5 What ensured Shakespeare's lasting fame? EVIDENCE

🎭 SPOTLIGHT

6 Identify three features of a biography in this extract. OPINION REASON EVIDENCE
7 Where would you expect to find a biography like this one? OPINION REASON
8 What aspect of the writer's life is considered in paragraph two? OPINION REASON EVIDENCE
9 From reading this biography, are you impressed with Shakespeare's achievements? OPINION REASON EVIDENCE
10 How reliable do you think this biography is? OPINION REASON

🎩 CENTRE STAGE

My Hero
Using the biography checklist, write a short biography of someone you admire. Use a paragraph for each area of the person's life.

- Structure your answer through paragraphs.
- Start with birth and background.
- Make a list of achievements.
- Explain why the character is a hero.
- Use a quotation from the character.

Your hero could be unusual or made up. If you want to have some fun, you could even write about yourself, or perhaps your hero is one of your teachers?

IN YOUR OWN WORDS

BIOGRAPHY:

Autobiography

> JACK TO THE FUTURE: THE AUTOBIOGRAPHY

> JACK WHITE: WHAT I READ

> NOT SO BLACK AND WHITE

An **autobiography** is the story of a person's life told by the person who lived that life. It usually takes in the length of a person's life up to the time of writing, from early childhood to late adulthood. It is always written in the first person.

The following extract is from a type of autobiography called a memoir. *A* memoir *is an autobiography written about a special part of a person's life. It could be about the time a person spent in a particular job or career, such as in sport or politics, or it could be about a stage in their life, such as childhood.*

The Speckled People
Hugo Hamilton

When you're small you know nothing. You don't know where you are, or who you are, or what questions to ask.

Then one day my mother and father did a funny thing. First of all, my mother sent a letter home to Germany and asked one of her sisters to send over new trousers for my brother and me. She wanted us to wear something German – lederhosen. When the parcel arrived, we couldn't wait to put them on and run outside, all the way down the lane at the back of the houses. My mother couldn't believe her eyes. She stood back and clapped her hands together and said we were real boys now. No matter how much we climbed on walls or trees, she said, these German leather trousers were indestructible,

READING

4

LEDERHOSEN
traditional leather
dungarees worn in
Germany

INDESTRUCTIBLE
can't be broken

124 WORDPLAY 2

and so they were. Then my father wanted us to wear something Irish too. He went straight out and bought hand-knit Aran sweaters. Big, white, rope patterned, woollen sweaters from the west of Ireland that were also indestructible. So my brother and I ran out wearing lederhosen and Aran sweaters, smelling of rough wool and new leather, Irish on top and German below. We were indestructible. We could slide down granite rocks. We could fall on nails and sit on glass. Nothing could sting us now and we ran down the lane faster than ever before, brushing past nettles as high as our shoulders.

When you're small you're like a piece of white paper with nothing written on it. My father writes down his name in Irish and my mother writes down her name in German and there's a black space left over for all the people outside who speak English. We're special because we speak Irish and German and we like the smell of these new clothes. My mother says it's like being home again and my father says your language is your home and your country is your language and your language is your flag.

But you don't want to be special. Out there in Ireland you want to be the same as everyone else, not an Irish speaker, not a German or a Kraut or a Nazi. On the way down to the shops, they call us the Nazi brothers. They say we're guilty and I go home and tell my mother I did nothing. But she shakes her head and says I can't say that. I can't deny anything and I can't fight back and I can't say I'm innocent. Instead, she teaches us to surrender, to walk straight by and ignore them.

We're lucky to be alive, she says. We're living in the luckiest place in the world with no war and nothing to be afraid of, with the sea close by and the smell of salt in the air. There are lots of blue benches where you can sit looking out at the waves and lots of places to go swimming. Lots of rocks to climb on and pools to go fishing for crabs. Shops that sell fishing lines and hooks and buckets and plastic sunglasses. When it's hot you can get an ice pop and you can see newspapers spread out in the windows to stop the chocolate melting in the sun. Sometimes it's so hot that the sun stings you under your jumper like a needle in the back. It makes tar bubbles on the road that you

can burst with the stick from the ice pop. We're living in a free country, she says, where the wind is always blowing and you can breathe in deeply, right down to the bottom of your lungs.

*The **style** of writing is the way in which a writer uses language. If the writer uses a lot of facts and figures, it is called a **factual style**. If a writer tells a story without many facts, then we call it a **narrative style**. A writer can often use a blend of different styles. Other styles that a writer can use include a comic style, an informative style, a poetic style or a descriptive style.*

▲ OPENING ACT

1 What did the writer's mother have sent from Germany to Ireland? **EVIDENCE**
2 With their indestructible clothes, what could the brothers now do? **EVIDENCE**
3 What simile does the writer use to describe being small? **EVIDENCE**
4 What does the mother ask her boys to do when they are being teased? **EVIDENCE**
5 What does the boy's mother think of Ireland? **EVIDENCE**

▣ SPOTLIGHT

6 Write two paragraphs explaining how the boys' parents influenced their lives, using a paragraph for each parent. **OPINION** **REASON** **EVIDENCE**
7 Why does the young boy not want to be 'special'? **OPINION** **REASON** **EVIDENCE**
8 'When you're small you're like a piece of white paper with nothing written on it.' *What do you think the writer meant by this?* **OPINION** **REASON**
9 Can you find any examples of vivid descriptive writing in this extract? **OPINION** **REASON** **EVIDENCE**
10 What style or styles of writing can you find in this extract? **OPINION** **REASON** **EVIDENCE**

🎩 CENTRE STAGE

My Memoir: A Chapter from My Childhood

Write a short memoir about a time or incident in your early childhood life. It could be a trip, a holiday, a birthday or something you remember clearly.

Step 1: to begin with, have a five-minute group or paired discussion about how your life and the world have changed since you were a child.

You can start the conversation by talking about the oddest or silliest thing you believed in when you were young. Don't forget to include your teacher in the discussion.

Step 2: now concentrate on one incident. Structure it into a story with a beginning, middle and end.

Include details from your childhood when you are writing. You can mention such things as:

- family;
- school;
- clothing;
- hobbies;
- habits;
- misunderstandings about the world.

Step 3: for your last paragraph, include your reflections on the incident. Explain how the outcome of the incident affected you and explain what you learned from it. *You can also find a childhood photograph to accompany your memoir.*

IN YOUR OWN WORDS

AUTOBIOGRAPHY:

MEMOIR:

STYLE:

diary

A **diary** is a **record** written by a person about their **daily life**. A diary allows the reader to see exactly what a diarist is thinking and feeling as events happen. It is written in the first person. A diary contains:

- **personal feelings and emotions;**
- **information about the diarist's lifestyle;**
- **details about family and friends;**
- **key moments in the diarist's life;**
- **opinions on events that happen.**

This is a diary written by an Irishman and a Canadian woman who rowed across the Atlantic. Their perspective gives us an insight into how difficult their achievement was. This extract was written by Tori Holmes, the Canadian woman.

Little Lady, One Man, Big Ocean

Fifty-foot Waves, Day 36, 4 January 2006
Tori Holmes

In the past week we had been at the mercy of Mother Nature and discovered she has no mercy. I wrote in my diary on 29 December, 'How low can you go?' We had no water and then devastating amounts of water. And we came through.

4

We were two non-rowers who took on rowing the Atlantic; a student and a financial adviser who became adventurers. Could our relationship survive? Could we get across the Atlantic? Through these days the question was simpler: would we live or die?

Our water maker started to fail on us. It went from producing 16 litres of water in an hour to none. Not long after Christmas our satellite phone had run out of credit and the phone company's head office was closed for the holidays. So we could not ring the water-maker technician to sort it out. The filters looked a little brown. We convinced ourselves this was the problem and took the water maker apart to get at the filters, which were screwed into a plastic container. All we would have to do is open the container, replace the filters and that would be the end of our problem.

Unfortunately nothing in this row was ever that straightforward. The bloody plastic container would not open. We spent about 30 minutes trying to open the container before I remembered a rhyme my Dad had taught me as a child when I would help him build his motorcycles: 'Tighty righty, lefty loosy.' We had been turning the container as hard as we possibly could … in the wrong direction. I sat there trying to open the container with all my might, fearing I would thirst to death if we could not open it. My hands, like those of an 80-year-old after a month and a half at sea, just would not work. It was strange to be surrounded by water and be so thirsty, to have a fear you might die of thirst. I remember wishing the water maker was broken with a problem out of our control because if we were to die due to being too weak to open this bloody container it would feel like we had been subjected to the most evil torture.

This led to one of our major meltdowns. Dehydration really started to affect our coping skills. We lay on the deck of our small boat trapped in the ocean and just sobbed. At that moment I was the tiny child who had been denied what she most wanted. I really believed my world was coming to an end.

We had fresh water on board but it was ballast – and under the rules of the race once we broke into it we would be penalised. We decided to continue rowing, limiting ourselves to 5 litres of water a day. This was truly torturous. You rowed for two hours in the blistering heat allowing yourself less than one-eighth of a litre (we're talking sips here) per shift. All I wanted to do was grab the whole bottle and chug it down. The inside of my mouth was like a desert. With every sip you could feel it rush through your body. For a few seconds you would have renewed strength, not just in the body but, most importantly, in the mind. After those few seconds of bliss you came crashing down, already waiting till the hour passed so that you could have another sip.

Because we had so little water we also had to sacrifice meals. We ate biscuits and energy bars. We could have cooked using seawater but you can get quite ill from that, so we decided against it, at least in the short term.

Our spirits started to suffer. Emotionally, mentally and physically we were slowly breaking down from the inside out. We had no water to drink, or for sanitation and washing. Just when we thought it could not get any worse I developed a kidney infection as a result of not drinking enough water to flush the bacteria out of my system. How do you get rid of a kidney infection? Same way as you prevent it – drink water. Since that was not possible, I took antibiotics for three days and the infection eventually cleared.

BALLAST

weight in the bottom of a ship to keep it upright

CHUG

to drink quickly

Three painful days into our drought the phone rang. It was the best sound I had ever heard in my life – we had contact with the outside world! It was Eamonn Kavanagh, our mentor back in Ireland. He told us all the teams were finding the race difficult. Teams were struggling with their steering lines and many of the water makers had broken down. We were not alone. We did not wish misfortune on any other team but we found comfort in knowing they were struggling too, and pushing through it. It meant we could as well. The sound of Eamonn's voice was comforting. To hear his support for us meant a lot, as we had spent the last year trying to prove to him we could handle anything; we could take on an ocean. In our eyes Eamonn was the master of the ocean. His advice completely refocused us – now we were ready to fight back.

Diaries often contain **reflections** *on incidents or events that happened. To reflect on an incident or event is to think deeply about what happened. When we reflect we ask questions about the world and ourselves and try to figure out the reasons why things happen as they do.*

♟ OPENING ACT

1 What were the two rowers before they became adventurers? `EVIDENCE`

2 What happened to their water maker? `EVIDENCE`

3 How much water did they limit themselves to? `EVIDENCE`

4 What does the writer mean by a 'major meltdown'?

5 What illness did the diarist suffer from? `EVIDENCE`

6 What news did Eamonn Kavanagh tell them when he rang? `EVIDENCE`

📷 SPOTLIGHT

7 Identify two qualities you think a person needs to succeed in an adventure like the one described. Use a separate paragraph to explain each quality, giving reasons based on the text. `OPINION` `REASON` `EVIDENCE`

8 Why did the two rowers' spirits suffer? `OPINION` `REASON` `EVIDENCE`

9 What reflections helped the diarist to continue? `OPINION` `REASON` `EVIDENCE`

10 Of all the challenges the diarist faced, which one would you least like to meet? `OPINION` `REASON`

11 'Sharing your adventure experiences can be an inspiration for others.' Would you agree or disagree with this statement, using the extract as an example? `OPINION` `REASON` `EVIDENCE`

CENTRE STAGE

Rowing the Atlantic

Use your imagination to write two diary entries for your own rowing adventure. Here is a checklist of details for you to explore:

- **weather;**
- **your team;**
- **difficulties;**
- **family at home;**
- **hopes for the future;**
- **the training involved;**
- **food;**
- **inspiration for doing it.**

As a class group, add four more detail areas to this list. Remember, you can mention each detail more than once.

1 Decide on how many days apart you are going to space the two diary entries and put a date on each entry.

2 Remember to show how things have changed between the two diary entries. For example, the mood or weather could change from one day to the next. This is called continuity.

Continuity is when details change in a story to show the passage of time or events. *Continuity gives us an understanding of how circumstances have changed as time has passed and makes a story more realistic.*

IN YOUR OWN WORDS

REFLECTION:

CONTINUITY:

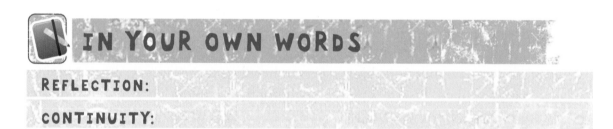

Anecdote

An **anecdote** is a short story about an interesting moment or event in a person's life. Anecdotes are usually told orally and can be exaggerated so that they become more humorous or exciting. Anecdotes can also be used to make a point, for example you could argue that crime is rising by telling an anecdote about a crime that you witnessed.

The following anecdote has an **ironic outcome**. **Irony** is when unusual or unlikely events coincide to give us an outcome that fits in a surprising way. See if you can explain why these situations are ironic, and see if you can think of an example of your own.

- An outbreak of fire in a fire station.
- A riot at a peace rally.
- A worker sustaining an injury by tripping over a safety notice.

This anecdote was told by a veteran of the Second World War.

August 1945

Robert C. North

We were being briefed by the colonel for another mission. It would be our seventh since arriving in the Pacific theatre six months ago. Intelligence described it as extremely risky, involving invasion of the mainland Japan, and reports suggested that the Japanese had advance knowledge of our plans and were preparing a massive resistance. Stunning as this information was, we took in the details as though it were a routine briefing. We figured we'd gambled our last survival chips months before anyway.

"This is a volunteer mission," barked the colonel. "Any man who doesn't want to undertake this mission just needs to report to my quarters, stand at attention, look me in the eye, and say, 'Colonel, I'm yeller, sir!' And you'll be shipped out, back to base at Oahu on the next ship. Is that clear? Dismissed!"

After dozens of missions, we were exhausted. Although none of us said it out loud, each knew what the other was thinking. It was what I was thinking, too. I wished I had the guts to go in there and tell the colonel I was yellow. We were too tired to admit fear, too proud. We were seasoned soldiers, veterans of the many battles that would eventually end as battle stars on our uniforms and hang in our closets until the moths ate holes in our lapels or until some kid took the jacket off the hanger for Halloween. And we knew enough of battle to have real fear. But I feared something more than looking into the colonel's eyes and telling him I was afraid. I feared looking into my own eyes, even though in the middle of the Pacific we didn't have mirrors, and I knew that,

CHIPS
special plastic coins for gambling in a casino

LAPELS
fabric on the collar and shoulder of jackets

READING

4

battle-fatigued and frightened as I was, I could never bring myself to walk into the colonel's tent.

But one man, Symes, did go in to the colonel. The colonel was true to his word and transferred Symes out of the unit. His orders were to board the *Jasper*, a supply ship returning to Oahu to restock.

I resented Symes. I hated him. We all did. We knew that Symes had fought next to us throughout our tour, facing fire as well as any of us had, no better, no worse. But he was the only one who had the guts to say that he was a coward, and now he was going to get out of this hellhole. He was going to be shipped out, to eat at a table, to sleep in a bed with sheets, to smell fresh sea air instead of the constant stink of gunpowder and dead bodies, to hear the soothing rhythm of the ocean instead of the whistle of bullets and the gut-thumping blow of heavy artillery. And maybe he'd spend the rest of the war behind a desk or on the receiving end of a radio on a base. (And he'd still have the battle stars; who would know what he's said to the colonel but us? And in a week we might all be dead anyway.)

We all made sure we had other things to do while Symes packed his duffel and marched down to board the *Jasper*. Then we began to pack up for the next battle. We all wrote letters to our families, to our wives, to our girls, trying to tell them good-bye without letting them know where we were going and what we were thinking.

Then, on the morning we were preparing to board the transports, one of the Filipino truck drivers came running toward us, gesturing excitedly. "Never mind. No bother. Big bomb dropped. War over!" We turned on the radio and listened to the news of the bomb that had been dropped on Hiroshima.

As we all stood around soaking up the meaning of this news, we received a second message: the *Jasper* had been torpedoed at sea, all aboard lost.

🎬 OPENING ACT

1 What reasons made the mission that the men were to undertake incredibly risky?
EVIDENCE

2 How could the men avoid the mission? **EVIDENCE**

3 What were all the men thinking after the colonel's speech? **EVIDENCE**

4 What did the men think of Symes for avoiding the mission? **EVIDENCE**

5 What does the writer mean by 'gut-thumping blow'?

6 Why was the mission called off? **EVIDENCE**

🔦 SPOTLIGHT

7 What is the real reason why the narrator could not bring himself to avoid the mission? **OPINION** **REASON** **EVIDENCE**

8 How does the narrator of the story see the men being remembered long after the war is over? **OPINION** **REASON** **EVIDENCE**

9 Would you have chosen to go on the mission or would you have left with Symes? `OPINION` `REASON`

10 What is the ironic outcome of this story? Explain why it is ironic. `OPINION` `REASON` `EVIDENCE`

11 'But he was the only one who had the guts to say that he was a coward.' *Explain the contradiction in this statement.* `OPINION` `REASON` `EVIDENCE`

 ## CENTRE STAGE

Our Story: All Included

Everyone has an interesting story to tell. It may be your own or one belonging to a family member or friend. Write down an anecdote to share with the class. Here are some categories to help you.

1 A strange encounter.
2 The perfect moment.
3 Wild creatures.
4 The people you meet.
5 It made me think.

Tips

• Use paragraphs to structure your story.
• Use descriptive writing.
• Don't write about anything too sensitive or that you wouldn't like to share.

When your stories are finished, remember to read some out. Does listening to other people's anecdotes remind you of more stories you could share?

IN YOUR OWN WORDS

ANECDOTE:

IRONY:

Human Interest

Human interest is writing that explores the **variety** of **human experience**. People like to read about experiences that are different from their own, and people who have unique or extreme experiences often have interesting and valuable reflections to share.

This next extract is taken from a book written by a Jewish survivor of the Auschwitz concentration camp in Poland. Those who were taken to these camps suffered great hardship, with many not surviving. This book is part autobiography, describing what happened to the inmates of the camp. It is also contains deep reflections on human nature and the meaning of existence.

Man's Search for Meaning
Victor E. Frankl

In camp, too, a man might draw the attention of a comrade working next to him to a nice view of the setting sun shining through the tall trees of the Bavarian woods (as in the famous water colour by Dürer), the same woods in which we had built an enormous, hidden munitions plant. One evening, when we were already resting on the floor of our hut, dead tired, soup bowls in hand, a fellow prisoner rushed in and asked us to run out to the assembly grounds and see the wonderful sunset. Standing outside we saw sinister clouds glowing in the west and the whole sky alive with clouds of ever-changing shapes and colours, from steel blue to blood red. The desolate grey mud huts provided a sharp contrast, while the puddles on the muddy ground reflected the glowing sky. Then, after minutes of moving silence, one prisoner said to another, "How beautiful the world *could* be!"

BAVARIAN
an area in Germany

MUNITIONS
bullets and bombs

SINISTER
evil-seeming, of bad intention

*It is important to **document** significant events in a variety of ways. A narrative style helps us to understand what happened to individual people. We can see what happened from one person's point of view and feel some of the emotions that they went through.*

 # OPENING ACT

1 What did the men have to build in the woods? `EVIDENCE`

2 Where were the men and what were they doing when a prisoner rushed in from outside? `EVIDENCE`

3 How does the author describe the clouds in the west? `EVIDENCE`

 # SPOTLIGHT

4 What is the mood of this text? `OPINION` `REASON` `EVIDENCE`

5 What do you think is the central message of this text? `OPINION` `REASON` `EVIDENCE`

6 What sense is appealed to most in the descriptions? `OPINION` `REASON` `EVIDENCE`

7 This extract could also be put in a historical interest category or a biographical category of writing. Which category do you think suits it best? `OPINION` `REASON`

8 Do you think people should record or forget experiences of their suffering? `OPINION` `REASON`

 # CENTRE STAGE

Postcard from the Edge

Design a postcard to remind people of one of the following.

1 Their responsibility to their fellow people.

2 What happened in our past.

3 The wonder of existence.

You can buy blank postcards or make one out of cardboard.

You can use any or a number of the following:

• a title;

• a suitable quote;

• a drawing;

• colour;

• images cut out of magazines;

• a photograph;

• a message.

Can you think of anyone to send it to? You could also put a collection of them on the wall of your class.

IN YOUR OWN WORDS

HUMAN INTEREST:

Historical Interest

Historical interest takes the **past** as its subject. It presents us with **factual details** about the past in a way we can understand. Writers need to **research** the details of a subject before they can write about it.

Types of research:
- **Numbers: dates and quantities.**
- **Facts: documented evidence and accepted details of what happened.**
- **Names: individuals and groups involved.**
- **Place names: countries, places and regions involved.**
- **Narratives: anecdotes or personal stories that can be proven.**
- **Consequences: the results of an event.**

Research information can be found in **documentary evidence.** This is evidence that can be used to prove and show how an event happened. Documentary evidence can be records kept by organisations such as the government, army or schools. It can also be records kept by individuals, such as letters, official documents and photographs.

When you are reading the following extract, compare its factual style to the narrative style of the previous extract, Man's Search for Meaning. *The following extract examines the role of women in the First World War. Some people argue that too much is written about men in war and too little is written about the role of women. Have you ever seen a film or read a book from the point of view of a woman in wartime?*

Women and War

Ann Kramer

TYPES OF WORK

Women did virtually everything that men had done. Women in Britain, France, Germany, Austria and North America entered the chemical and metalworking industries. They worked in munitions factories, built aircraft and worked in construction. They were employed in communications and as police. More women entered the transport industries than ever before. In Britain in 1914, around 12,000 women worked in transport, but by 1918 numbers had increased to 61,000. Women worked on trains as ticket collectors and guards and drove buses and trains. Women also worked in banking and postal services.

DIFFICULTIES

Many newspapers and organisations praised women's wartime work. But there was also opposition to employing women in what had been seen as men's jobs. Male trade unions were hostile. They thought women would steal jobs or undercut wages. The public could be critical, too, because it was feared that women would abandon their roles as wives and mothers.

For working-class women war work meant higher wages and greater opportunities. Many left low-paid work for better jobs. Nevertheless, women were still paid less than men and working conditions were often harsh. Later in the war, some crèches and childcare facilities were provided, but most married women had to combine waged work with looking after their home and children. In spite of this, war work gave women not only an income but also the satisfaction of doing what they saw as their duty for the war effort.

OPPOSITION
people against

TRADE UNION
organisation to protect workers' rights

HOSTILE
angry and against

WORKING CLASS
people who worked low-paid, physical jobs

CRÈCHE
place for child-minding

READING

4

*A **factual** style **contrasts** with a **narrative** style because it allows us to see what happened to large groups, societies and whole countries. Factual details help us to realise the scale of major historical events. It can help us to see how our society, country and world were formed.*

👑 OPENING ACT

1 In what countries did women enter the chemical and metalworking industries? `EVIDENCE`

2 By 1918, how many women worked in transport in England? `EVIDENCE`

3 What other jobs did women in England do? `EVIDENCE`

4 What did male trade unions think of women's wartime work? `EVIDENCE`

5 What did wartime work bring for working-class women? `EVIDENCE`

💡 SPOTLIGHT

6 Was there anything about people's attitudes to women working during the war that surprised you? `OPINION` `REASON` `EVIDENCE`

7 What advantages did women gain from the war? `OPINION` `REASON` `EVIDENCE`

8 Did you find this extract interesting? `OPINION` `REASON` `EVIDENCE`

9 If you were alive during the war, do you think you would have wanted women to work or not? Explain your answer. `OPINION` `REASON`

10 Do you think attitudes to women working have changed since the First World War? `OPINION` `REASON`

🎩 CENTRE STAGE

The Right to Rights!

A right is something that you should be allowed to have or allowed to do. It can also be called an entitlement.

As a class, choose one of these groups:
• teenagers;
• students;
• women.

Write out a list of ten rights that you think your chosen group should have. You can work on this in pairs, if suitable, discussing possible rights until you can both agree on them.

Example:

1 Teenagers should have the right to privacy.

When you are finished, you can have a class debate and adopt a list of ten rights for your chosen group.

READING

4

How to debate:

1 Let each pair read out their favourite right in turn.

2 If there is anyone who disagrees with the right that has been read out, they can put up their hand and present an argument against it. Then the pair who proposed the right must defend it.

3 The class can have a show of hands when they have heard both sides of the argument. If the right is accepted by the majority, it goes on the list.

4 Keep debating your rights until you have a group list of ten rights.

IN YOUR OWN WORDS

DOCUMENTARY EVIDENCE:

Travel Feature

Travel writing is common in books, newspapers and magazines. Writers can focus on exotic places, regions of their own country or whole continents. They can explore different methods of travelling, such as horseback, boating or walking.

The next writer uses a **comic style**.

Features of comic writing include:

- **comic irony;**
- **exaggeration;**
- **understatement and hyperbole;**
- **sarcasm;**
- **comparisons and unusual similes.**

Comic irony: a type of irony where the writer says one thing but the reader is aware that the writer means something else.

Example: I was delighted to find a slug in my salad, as my doctor told me I needed more protein in my diet.

Understatement: when the writer exaggerates something as less significant or less important than it actually is.
Example: I didn't mind burning a hole in my new suit, but setting the winning lottery ticket on fire was a real nuisance.

Hyperbole: when the writer exaggerates something in a far-fetched or sensational way.

Example: The train carriage I stepped onto must have been a hundred years old, and the ticket inspector at least twice that.

The following extract is an example of autobiographical travel writing. In the book, the writer describes hiking along the Appalachian Trail, a 2,200-mile walking trail in North America. Can you see the understatement in the title of the extract?

A Walk in the Woods

Bill Bryson

EXQUISITE
very fine, excellent

CUSTOMARY
usual

CHRONICALLY
persistently, constantly

BANALITIES
boring everyday conversation

On the fourth evening we made a friend. We were sitting in a nice little clearing beside the trail, our tents pitched, eating our noodles, savouring the exquisite pleasure of just sitting, when a plumpish, bespectacled young woman in a red jacket and the customary outsized pack came along. She regarded us with the crinkled squint of someone who is either chronically confused or can't see very well. We exchanged hellos and the usual banalities about the weather and where we were. Then she squinted at the gathering gloom and announced she would camp with us.

Her name was Mary Ellen. She was from Florida, and she was, as Katz for ever after termed her in a special tone of awe, a piece of work. She talked non-stop, except when she was clearing out her Eustachian tubes, which she did frequently, by pinching her nose and blowing out with a series of violent and alarming snorts of a sort that would make a dog leave the sofa and get under a table in the next room. I have long known that it is part of God's plan for me to spend a little time with each of the most stupid people on earth, and Mary Ellen was proof that even in the Appalachian woods I would not be spared. It became evident from the first moment that she was a rarity.

'So what are you guys eating?' she said, plonking herself down on a spare log and lifting her head to peer into our bowls. 'Noodles? Big mistake. Noodles have got like no energy. I mean like zero.' She unblocked her ears. 'Is that a Starship tent?'

I looked at my tent. 'I don't know.'

'Big mistake. They must have seen you coming at the camping store. What did you pay for it?'

'I don't know.'

'Too much, that's how much. You should have got a three-season tent.'

'It is a three-season tent.'

'Pardon me saying so, but it is like seriously dumb to come out here in March without a three-season tent.' She unblocked her ears.

'It is a three-season tent.'

'You're lucky you haven't frozen yet. You should go back and like punch out the guy that sold it to you because he's been like, you know, negligible selling you that.'

'Believe me, it is a three-season tent.'

She unblocked her ears and shook her head impatiently. 'That's a three-season tent.' She indicated Katz's tent.

'*That's* exactly the same tent.'

She glanced at it again. 'Whatever. How many miles did you do today?'

'About ten.' Actually we had done eight point four – but this had included several formidable escarpments, including a notable wall of hell called Preaching Rock, the highest eminence since Springer Mountain, for which we had awarded ourselves bonus miles, for purposes of morale.

'Ten miles? Is that all? You guys must be like *really* out of shape. I did fourteen-two.'

'How many have your lips done?' said Katz, looking up from his noodles.

She fixed him with one of her more severe squints. 'Same as the rest of me, of course.' She gave me a private look as if to say, 'Is your friend like seriously *weird* or something?' She cleared her ears. 'I started at Gooch Gap.'

So did we. That's only eight point four miles.

She shook her head sharply, as if shooing a particularly tenacious fly. 'Fourteen-two.'

'No, really, it's only eight point four.'

'Excuse me, but I just *walked* it. I think I ought to know.' And then suddenly: 'God, are those Timberland boots? *Mega* mistake. How much did you pay for them?'

And so it went. Eventually I went off to swill out the bowls and hang the food bag. When I came back, she was fixing her own dinner, but still talking away to Katz.

'You know what your problem is?' she was saying. 'Pardon my French, but you're too fat.'

Katz looked at her in quiet wonder. 'Excuse me?'

'You're too fat. You should have lost weight before you came out here. Shoulda done some training 'cause you could have like a serious, you know, heart thing out here.'

'Heart thing?'

'You know, when your heart stops and you like, you know, die.'

'Do you mean a heart attack?'

'That's it.'

FORMIDABLE
difficult to overcome

ESCARPMENT
long and steep slope

EMINENCE
a piece of high ground

MORALE
courage and spirit

TENACIOUS
staying or holding firmly

Bill Bryson is liked for his humorous skills of **observation**. *This is when the writer notices something unusual or ridiculous in an everyday situation.*

🎭 OPENING ACT

1   What was the author doing when he met Mary Ellen? `EVIDENCE`
2   What is 'God's plan' for the author? `EVIDENCE`
3   What does Mary Ellen think of the author's tent? `EVIDENCE`
4   How far does the author think Mary Ellen has walked? `EVIDENCE`
5   Why did the author award himself 'bonus points'? `EVIDENCE`

📷 SPOTLIGHT

6   What features of comedy can you find in this extract? `OPINION` `REASON` `EVIDENCE`
7   Do you think this extract is written in a narrative style or a factual style? `OPINION` `REASON` `EVIDENCE`
8   Would you like to walk the Appalachian Trail with Mary Ellen? `OPINION` `REASON` `EVIDENCE`
9   What part of this extract did you find the most humorous? `OPINION` `REASON` `EVIDENCE`
10 Why do you think Bill Bryson is a popular travel writer? `OPINION` `REASON`
11 If you could travel anywhere, where would you like to travel to and why? `OPINION` `REASON`

🎩 CENTRE STAGE

Right of Reply

The right of reply is the right to reply to accusations or comments made about you.

Write a letter to Bill Bryson from the perspective of Mary Ellen.

Beginning
• Introduce yourself and explain who you are.
• Outline why you are writing.

Middle
• Outline the three things that you felt were most unfair.
• Explain why they were unfair.

End
• Say what you think of him and explain why.
• Ask for an apology.

Try to put yourself in her walking boots!

IN YOUR OWN WORDS

COMIC IRONY:

OBSERVATION:

UNDERSTATEMENT:

cultural interest

Culture is the artistic achievements, traditions and customs of a country or society. Culture is the way in which groups of people artistically express themselves differently from other groups or nations. Culture influences how we look at the world and how we think, act and express ourselves in it.

Cultural subjects include:
- **language;**
- **art;**
- **music;**
- **fashion;**
- **fiction;**
- **poetry;**
- **drama;**
- **film;**
- **architecture;**
- **food.**

The following extract explores the culture of the English language. In particular, it explores idioms. These are expressions we use that have a meaning that is not directly obvious from the words themselves. They are often historical expressions whose origins have been forgotten.

Red Herrings and White Elephants

Albert Jack

REFINED
advanced

EXHUMED
to dig up a corpse

GENTRY
the rich and powerful

PREMATURELY
before its time

A **Dead Ringer** is somebody who looks just like another. In medieval Britain the medical profession was not quite as refined as it is now, and often anybody found not to show signs of life was regarded as dead, when they might have been simply unconscious. (This was also before comas were fully understood.) It was not uncommon for bodies to be exhumed later and corpses found with their fingers worn to the bone, an obvious indication somebody had returned to consciousness and tried to claw their way out of a coffin. So horrific was this image that the English gentry began mistrusting medical opinions and buried their loved ones with string attached to their wrists, connected to a bell above the grave. Anybody who returned to consciousness and found themselves prematurely buried could attract attention by ringing the bell and it has been recorded this actually worked. Many 'bodies' were exhumed after bells were rung and some people carried on with their normal lives. But when spotted in the street startled acquaintances would cry to each other, 'That looks just like Jack Jones – I thought he was dead' to which they would receive the reply, 'Yes, he must be a dead ringer.' And that, believe it or not, is true.

TETHER
to tie up

TRAUMATISED
suffering

At the end of My Tether means I am at the very limit of my patience and self-control. In the Middle-Ages a grazing animal would often be tethered to a post, ensuring it didn't stray beyond a certain small area. But, once the animal arrived at the limit, unable to quite reach pastures new, it would become frustrated, irritable and sometimes traumatised to the point of despair.

OPENING ACT

1 What does the idiom 'dead ringer' mean? `EVIDENCE`
2 What indicated that people had woken up in their coffins? `EVIDENCE`
3 What solution was found to this problem? `EVIDENCE`
4 What happened if a bell was rung from a grave? `EVIDENCE`
5 Why were animals tethered to posts? `EVIDENCE`
6 What happened to the animal when it reached the limit of its rope? `EVIDENCE`

 SPOTLIGHT

7 Of the two explanations, which do you find the most interesting? OPINION
REASON EVIDENCE

8 Do you believe the explained origins of the term 'dead ringer'? OPINION
REASON EVIDENCE

9 What drives you to the end of your tether? OPINION REASON

10 Identify an idiom you use and explain what it means.

CENTRE STAGE

Animal Idioms

There are many animal idioms!
- If I called you a chicken or a sheep, would you know what I meant?
- Are you bird-brained?
- Have you ever flogged a dead horse?
- Were you ever knee-high to a grasshopper?

Below are five animal idioms. You have to research and explain the origins of each idiom. You can use a library or the Internet to help. If you are allowed, you might also take the option of making up your own origin. Then you can listen to explanations in class and try to figure out which ones are genuine!

1 Sing like a canary.
2 Smell a rat.
3 A red herring.
4 Raining cats and dogs.
5 A frog in your throat.

 IN YOUR OWN WORDS

IDIOMS:

curtain call

In this unit we focused on **reading non-fiction**. This included the **stories of people's lives** as told through **biography, autobiography, memoir, diary** and **anecdotes**. These texts used **narrative details** that we recognised from Unit 1, such as descriptive writing, a first person narrator and characters.

The stories of people's lives often include the following elements.

- **Background and early life: who are they and where did they come from?**
- **Achievements and profession: what are they known or remembered for?**
- **Personality, opinions and personal emotions: how did they feel inside?**
- **Key moments and life-changing events: what happened to them?**
- **Family, friends, heroes and enemies: who influenced the person's life?**

We also learned about **feature** and **special interest writing**, which often uses a more **factual style** of writing. Writers need to **research** a **factual subject** before they can write about it, using **documentary evidence**.

Research includes the following:

- **Numbers: when, how much and how many?**
- **Facts: what evidence is there about the subject?**
- **Names: who is or was involved?**
- **Place names: where does or did it happen?**
- **Narratives: are there any individual or personal stories?**
- **Consequences: what is the result?**

Writers will often use a blend of different styles of writing, including narrative and factual styles.

Here is a factual interest feature about the origins of pizza delivery. Factual interest features often research subjects that we wouldn't normally think about. Many of us have had pizzas delivered, but how many of us know the history of this useful service?

Century Makers: Pizza Delivery

Second only to the hamburger as the world's favourite fast food, the pizza has the unique distinction of usually being eaten at home, although prepared and cooked at the local pizzeria. With companies falling over themselves to promise ever-shorter delivery times, a telephone call will bring the pizza you desire to your door in a few minutes.

Pizza deliveries almost certainly started in the late 1950s in New York, home of the Italian immigrant and also the place where the first pizzeria opened in 1905. Pizza had already become a favourite takeaway, remaining hot and not becoming too soggy on the journey home. So, in a city where businesses have a tradition of delivering most anything the customer wants, enterprising pizzerias began to include home delivery. Many pizza companies now do nothing else. The world's largest pizza delivery company is Domino's, which has 6,000 outlets in 60 countries and in 1996 had record sales of $2.8 billion.

The modern pizza – and the first pizza delivery – are attributed to a baker called Raphael Esposito, in Naples, who created a special version of what was then a simple peasant dish for the visit of King Umberto and Queen Margherita in 1889. Called pizza margherita to this day, it consisted of red tomatoes, white mozzarella and green basil, which are the colours of the Italian flag.

Pizza migrated to the USA with the Italians, but it was after the Second World War, when returning GIs created a nationwide demand for the food they had loved so much

DISTINCTION
something marked out as different or special

ENTERPRISING
acting in a business-minded way

ATTRIBUTED
the reason or cause behind something

READING

in Italy, that it became such big business. American pizzas are now a far cry from their Italian ancestors. All sorts of different crusts – thin, deep dish, stuffed – are loaded with toppings of every imaginable complexion and derivation, including Indian, Mexican and Chinese.

DERIVATION
originally found or used somewhere else

OPENING ACT

1 When and where did pizza deliveries start? **EVIDENCE**
2 What does 'falling over themselves to promise' mean?
3 According to the writer, what tradition do businesses in New York have?
4 How big is Domino's pizza business? **EVIDENCE**
5 Who is the first pizza delivery attributed to? **EVIDENCE**
6 What is the anecdote that tells us how pizza margherita got its name?
7 How and when did pizza become 'big business' in America?

SPOTLIGHT

8 Do you think this feature is interesting? **OPINION** **REASON** **EVIDENCE**
9 What did you learn in the second paragraph? **OPINION** **REASON** **EVIDENCE**
10 What narrative features can you find in this extract? **OPINION** **REASON** **EVIDENCE**
11 Can you identify examples of two different types of research in this feature? *Use a separate paragraph to explain why each type of research was used.* **OPINION** **REASON** **EVIDENCE**
12 How have pizzas changed from their origins? **OPINION** **REASON** **EVIDENCE**

CENTRE STAGE

Feature Creature

Write your own factual interest feature. You can do this in groups, with each person researching a different area of the same subject, or on your own.

Step 1: decide on the subject. *You could choose a subject that you have come across in a play, poem or novel. You could choose a subject based on sport or personal interest, such as the history of a local football team, facts about a type of horse or the wildlife of a local river.*

Step 2: research the subject. *Examples of research include interviewing people, exploring the internet, visiting your library or reading books.*
You can divide your subject into areas. For example:
• numbers and dates;
• individuals involved;

- interesting anecdotes;
- facts of what happened;
- present and future developments.

Step 3: structure your research into paragraphs. *Each subject area can be a paragraph in itself.*

Step 4: write your interest feature. *If you can, type it out and find images to use with it. When you are finished, you can put it up on the wall.*

Punctuation Station

Quotation Marks

Quotation marks have a number of important uses. They are used to indicate:

- **dialogue;**
- **extracted text;**
- **titles;**
- **highlighted text.**

Dialogue

Dialogue uses quotation marks to indicate where a person is speaking. If there were no quotation marks in a text, you would have difficulty figuring out who is speaking and when.

You can use single ʹʹ or double ʺʺ quotation marks. The important thing is to be consistent.

Examples:

ʺWithout quotation marks, where would we be?ʺ Mr Byrne asked us.

ʺI never knew what they were before today and I've done okay,ʺ replied Timmy.

ʺAnd cavemen didn't have them and did all right,ʺ Anna observed.

ʺTimmy and cavemen are survival specialists,ʺ replied Mr Byrne. ʺFor us ordinary mortals, quotation marks are a useful and necessary tool.ʺ

There is another section on dialogue after the next unit.

Extracted Text

If you are extracting and using text directly from another source, you must use quotation marks to show this.

Example: Dill is my favourite character in the novel because he is spontaneous and unpredictable. From the moment we are introduced to him we realise that he is going to be a source of unexpected twists and turns. In the first chapter Harper Lee writes, "Thus we came to know Dill as a pocket Merlin, whose head teemed with eccentric plans."

Titles
We also use quotation marks for the titles of texts.
"Mother of the Groom" is my favourite poem by Seamus Heaney.

Highlighted Text
We can also use quotation marks to highlight text. We use it when we want to indicate that something is other than as it appears, or that special attention should be paid to what we mean.

Comic irony: my "dinner" consisted of two slices of badly burnt toast, a few soggy leaves of lettuce and a soapy slice of what may have been ham at one stage in the food cycle.

To signal a code: meet me at the "shop" so we can discuss our plans for later.

When not being literal: this ordinary "Joe" is the most important person in politics today.

This type of quotation mark is also called **parenthesis**.

DRAMA

5

I AM THE ACTOR AND DIRECTOR RICHARD REDGRAVE. I will be your guide for the drama units. Together we will learn about what is needed to stage a drama and how the actors can prepare for their parts. We will study the features of successful drama and you will learn the terms needed to discuss it. Drama has similar narrative features to novels and stories, including characters and dialogue, and also uses familiar techniques, such as tension.

You will learn about the following:

HOW TO STAGE A PLAY;
STAGE SETTING;
RELATIONSHIPS;
KEY SCENE;
SUSPENSE;
RESOLUTION.

There is a second drama unit later in the textbook, focusing on Shakespearean drama (see Unit 11).

It is very important that you act out some of these scenes to see how drama comes to life from words on the page. Drama is put together from many parts and requires teamwork.

You will also learn about **dialogue** at the **Punctuation Station**.

How to stage a Play

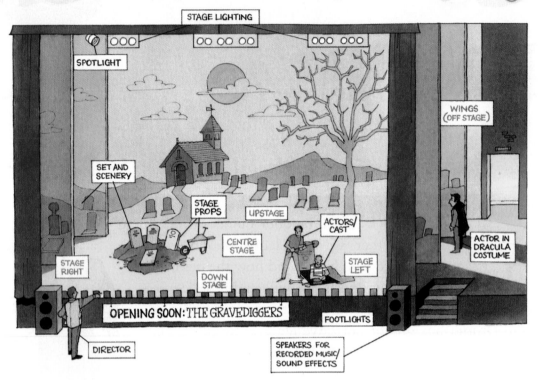

Here is what you need to **stage** *a play.*

Cast: this is what we call the group of actors.

Director: this is the person who organises, instructs and advises the cast.

Set and scenery: the set is the collection of mock buildings and objects that are on the stage. The scenery is the background painting and images that give the play its sense of place.

Costumes and props: costumes are the clothes the actors wear. 'Props' is short for properties, the objects characters use to act out the drama.

Lighting: there are many lights directed onto a stage. They create mood and atmosphere. They also help to focus audience attention with special lights, such as a spotlight.

Sound: music and sound effects also help to create mood and atmosphere.

Terms to describe **positioning**, *i.e. where an actor is on the stage.*

Centre stage: the centre or middle point of the stage, where most of the acting occurs.

Upstage: the background area of the stage furthest from the audience.

Downstage: the foreground area of the stage closest to the audience.

Stage left: the area of the stage to the actors' left when facing downstage.

Stage right: the area of the stage to the actors' right when facing downstage.

Wings: the area to the side of the stage, where the audience can't see the actors.

A director gives advice to an actor.

The cast rehearse their script.

Set and scenery create a sense of place.

Actors in costume lit up on stage.

SPOTLIGHT

1 If you were an actor making an important speech in a play, where on the stage would you stand? Explain why.

2 What set and scenery would you use if you were setting a stage for a scene in a port or harbour? Explain why.

3 What props and costume would you use for actors acting out a scene in a busy restaurant? Explain why.

4 What lighting and sound effects would you use for a scene set on a boat in a stormy sea? Explain why.

PROPS:

POSITIONING:

UPSTAGE:

DOWNSTAGE:

WINGS:

Stage Setting

The opening scene of the play introduces the audience to the **stage setting**. This includes the **set** and the **scenery** of the play. These indicate **where** and **when** the story of the play is taking place. Other aspects, such as the **costumes** worn by the characters and the **props** they use, establish the stage setting.

Features of stage setting: *it might help to look at an extract from a film or play and discuss the different features you can spot.*

- Set.
- Scenery.
- Costume.
- Props.
- Lighting.
- Sound.
- Positioning.

The following extract is from a play about three men who are kidnapped and taken hostage. It is set in a prison cell in the Lebanon. In this opening scene we are introduced to two of the men, Edward and Adam, an Irishman and an American. The writing in italics that describes the setting and gives instructions is called the **stage direction**.

Someone to Watch Over Me

Frank McGuinness

Complete light. Ella Fitzgerald sings 'Someone to Watch Over Me'.
EDWARD *and* **ADAM** *are together in the cell. They are separately chained to the walls.* **EDWARD** *is centre stage;* **ADAM** *is stage right.*
The chains are of sufficient length to allow freedom of movement for both men to exercise.
EDWARD *is dressed in a loose blue T-shirt and white football shorts.* **ADAM** *is dressed in black T-shirt and grey shorts.*
They exercise in silence. **ADAM**'s *exercises are rigorous;* **EDWARD** *moves through his paces more sluggishly.*

EDWARD: That was Ella Fitzgerald singing, 'Someone To Watch Over Me'.

ADAM: What was?

EDWARD: My eighth and final record for *Desert Island Discs*. It is also my single choice of record. Good old Ella. Did you have *Desert Island Discs* in America?

ADAM: No. What is it?

EDWARD: You pick eight records and your favourite among the eight. Then you choose a luxury. Then a book, apart from the Bible and Shakespeare. They're already on the desert island. My book is a guide to home-brewing beer, and my luxury is a beer-making kit. And Ella Fitzgerald would sing to me. I'd be happy on a desert island. Easy pleased, that's me. An easy-going man.

(Silence.)

Jesus, the boredom, the boredom, the bloody boredom. And they're coming up the hill at Cheltenham and Dawn Run is fading, she is fading, the great Irish mare will not complete the unique double of the Cheltenham Hurdle and the Gold Cup, she's tiring and she jumps the fence, she's gaining strength in the air, she's wearing them down, she passes one, she passes two, a third she passes and the winning post's in sight, she's done it, she's won. Dawn Run for Ireland, mighty woman. She's won the Gold Cup.

(Silence.)

Jesus, it was a real pity I didn't have any money riding on her. Dawn Run. Did I ever tell you about Dawn Run?

ADAM: She was your favourite horse. She won both her great races. She was magnificent. You loved her and would have married her, but it couldn't have worked out. She was a horse and you were human. Besides, she was

SLUGGISHLY
moving slowly, with tiredness

Protestant, you were Catholic, and you were already married. You've told me about Dawn Run.

EDWARD: Sarcastic Yankee. She was a hero, that horse.

ADAM: So were Glasgow Celtic when they won the European Cup, and I don't want to hear about them, either.

(Silence. ADAM exercises strenuously.)

STRENUOUSLY
with great effort

How many press-ups did you do?

EDWARD: Didn't count.

ADAM: How many?

EDWARD: Twenty.

ADAM: You did not.

EDWARD: Fifteen.

ADAM: You did not.

EDWARD: Twelve.

ADAM: Eleven. One more than yesterday.

EDWARD: Yes.

ADAM: Come on, Edward, we've got to keep going. I got to get you into condition. You know that, you agreed to it. We can have competitions when you're in condition.

EDWARD: I don't care about competitions or about my condition.

(Silence.)

ADAM: Yea, yea, I know what you mean. Who am I fooling? Who the hell am I fooling? Me. That's who. No, no brooding. No blaming myself. That way I go under. I will not go under.

(Silence.)

BROODING
thinking about something that makes you unhappy

EDWARD: The boredom, the boredom, Jesus, the boredom.

(Silence.)

I'm going to start to brood.

ADAM: I will not brood.

EDWARD: I'm going to start to blame myself.

ADAM: Don't.

EDWARD: I'm imagining where I would be, if I hadn't come to this country.

ADAM: Where would you be if you hadn't come here?

EDWARD: At home wondering what it would be like to be here.

ADAM: Yea.

OPENING ACT

1 What situation do we find the characters of this play in?
2 Who does Edward imagine winning the Gold Cup?
3 How many press-ups did Edward do?
4 Where would Edward be if he hadn't come to the Lebanon? **EVIDENCE**
5 What kind of lighting would you use for a prison scene like this?

SPOTLIGHT

6 What do we find out about the situation from the stage directions at the beginning? **OPINION** **REASON** **EVIDENCE**
7 How would you organise the stage for this play? Mention set and scenery, costume and props, lighting and positioning. **OPINION** **REASON**
8 Is there potential for tension in the situation that the characters find themselves in? **OPINION** **REASON** **EVIDENCE**
9 Can you think of any sounds that could be used in this scene? **OPINION** **REASON**
10 Following the rules above, make out a list of what you'd bring to your desert island.

CENTRE STAGE

Improve Your Improvisation
Improvisation *is when you think up lines for a character on the spot.*

Here are some tips for improvisation:
• decide on one or two traits for your character (*e.g. anger/jealousy*);
• start politely, but increase conflict and tension if appropriate;
• slowly reveal your character;
• try to get what you want from the other character;
• avoid giving the other character what they want;
• think of the costume and props you could use.

In pairs, discuss how you would improvise the following situations. At first it can be difficult to improvise completely, so you can write down some dialogue to help you. When you have enough ideas, act it out.

1 A police chief and a thief step into a lift, then the lift breaks down. Slowly reveal who the characters are and what conflict occurs.
2 A presenter on a TV show is interviewing a teacher about poor discipline in schools (*the class can be the audience!*). A student or the teacher's parents could be brought on as a surprise guest.

3 Two family members were separated at birth and don't know each other. One is interviewing the other for a job and is looking through his CV. The interviewer begins to notice coincidences in their lives, but the interviewee is slower to realise the truth.

4 A student who is skipping class meets a parent of a friend. Perhaps the parent or friend is also skipping work or class. Do they discuss the situation openly?

5 Two spies who work for the same government meet each other. They are in disguise and don't recognise each other. They are suspicious of each other and each tries to find out who the other is.

 IN YOUR OWN WORDS

STAGE DIRECTION:

IMPROVISATION:

Relationships

Characters in plays interact with each other through dialogue and action. Our understanding of each character is developed by understanding their relationships with the other characters. Changes in relationships create interest, curiosity and tension in the audience.

Focus on acting: when characters are put into situations with other characters, we see how they **react** to each other. This **reveals** who they are and what they are feeling.

We look for:
- costume;
- gestures and body language;
- facial expressions;
- posture;
- use of props;
- positioning of characters.

We listen for:
- tone of voice;
- changes in speech, such as volume or speed;
- words and meaning.

The following drama is a fictional drama based on a real story. It is about a famous English writer, Rudyard Kipling, and his family. In the play Rudyard persuades and helps his only son to fight in World War One, even though his son is not fit to be a soldier because he has very poor eyesight. Rudyard believes that it is important and noble to fight for one's country. His son is soon reported missing in battle, and later confirmed dead. Carrie is Rudyard's wife, Caroline.

My Boy Jack

David Haig

TELEGRAM
written message

RUDYARD *walks to the table, he makes a couple of notes. The telegram is still in his hand, unopened. Eventually* **RUDYARD** *puts down his pen and looks at the telegram.*

RUDYARD: Jack…
He opens the telegram.

> No. No. No. No. No. No…Oh no.

He is very still.

> Please, if there is a God, let Jack live. *(Shouting.)* Carrie! Carrie!

CARRIE *is at the door, frightened.*

> Sit down.

CARRIE: Rud…?

RUDYARD: Sit down please. *(**CARRIE** sits.)* John…

CARRIE *(a scream)*: No!

RUDYARD: Is not dead.

CARRIE: What's happened?

RUDYARD: John is not dead.

CARRIE: Give me that.

RUDYARD: He is missing.

CARRIE: Give me that. *(Grabs the telegram.)*

RUDYARD: He is missing, believed wounded.

CARRIE: …Jack…

RUDYARD: Carrie.

CARRIE: My child. My little child.

RUDYARD: He may very well have strolled into H.Q. by now. He may have got lost. That happens fairly frequently you know.

Jack Kipling

Rudyard Kipling

H.Q.
headquarters

CARRIE: Two weeks, he's been out there two weeks. (*Silence.*) Why did you do it?

RUDYARD: Why did I do what? ...Carrie, why did I do what?

CARRIE (*unable to resist*)**:** Why did you push him? You could have changed his mind.

RUDYARD: I had no desire to change his...(*Desperately angry.*) This is not the moment.

CARRIE: I knew it would happen. He should never have gone, and you should never have bullied him.

RUDYARD: Stop this.

CARRIE: Pushing, never letting up.

RUDYARD: This is so wrong of you.

CARRIE: Could he be captured? Could he? If they find out he's your son...would they know he's your son? When did we send his new I.D. disk?

RUDYARD: I'm not sure.

CARRIE: It was over a week ago, over a week, he'll be wearing it, they'll know, they'll torture him.

RUDYARD: Calm down.

CARRIE: They hate you so much, they'll torture him...

RUDYARD: Be quiet! For one moment.
Silence.

CARRIE: I'd like a whisky.

RUDYARD: Right. (*He organizes two whiskies.*)

CARRIE: I can't bear to think of him in pain.

RUDYARD: No.
Silence.

Do you really blame me for this?...Do you?...You do...do you Carrie?

CARRIE: You should have stopped him.

RUDYARD: All of Jack's friends, to a man, every one of them, is in France. Do you think for one moment that I could have dissuaded him?

CARRIE: The point is, that you never tried.

RUDYARD: No I didn't.

CARRIE: Nor did you want to stop him.

RUDYARD: No...Why should I? Why should I stop him? If I had, he would have suffered a living death here, ashamed and despised by everyone. Could you bear that?...It's true. How would he hold his head up, whilst his friends risked death in France? How would he walk down the high street,

---

DISSUADED

persuaded not to do

DRAMA

5 ✦
✦ ✦

160 WORDPLAY 2

or into a shop? He wouldn't. He would stay indoors, growing weaker and quieter by the day. Unable to leave his room. And he would wish he was dead.

CARRIE: People would understand.

RUDYARD: No they would not. They know what we are fighting for. They know we must go forward, willing to sacrifice everything to deliver mankind from evil.

CARRIE: Yes, that's very fine. But will you believe that tomorrow? Today is the last day you can believe that.

RUDYARD: Carrie, if by any chance Jack is dead, it will have been the finest moment in his young life. We would not wish him to outlive that.

CARRIE: You don't believe that Rud. I know you don't. There's no need to say that to me.

Long pause. **RUDYARD** *says nothing.*

Rudyard Kipling wrote a poem called 'My Boy Jack' about his feelings for his son after he went missing. Can you find the poem in a library or on the Internet? If you can, bring it in and share it with the class. Does reading the poem change your view of Rudyard Kipling?

OPENING ACT

1 Who are the characters in this extract and what is their relationship to each other?

2 What information is in the telegram?

3 How do we know Rudyard is upset when he opens the telegram? `EVIDENCE`

4 How does Carrie, Jack's mother, react to the information? `EVIDENCE`

5 What actions tell us that that the characters are upset? `EVIDENCE`

SPOTLIGHT

6 What scenery and set would you use in this scene? `OPINION` `REASON` `EVIDENCE`

7 What major change happens in the relationship between Rudyard and Carrie in this scene? `OPINION` `REASON` `EVIDENCE`

8 Do you think Carrie blames Rudyard for what has happened to her son? `OPINION` `REASON` `EVIDENCE`

9 For the character of Carrie, how could an actress show her emotions in:
   i) voice;
   i) body language;
   iii) use of props?
   `OPINION` `REASON` `EVIDENCE`

10 Do you think this scene would be an important one in the play? Why?
OPINION REASON EVIDENCE

10 For each of the following three images, identify:

    i) The mood of the actors.

    ii) What their costumes and props tell us about who they are.

    iii) What you think the relationships between the characters might be.

In each case, explain your answer with reference to features of acting and stage setting.

 CENTRE STAGE

Prime Mime

Miming *is acting without words.*

1 In pairs, look back over the texts you have read so far this year. Choose a text to mime out in front of the class. It can be a poem or a story or even an advertisement! Keep your choice a secret.

2 Discuss how you will mime your text. Pay attention to gestures, facial expressions, posture, positioning and props.

3 Mime your text in front of the class. When you are finished, see if anyone can guess what your text is.

Key Scene

A play is divided into acts, and each act is divided into scenes. When we discuss a key scene, however, we can mean a full scene *or* a part of a scene. A **key scene** is the section of a play where an important event occurs. It could be the introduction of an important character, a moment of tension or a twist that reveals a secret fact to the audience.

Focus on sound

- Music can create mood and atmosphere. For example, lightly playing classical music might create a gentle and peaceful mood.
- Harsh sounds, such as drums or banging, can emphasise conflict, tension or excitement.
- Recorded sounds or sound effects, such as birds singing or children playing, can create a sense of time or place.

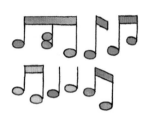

This following extract is from a play about a family of sisters who do not fit into their small Donegal community. One of the sisters, Christina (Chris), has a child with a Welsh man called Gerry Evans. Gerry has not visited her in over a year. In this key scene Gerry is introduced into the play. We also see the different attitudes the sisters have to Gerry. One part of this scene, with the sisters, takes place indoors, while the other part, with Chris and Gerry, takes place in the yard outside. Can you think of any sounds or sound effects you could use in this country scene?

Dancing at Lughnasa

Brian Friel

(Chris and Gerry are out in the yard. The sisters Maggie, Kate and Agnes are watching from the house.)

GERRY: You have a gramophone! I could have got it for you wholesale.

CHRIS: It's a wireless set.

GERRY: Oh, very posh.

CHRIS: It doesn't go half the time. Aggie says it's a heap of junk.

GRAMOPHONE
an old style of record-player

A WIRELESS SET
a radio

DRAMA

5

GERRY:	I know nothing about radios but I'll take a look at it if you—
CHRIS:	Some other time. When you come back.

(*Pause.*)

GERRY:	And Agnes is well?
CHRIS:	Fine – fine.
GERRY:	Of all your sisters Agnes was the one that seemed to object least to me. Tell her I was asking for her.
CHRIS:	I'll tell her.

(*They listen to the music.*)

GERRY:	Good tune.

(*Suddenly he takes her in his arms and dances.*)

CHRIS:	Gerry—
GERRY:	Don't talk.
CHRIS:	What are you at?
GERRY:	Not a word.
CHRIS:	Oh God, Gerry—
GERRY:	Shhh.
CHRIS:	They're watching us.
GERRY:	Who is?
CHRIS:	Maggie and Aggie. From the kitchen window.
GERRY:	Hope so. And Kate.
CHRIS:	And Father Jack.
GERRY:	Better still! Terrific!

ELEGANTLY
gracefully

(*He suddenly swings her round and round and dances her lightly, elegantly across the garden. As he does he sings the song to her.*)

MAGGIE:	(*Quietly*) They're dancing.
KATE:	What!
MAGGIE:	They're dancing together.
KATE:	God forgive you!
MAGGIE:	He has her in his arms.
KATE:	He has not! The animal!

(*She flings the paper aside and joins MAGGIE at the window.*)

MAGGIE:	They're dancing round the garden, Aggie.

DRAMA

5

KATE:	Oh God, what sort of fool is she?
MAGGIE:	He's a beautiful dancer, isn't he?
KATE:	He's leading her astray again, Maggie.
MAGGIE:	Look at her face – she's easy led. Come here till you see, Aggie.
AGNES:	I'm busy! For God's sake can't you see I'm busy!

(*MAGGIE turns and looks at her in amazement.*)

KATE:	That's the only thing that Evans creature could ever do well – was dance. (*Pause.*) And look at her, the fool. For God's sake, would you look at that fool of a woman? (*Pause.*) Her whole face alters when she's happy, doesn't it? (*Pause.*) They dance so well together. They're such a beautiful couple. (*Pause.*) She's as beautiful as Bernie O'Donnell any day, isn't she?

(*MAGGIE moves slowly away from the window and sits motionless.*)

GERRY:	Do you know the words?
CHRIS:	I never know any words.
GERRY:	Neither do I. Doesn't matter. This is more important. (*Pause.*) Marry me. (*Pause.*) Are you listening to me?
CHRIS:	I hear you.
GERRY:	Will you marry me when I come back in two weeks?
CHRIS:	I don't think so, Gerry.
GERRY:	I'm mad about you. You know I am. I've always been mad about you.
CHRIS:	When you're with me.
GERRY:	Leave this house and come away with—
CHRIS:	But you'd walk out on me again. You wouldn't intend to but that's what would happen because that's your nature and you can't help yourself.
GERRY:	Not this time, Chrissie. This time it will be—
CHRIS:	Don't talk any more; no more words. Just dance me down the lane and then you'll leave.
GERRY:	Believe me, Chrissie; this time the omens are terrific! The omens are unbelievable this time!

OMENS

signs for the future

(*They dance off. After they have exited the music continues to play for a few seconds and then stops suddenly in mid-phrase. MAGGIE goes to the set, slaps it, turns it off. KATE moves away from the window.*)

![] OPENING ACT

1 What does Gerry say about Agnes? EVIDENCE
2 Who is watching Chris and Gerry from the window?
3 What does Kate call Gerry when she hears he's dancing with Chris?
4 What does Gerry want Chris to do in two weeks' time? EVIDENCE
5 What sound effects could you use in this scene that would help to set it in the country?

![] SPOTLIGHT

6 What sort of mood do you feel is created in this scene? OPINION REASON EVIDENCE
7 What sound and lighting effects could you use to help create the mood? *Write a short paragraph for each.* OPINION REASON
8 What character would you like to play in this scene? OPINION REASON
9 This set calls for two locations to be on the stage at the one time: the yard and the interior of the house. Do you think this would work well on stage? OPINION REASON
10 Can you see any humour or comedy in this scene? OPINION REASON EVIDENCE

CENTRE STAGE

Proper Act

This is a scene to act out. This can take two or three classes to prepare.

In the first class…

1 Divide the class into four or five groups.

2 Each group reads through each part, with everyone trying out different roles.

3 If there is an extra person in the group, let one person be the director. We remember the director is the person who organises and instructs the actors.

4 Decide on your roles.

For homework …

5 Think about what you can use as props. If you can find props at home, bring them in.

6 Draw a map of the stage showing how you would lay out the set.

For the next class …

7 Discuss how you will set up the stage. Share out and discuss your props.

8 Arrange the room as a stage, or if you have a theatre see if you can use it.

9 Act out the scene.

 IN YOUR OWN WORDS

KEY SCENE:

Suspense

Suspense is the nervous or tense feeling we get when we feel that an exciting moment is going to happen. Suspense usually **escalates**, or builds up, over a number of scenes. When it reaches its highest point, it usually results in an important event or action occurring, such as a fight, capture or accident. This is the **climax**, the highest point of suspense, tension and action.

Suspense is often created by **conflict**, when two or more characters disagree with each other. A conflict can be verbal, shown in words and tone. It can also be physical, shown through action or body language. Conflict, like suspense, often escalates over a number of scenes.

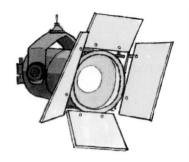

Focus on lighting
- Spotlights focus the audience's attention for an important event, such as an argument.
- Footlights are at the front of the stage, lighting the actors from below. A flickering footlight can create confusion or a tense atmosphere.
- Coloured lights can give a sense of place, such as blue for water, or a sense of time, such as orange for sunset.
- Flashing lights can create confusion or emphasise conflict. Shadows can create suspense or hide a character.

The following extract contains two scenes from a play about love, identity and freedom. The play features conflict between two brothers, Orlando and Oliver. The following two scenes are set in the city. In the play there are two settings. One is the urban setting of the city, where conflict occurs. The urban setting contrasts with the freedom of the garden allotment setting, where Orlando flees to so he can avoid his brother's scheming. The play is a modern drama based on an older Shakspearean drama, As You Like It. Adam is a young friend of Orlando.

Arden City

Timberlake Wertenbaker

SCENE ONE

ORLANDO: When my father was dying, he told him to look after me. The first thing he did was take me out of school. He said it was too expensive. He doesn't give me any money to do anything, not even to buy trainers.

ADAM: Why are you telling me this?

ORLANDO: I want you to know.

ADAM: Knowing doesn't help. I have to work for him.

ORLANDO: He looks after those big dogs of his better than me. All I do is walk the streets, hang around. I've forgotten anything I knew. I'm even forgetting who I am.

ADAM: Look, here he comes.

ORLANDO: Keep yourself hidden and listen.
Adam leaves. Oliver comes on.

OLIVER: What are you doing here?

ORLANDO: Nothing, I don't know how to do anything.

OLIVER: Then get out of the way.

ORLANDO: The streets are free.

LOITERING

hanging around
for no reason

OLIVER: I'll have you arrested for loitering.

ORLANDO: I wouldn't loiter if I had something to do. Oliver – our father told you to look after me.

OLIVER: I feed you and house you, that costs.

ORLANDO: Give me some of the money my father left. I'll go to another city and you won't ever see me again.

OLIVER: He left you in my care.

ORLANDO: How have you cared for me? You've turned me into a yob.

OLIVER: That's what you are, Orlando. Now move or you'll get yourself into more trouble. Out of my way!

ORLANDO (*physically threatening*): I'm stronger than you—

OLIVER: Are you threatening your brother?

ORLANDO: No. Our father never hurt anyone. I am still my father's son.
He goes.

OLIVER: No way you're getting anything out of me, little brother. The sooner you're out of the way the better.

SCENE TWO
Che, a professional kick-boxer, comes on.

CHE: I've been looking for you. I've heard your brother is going to challenge me in a kick-boxing contest. Now look, I don't practise Peacenik Judo but the real thing. This is Sanshou and it's tough. A kid can get hurt. So you've got to convince your brother to forget it and fight with people his own age.

OLIVER: He won't Che. He's stubborn and vicious. I've done everything I can for him and all he does is threaten me.

CHE: OK, I'll teach him a lesson.

OLIVER: Watch out. He'll probably have a knife, and when you're not looking

	he'll take it out and kill you. I won't hold it against you if you have to do the same in self-defence.
CHE:	I won't need a knife, there are places you can kick – and it's all over. It's against the rules, but it can happen by accident.
OLIVER:	I don't like to say this, because he's my brother, but if you win, he'll never forget it and he'll find a way to kill you.
CHE:	OK.
OLIVER:	Whatever you do, make it quick. And final. I don't want him to linger in pain.

Che leaves.

I'm going to be rid of the little brother at last. I hate him. I don't know why. He always reminds me—

Adam comes on.

How good is Orlando at kick-boxing?

ADAM:	I don't know.
OLIVER:	Well: go and find out.

They leave.

OPENING ACT

1 Why does Adam not want to know about how Oliver treats Orlando?
2 What did the brother's father tell Oliver to do before he died?
3 How does Oliver treat Orlando?
4 What does Oliver say to Che to convince him to kill his brother?
5 What kind of stage set and scenery would you use for these scenes?

SPOTLIGHT

6 What type of sound and lighting would you use for this scene? `OPINION` `REASON`

7 Describe the relationship of Orlando and Oliver, based on these scenes. `OPINION` `REASON` `EVIDENCE`

8 How is suspense developed in these two scenes? `OPINION` `REASON`

9 Which way of reading the play do you think is most enjoyable:
i) read the play to yourself in silence;
ii) read it aloud with class members;
iii) act it out in your classroom?
Explain your answer. `OPINION` `REASON`

10 What would you like to see happen as a climax to the conflict between Orlando and Oliver? Explain why. `OPINION` `REASON`

11 If you had to play the part of Oliver, how would you play it with regard to:

i) costume;

ii) tone of voice;

iii) body language?

Explain your answers. **OPINION** **REASON**

CENTRE STAGE

Following Up

1 It might help to start this exercise at the beginning of a class.

Write a follow-up scene in groups of two or three, with all students making a copy of the scene. In this scene Adam tells Orlando about Oliver's plans with Che. Decide where to set the scene and remember to include stage directions.

If possible, you can discuss some scenarios in class before you begin this exercise. A scenario is the outline of a dramatic situation or scene.

Here are some possible suggestions.

• Adam has to meet Orlando in secret.

• Orlando is upset and doesn't believe Adam at first.

• Adam has to convince Orlando that he can't fight Che.

• Orlando decides to confront Oliver.

• Adam disagrees with this idea because it is dangerous.

• Orlando decides to write Oliver a letter.

• Make a plan of escape for Orlando.

• Oliver will realise Adam has betrayed him.

• Adam decides to escape with Orlando because he doesn't trust Oliver.

If you want to add suspense, another character, for example Orlando or Che, could arrive towards the end of the scene. What would happen then?

2 For the next class.

You can rehearse the scene and act it out. If you have the time, act out a number of different scripts and discuss the scenarios and ideas that you feel work the best.

3 Possible follow-up lesson.

Warning: *one person will have to do some extra typing work for this! It might be an idea to do it over a weekend so the person typing can do it while other students are doing another exercise, perhaps even preparing costumes or some scenery.*

If someone has access to a computer, they can type out a printed version of the script with the best ideas and features taken from each script in it. If possible, photocopy the new scene for everyone in the class. Now act out the three scenes in a row!

Resolution

We've learned how to prepare for a play by putting together the right **stage set and scenery**. Then we use **lighting and sound** to create different moods, atmospheres and effects. The actors must use appropriate **costumes and props**.

The actors bring the characters to life by using **body language**, such as **gesture** and **posture**. They also use **facial expressions** to convey mood. They can use **tone of voice** or changes to voice, such as **volume**, to express emotion and create tension.

We learned about the various features of plays, such as **relationships, key scenes, suspense, conflict** and **climax**. The **resolution** is the final part of a drama, where the results of the plot become clear. The main parts of the story are resolved and the consequences of the climax are made known to the audience. The suspense and tension have gone.

This following extract is set in a pub at the end of the play. Bull and his son, Tadhg, waited along a quiet road to intimidate a man who was trying to buy a field they wanted. They kill him during a fight, with Tadhg dealing the fatal blow. The local priest and garda sergeant visit the two men, looking for information. Mick is the owner of the pub and Leamy is his son. This play was made into a film, but the resolution of the film is different from that of the play.

The Field

John B. Keane

LUGGED
dragged

BULL: Christ had no guard's uniform and He had no white collar around His neck. But he picked a gang of small farmers and poachers. They had their cross like all poor people, and that held them together. If a poor man does something wrong he gets a guard's baton on the poll and he's lugged up to the barracks. But, if 'tis the doctor or the schoolmaster or the lawman, they say, 'tis tough on them but there's a way out and the law is law no more.

SERGEANT: See here now …

FR MURPHY: Let him go on!

BULL: I seen an ould priest last year, as called to our house outside. He sat down near me and spoke to Tadhg and me about hard luck, about dead-born calves and the cripples you meet among dropped calves. He ate with us and he got sick after it… fat mate but he ate it and by God, he had a shine of us and said he wished was like us. I gave him a pound and Tadhg gave him seven and a tanner and if he wanted to stay with us for a year, we'd have kept him. But I won't pay you no Christmas dues, Father… not no more… and there's no law against that… Were we fond of him, Tadhg, of that ould priest?

TADHG: We were, Da, we were. He was one of our own.

MICK: I'll have to ask you to go now, Father. What will the village think if ye don't leave? We have a family to think of.

SERGEANT: You're a cleverer man than I took you for, Bull!

BULL: The likes of us that's ignorant has to be clever.

SERGEANT: Did you see the dead man's widow at the funeral, Bull?

BULL: I saw her… wasn't Tadhg and myself the first to sympathise?

FR MURPHY: We can't beat the public, Tom.

SERGEANT: It's what the public wants.

FR MURPHY: But they never get what they want.

BULL: Don't we now. You're wrong there, Father. You have your collar and the Sergeant, his uniform. I have my fields and Tadhg, [*To TADHG*] remember this. There's two laws. There's a law for them that's priests and doctors and lawmen. But there's no law for us. The man with the law behind him is the law… and it don't change and it never will.

FR MURPHY:	Do you ever think of God… any of you?
BULL:	He's the man I says my prayers to, and I argues with Him sometimes.
FR MURPHY:	About what?
BULL:	Same as you, 'cos I'm the same kind of creature as you.
FR MURPHY:	The Sergeant asked you if you spoke with the widow and you said you did. Did you feel pity for her?
BULL:	I'm like you. I can't support her 'cos I'm married myself and you'll hardly throw off the collar and marry her… When you'll be gone, Father, to be a Canon somewhere and the Sergeant gets his wallet of notes and is going to be Superintendent, Tadhg's children will be milking cows and keeping donkeys away from our ditches. That's what we have to think about and if there's no grass, that's the end of me and mine.
FR MURPHY:	God will ask you questions about this murder one day.
BULL:	And I'll ask God questions! There's a lot of questions I'd like to ask God. Why does God put so much misfortune in the world? Why did God make me one way and you another?
SERGEANT:	Let's go, Father, before I throw up!
FR MURPHY:	You'll face the dead man's widow some day, McCabe… not here, but in another place.
BULL:	Indeed I won't, Father, because she'll have her own facing to do with another man by her side.

[*Exit FR MURPHY and SERGEANT*]

BULL:	[*Louder… after them*] No, I won't face her because I seen her and she's a pretty bit and the grass won't be green over his grave when she'll take another man… A dead man is no good to anyone. That's the way of the world. The grass won't be green over his grave when he'll be forgot by all… forgot by all except me! [*To MICK*] There's your other twenty. C'mon Tadhg.

[*BULL pauses a moment. Then gathering himself, he throws back the remainder of his drink and leaves the pub. MICK gives the counter a wipe and returns upstairs. Silence.*]

The half-door of the cubbyhole we saw in the first act swings open, revealing LEAMY. He has been there throughout the scene. He climbs out and stands centre stage. We feel that he is in the grip of torturous indecision, but finally he turns reluctantly to the table and begins clearing the drinks away]

[The End]

CANON
a member of the clergy

CUBBYHOLE
an enclosed space

TORTUROUS
very difficult, painful

INDECISION
unable to choose or decide

DRAMA

5

OPENING ACT

1 According to Bull, what happens to the poor man who commits a crime? **EVIDENCE**

2 What happens to a wealthier person who commits a crime? **EVIDENCE**

3 Does Bull ever think of God? **EVIDENCE**

4 According to Bull, who is the only person who won't forget the dead man? **EVIDENCE**

5 What characters are in conflict in this scene? **EVIDENCE**

SPOTLIGHT

6 If you had to play the part of Bull, how would you play it with regard to:
   i) costume;
   ii) tone of voice;
   iii) body language?

7 What type of sound effects would you use to set this scene? **OPINION** **REASON**

8 How could you use different types of lighting to give the scene tension? *Refer to particular moments in the scene.* **OPINION** **REASON**

9 Do you think Bull feels guilt for what happened? **OPINION** **REASON** **EVIDENCE**

10 Have you any sympathy for Bull? **OPINION** **REASON** **EVIDENCE**

11 'The likes of us that's ignorant has to be clever.' *Explain what you think Bull means by this.* **OPINION** **REASON**

CENTRE STAGE

End Scene

Write a new end scene for this play, to happen after the scene above. In this new end scene Leamy decides to reveal important information about the crime.

You can set the scene:
• outside the pub;
• in a confession box a week later;
• in the future, at Bull's funeral.

Tips to help you:
i) Identify the characters you will use.
ii) Write out a plan for the scene.
iii) Identify a source of conflict or tension to use in the scene.
iv) Include stage directions.
v) Model the dialogue and layout on the extract above.

Or

Watch the film version of *The Field*.

After you watch it, you can discuss it in class. Here are some points for discussion.
  i)   How did the resolution of the film contrast with the resolution of the play?
  ii) Who was your favourite actor in the film and why?
  iii) At what point did you feel the most suspense?
  iv) What sources of conflict did you find in the film?
  v)   Was there any humour in the film? Why was it funny?
  vi) Did you enjoy the film? Why? *Refer to features and techniques of writing, drama and staging.*

You could also write a review of the film and in it include:
• a brief summary of the plot;
• a paragraph on set, scenery, props and costume;
• a paragraph on one main character and how the character was acted;
• a paragraph on the key moment;
• a paragraph on the causes and results of any conflict;
• a paragraph on the resolution.

 IN YOUR OWN WORDS

RESOLUTION:

Punctuation Station

Dialogue

When you are writing dialogue, you need to make it **clear who is speaking** so that characters don't become confused. It also needs to be **clear when a character is speaking**. This is why we need to punctuate dialogue properly. There are five rules below to help you.

There are many ways of writing dialogue. The most important thing is to be **consistent**.

Here are some simple rules.

DESTINATION: DIALOGUE

1 Always use quotation marks at the opening and closing of a character's speech.
   "Hello," said Mark.

2 Always place punctuation inside the closing quotation marks, e.g. comma, exclamation mark, question mark.
   "This is fun!" Sarah yelled.
   "Can you ask the rollercoaster to stop?" asked Tom.

3 Always start a new paragraph each time you move from someone talking to normal text, or when a different character starts to speak.
   "Will you help me with my homework?" Mary asked.
   Mary always needed help with her homework, but at least she asked. She wasn't too proud to look for help, and she wasn't afraid of hard work.
   "Later this evening, but make an attempt at it first," her father replied.
   "Thanks Dad," said Mary.

4 When a character starts using speech after the opening of a sentence, use a comma before the opening quotation marks and a capital letter to start the dialogue. You can hear the pause in the sentence if you read it aloud.
   Mike looked out the window at the rain and laughed, "Tell me we aren't going running in that."
   "Fair enough," said Dylan. "I'll put the kettle on."

5 When a character stops speaking, close the quotation marks. Only open them up if a character speaks again. Use a capital letter to start all dialogue after a full stop.
   "Now what will we do?" I asked Cindy. "Will we go to the cinema?"
   There didn't seem like there was much to do in this town in the evening. I was beginning to regret visiting my cousin.
   "Not a bad idea," she replied. "Except it closed down ten years ago."

OPENING ACT

Write out the following dialogue in your copybook and punctuate it properly.

ok I said whats the problem

the problem is we have no money replied eoin

that was always the case we were broke constantly not a problem during the year

but in the summer it sometimes stopped you having fun

we could go for a swim i suggested

except i have no swimming togs he said

what happened to the small red ones i asked

i would be arrested by the fashion police if i wore them he laughed

he was right these had to be the funniest swimming togs on earth he got them in

DRAMA

5

france one summer when he was on holidays i fell off my chair when i saw them he told me they were big in paris i reminded him he wasn't in paris so he never wore them again

would you like lend of some shorts i asked him

i don t want to go for a swim he whined

what about a run i tried

this summer just gets more and more exciting he sighed

enough of the bad attitude we re young we can do anything we want i protested

don't give me the positivity lecture he complained

the world is our oyster think about it we only have limited time on this earth and we have to seize it the moment is ours i argued

do you want to play some computer games he asked

sounds like a plan i agreed

CENTRE STAGE

Dialogue Drama

Take a scene or extract from a play you have studied and transform it into a short story using dialogue and descriptive text.

Tips

- Use a new title.
- Plan your essay.
- Use modelling.
- Choose a scene with a climax.
- Explain background.
- Build tension.
- Use descriptive writing.

6

FUNCTIONAL WRITING

F UNCTIONAL WRITING IS WRITING THAT is used to communicate with people, groups or organisations in the real world. It is writing that is used for serious and necessary functions, such as sharing information, making an inquiry or writing a report.

Functional writing uses:

- **information;**
- **persuasion;**
- **argument.**

Language of Information

Information is factual knowledge that is used in reports, research, instructions, timetables and reviews. Information can be represented in facts, figures and graphics. You have already learned about information in Unit 4, Reading.

Language of Persuasion

Persuasive language is language that tries to convince the reader of a certain point of view or opinion. It is often used in advertisements, reporting and reviews.

Language of Argument

This is language that openly argues in favour of or disagrees with a point of view or opinion. It is often used in opinion columns, speeches and debates.

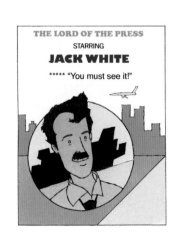

THE LORD OF THE PRESS
STARRING
JACK WHITE
***** "You must see it!"

FUNCTIONAL WRITING

6

In this unit you will learn about:

- PERSONAL LETTER
- FORMAL LETTER
- REVIEW
- SPEECH
- DEBATE
- CURRICULUM VITAE

PERSONAL LETTER;
FORMAL LETTER;
CURRICULUM VITAE;
REVIEW;
SPEECH;
DEBATE.

You will also learn about subject, verb and object at the Grammar Station.

Personal Letter

A **personal letter** is a letter written to close friends or family. When writing any letter you must decide on the **purpose** of writing it. The **purpose** is the reason for writing the letter, particularly what you hope to achieve by writing it. After you have decided on the purpose of the letter, you then choose the type of **language that is appropriate** for the purpose.

DEAR MARIE...

When you are writing a letter or note to a friend, you don't use a serious tone or many facts and figures. The purpose of a personal letter is to stay in touch, catch up on news, make plans and even gossip. For these purposes you use a casual type of language similar to everyday speech. The language can include slang, abbreviations and humour.

FUNCTIONAL WRITING

6

A letter should always have the sender's address in the top right-hand corner. The date goes beneath it.

> 15 Rockfield Close,
> Tramore,
> Co. Waterford.
>
> 24/4/2011

It is polite to start your letters with *Dear*, followed by the person's name.

Dear Samantha,

How are you? How is the big move to Cork going for you? Wait till you hear what happened to me. I was playing basketball the other day and I broke my arm. I was jumping up for a high ball and then: Splat-o! Disaster strikes! I was so dazed I couldn't remember what happened. I was told another player came in from the side and I fell over her shoulder and landed on my arm. I then bopped my head off the ground for good measure.

Sorry to jump in with such a drama but it's the biggest thing that's happened to me in a while. That's why I'm using the computer to write this. Tapping the letters out one at a time. I hope you appreciate it. So what else is new? Remember Simon, the guy I broke up with? Turns out his parents won half a million in the lotto last month. Am I bothered? Not me, no major regrets over a major loser. Still, I could do with a new pair of shoes.

School is going well, though I have to do all my homework on the computer. I am getting better at typing, though only with my left hand! I was training for the B-ball county finals when I broke my arm. It's a pity. I'm obviously out of the team for now. I got five As in my Christmas exams, legend! How is your new school going? Tried out for any of the sports teams?

OK. Better go now. Can't wait to catch up with you during the Easter break. You must visit. We'll have the greatest laugh ever! Remember the week you spent here during the Halloween midterm – it's going to be the same but better. You also have to write back to me soon, your letters are the funniest!

Your pal,

For a personal letter you can sign off casually with endings such as *your pal*, *your friend* or *best wishes*.

Kate

Other texts where you can use an informal register are e-mails, text messages, postcards and greeting cards. The important thing is that you only use it with friends because it is only appropriate to send an informal letter to someone you know well.

OPENING ACT

1 How would you describe the purpose of this letter?

2 Find an example of information in this text. `EVIDENCE`

3 Find an example of persuasion in this text. `EVIDENCE`

SPOTLIGHT

4 How would you describe the friendship of Kate and Samantha? `OPINION` `REASON` `EVIDENCE`

5 Do you think the language used in this letter would be appropriate for a letter to your bank manager asking for a loan? `OPINION` `REASON` `EVIDENCE`

6 Which would you prefer, e-mails or written letters? `OPINION` `REASON`

7 'The world is losing an important record of people's lives because we don't write personal letters anymore.'
Would you agree or disagree with this statement? `OPINION` `REASON`

CENTRE STAGE

Your Friend ...

Choose one of the following options to write a personal letter.

Someone who you haven't seen in:
• a week;
• a month;
• a year.

Now write them a personal letter. Structure your letter in paragraphs.

For example:
• what you are doing at the moment;
• news since you last talked;
• how school is going;
• how sport or a hobby is going;
• how your family are;
• questions about the other person;
• memories of times you shared;
• wishes for the future.

Formal Letter

A formal letter is a letter that uses a formal **register** and a serious tone. The register of a text is the type of language used. The register of formal language is polite and businesslike, with no slang words or casual remarks.

Formal letters can be used for purposes such as:
- **job application;**
- **complaint;**
- **letter of opinion to a newspaper;**
- **invitation;**
- **expressing gratitude or praise;**
- **information query;**
- **condolence—to express your sorrow for a death or loss.**

The structure of a formal letter

1 Sender's name, address, telephone details and date should be in the top right-hand corner; address of the letter recipient should be in the left-hand corner.

2 i) If you are writing to someone whose name and title you *do not know*, use the greeting Dear Sir or Dear Madam, and the ending Yours faithfully, followed by your first name and surname.

    ii) If you are writing to a *named or known person*, for example someone with the surname Jones, address them as Dear Mr Jones, Dear Mrs Jones or Dear Miss Jones, and end Yours sincerely, followed by your first name and surname.

3 Structure your letter into paragraphs. For example, for a job application letter include:
- introduction and background;
- skills and experience;
- personal attitude and character.

4 Express a polite note of gratitude at the end, if it is appropriate.

Job Application

The **register** of a job application should be appropriate to the task. You don't use slang or casual language for a formal purpose. The purpose of a job application letter is to express your interest in the job and to inform and persuade the employer of the reasons why you should be chosen.

Features of a formal register are as follows.
Polite: language should be respectful and serious.
Clear: language should be plain and easily understood.
Factual: all relevant and accurate information should be given.
Concise: language should use the least number of words to express its point.

Sender's name and address in top right-hand corner, with telephone number and date below that.

Harold Brophy,
23 Old Walk,
Baalincaher,
Co. Cork.

Ph. 089 4553225

12 June 2011

Address of recipient is on the left, often lower on the page.

General Manager,
A and B Stores,
Brook St.,
Glanville,
Co. Cork.

Dear Sir/Madam, **Sender doesn't know the name or gender of the employer, so uses Sir/Madam**

Introduction and background

I am applying for the job of general store assistant in A and B Stores in Glanville, as advertised in the *Cork Echo* on 4 June 2011. I am a sixteen-year-old transition year student in Glanville Community College. The details of my academic and personal achievements are included in my CV. I am available and looking for weekend and holiday work.

Skills and experience

I have six months of experience working in a local pet shop. My duties while working in the shop included stocktaking and ordering goods. I have studied basic accounting skills in school and I am part of the management team of our school canteen. I believe my experience and skills would be an asset to your business.

Personal attitude and character

I like to work with other people and I understand the importance of being a team player. I am a quick learner and I wish to gain experience in the retail trade. I am punctual and flexible with regard to time, and I am hardworking and professional in my attitude to all work duties.

Short note of gratitude

I would be very grateful if you would consider me for the advertised position. If you have any questions or queries, please contact me. Thank you for all time and consideration spent on this matter.

Yours faithfully,   **Use the correct ending for a person you don't know.**

_____

Harold Brophy   **When typing a formal letter, include your written signature and printed name.**

OPENING ACT

1 How would you describe the register of this letter?

2 Find an example of persuasive language in this letter. **EVIDENCE**

3 Find an example of information in this letter. **EVIDENCE**

SPOTLIGHT

4 Do you think this person used the appropriate register for a job application? Refer to the features of a formal register. **OPINION** **REASON** **EVIDENCE**

5 If you were the employer, which paragraph would you find most persuasive? Why? **OPINION** **REASON** **EVIDENCE**

6 Why do you think it is important to use a formal letter when applying for a job? **OPINION** **REASON**

CENTRE STAGE

Apply for one of the following jobs.

1 Dog-walker wanted. Weekends only. Must have experience with animals. References needed. Apply to: *Ann Phelan, Canine Care, 13 Green Ave., Navan, Co. Meath.*

2 Star Cinemas looking for cinema usher. Promotional opportunities available for the right candidate. Must be available nights. Apply to: *Manager, Star Cinemas, O'Connell St, Dublin 1.*

3 Rush Dance Group seeking young dancers for new show. Must be fit, active and enthusiastic. Dance styles range from ballet to breakdance. Apply to: *Head of Employment, Rush Dance, Dockside, Waterford City.*

Remember: use the correct register and include relevant information, using the advertisement to guide you.

 IN YOUR OWN WORDS

REGISTER:

Complaint

The following letter is a formal letter to a restaurant manager. The purpose of the letter is to complain to the restaurant about their service and food. Note how the letter uses a **consistent register**. This means it uses similar and appropriate language throughout the text. Note how the letter gives **information** about the experience and uses **argument** to say that it is not acceptable.

Jane Sprat,
23 Oak Street,
Naas,
Co. Kildare.

Tel. 073 8948884

21 October 2010

The Manager,
Happy Jacque,
Main Street,
Wicklow,
Co. Wicklow.

Dear Sir/Madam,

Background information

I am writing to you concerning a meal that I had at your restaurant on the evening of Friday the 14th of October. It was my grandmother's eightieth birthday and to celebrate we chose to eat at your restaurant as she loves French cuisine. We also saw that your restaurant got a five-star review in *The Wicklow Examiner*.

Food complaint

The food we had was of a poor quality. The frogs' legs looked suspiciously like chicken wings that had been dipped in green food colouring. The menu said that traditional French bread was baked on the premises but we were served a standard sliced pan. I asked the waiter to explain this and he laughed, saying that it was "Monsieur Brennan's Finest".

Service complaint

When we paid our bill the waiter took over fifteen minutes to bring us back our change. When I complained to him he told me that he was working to "put the wait back into waiter". I think you need to train your staff to a higher standard or replace them with politer staff.

How you want the matter dealt with

In total a meal for four cost us €160. Do you think this is good value? I think you need to bring your prices down to reflect the quality of your food and service. I am not asking for compensation as you can't return a birthday to an eighty-year-old woman. I am demanding a written apology however, and a promise to try harder in future.

Yours faithfully,

Jane Sprat

One of the features of argument that this text uses is the rhetorical question: 'Do you think this is good value?' We remember that a rhetorical question is a question that has an obvious answer or one that the writer answers immediately afterward. You will learn more about the language of argument in the next section.

 ## OPENING ACT

1 What is the background information in this letter?

2 What information is given in this letter about the meal and service?

 ## SPOTLIGHT

3 How would you describe the tone of this letter? `OPINION` `REASON` `EVIDENCE`

4 Do you think the woman expressed her complaints in an effective and correct way? `OPINION` `REASON` `EVIDENCE`

5 Do you think the quotations in the letter support the woman's argument? `OPINION` `REASON` `EVIDENCE`

 ## CENTRE STAGE

Learning about Letters

It is important to practise writing formal letters using the appropriate register.

Plan and write a formal letter using four paragraphs, choosing one of the following scenarios.

i) You are writing to the Minister for Education to complain about the lack of facilities in schools.

ii) You are the manager of the restaurant Happy Jacque and you are replying to Jane Sprat to apologise for the food and service she received.

iii) You are writing to the Minister for Health, arguing that it should be compulsory to wear a bicycle helmet when cycling.

iv) You are writing to ask your favourite author to come to your school to present prizes for a creative writing competition.

v) You are Seamus Heaney, writing to accept the Nobel Prize for Literature from the Nobel Prize Committee.

Remember:
• consistent register;
• structure ideas into paragraphs;
• formal opening and closing.

Letter to the Editor

The letter to an editor of a newspaper or magazine is an opportunity for the reader to have their opinions published. An opinion is a person's personal view on a topic or issue. Opinions are usually based upon a person's point of view, with their personal interpretation of circumstances and experience.

Note: *a statement based upon personal opinion and experience is* subjective. *A statement based upon proven fact is* objective. *When we argue, we often use objective facts to persuade people of our subjective opinions.*

Example: Carrying heavy schoolbags is not good for students' health (***objective fact***) and so I feel that schoolbags should be banned from schools (***subjective opinion***).

Letters to the editor often use the languages of argument and persuasion.

Features of argument include:
- **tone of certainty;**
- **direct appeals to the reader;**
- **statements of subjective opinion;**
- **statements of fact and supporting information, such as statistics;**
- **quotations;**
- **rhetorical questions;**
- **logic.**

Note: *logic is an argument that seems reasonable and correct. Logic is usually built upon a number of statements that link together.*

The following letter is giving an opinion. It is strongly trying to persuade the reader of a viewpoint. The purpose of an argument should be clear from the opening statement and paragraph.

3 Roseview,
Ballykill,
Co. Louth.

081 996965

25/07/2012

Letter to the Editor,
Daily Times,
32 Fleet St,
Dublin 1.

Dear Madam,

Outline of problem and central argument of letter

It is clear to me that we urgently need to adopt a new approach to environmental education. A recent government report on climate change found that "the consequences of climate change can no longer be avoided". I would argue that avoiding is exactly what Irish people are doing. The truth is we aren't properly prepared for this grave problem.

Proposed solution and specific details

Your readers need to know that our present school system doesn't teach environmental science as a subject. We need to change this. The subject could include topics such as pollution, climate change, conservation, planning and outdoor education. This would raise the environmental knowledge of students and, consequently, the public.

Appeal to the readers with logical argument

Readers will agree that a society that is educated properly is better placed to cope with problems and find solutions. How can we hope to adapt to climate change if we are not educated about it? Though we are highly skilled and educated in other areas, we cannot afford to be complacent about this.

Overview of problem, looking to the future

Over the next fifty years many of us will have to cope with the increasing effects of climate change. The answers to this problem will come in large part from those who are now young. An environmental education is a legacy that our present government must gift to future generations. If it hopes to avert disaster, it must gift it now.

Yours faithfully,

_____

Mike Thompson

GRAVE
serious, cause for alarm

COMPLACENT
careless

LEGACY
a gift handed down to the future

*The **closing statement** of this letter gives an urgent warning and repeats the **central message**. The last argument or appeal is often stated more strongly than before, so that the message makes a greater impact on the reader as they finish the letter.*

 ## OPENING ACT

1 What does the author of this letter find worrying? `EVIDENCE`

2 What solution does the author have to the problem outlined in the letter? `EVIDENCE`

  i) Identify two persuasive sentences in the text. `EVIDENCE`

  ii) What is the key persuasive word in each sentence?

3 What is the central message of this letter?

 ## SPOTLIGHT

4 Do you agree with the argument made in this letter? `OPINION` `REASON` `EVIDENCE`

5 Do you think the register of this letter is appropriate for its purpose? `OPINION` `REASON` `EVIDENCE`

6 Can you think of any way to make this letter more convincing? *Refer to features of argument.* `OPINION` `REASON`

7 What issue would you like to see debated more in society? `OPINION` `REASON`

 ## CENTRE STAGE

Dear Madam

Write a reply to this letter. You can agree further with the letter or you can argue against it.

• Plan and structure your reply into paragraphs.
• Use the correct opening and closing for the letter.
• Clearly outline your opinion in your opening statement.
• Summarise your opinion at the end and use a strong closing statement.
• Use details from the letter above to argue for or against the letter.
• Think about your own school experience and include it in your letter.
• Remember to use argument, persuasion and information where possible.

Or

You can write a letter to the editor based on one of the following topics.

• The Internet is not a social activity.
• Exams put too much pressure on young people.
• Cyclists should have right of way before cars.

You will learn more features of information, persuasion and argument in the following sections.

IN YOUR OWN WORDS

SUBJECTIVE:

OBJECTIVE:

LOGIC:

curriculum vitae

A curriculum vitae, or CV, is a short document used for job applications that outlines your personal details and your school, work and life experience. It comes from Latin, meaning 'the course of life'. It can also be called a résumé.

The purpose of a CV is to **inform** the employer of your personal details, education, skills, experience and pastimes. This is a lot of information to put into a short document. To fit in the necessary information, we apply what we have learned about functional writing.

Polite: language should be respectful and serious.
Clear: language should be plain and easily understood.
Factual: all relevant and accurate information should be given.
Concise: language should use the least number of words to express its point.

As the purpose is to inform, we know that we will be using the language of information, and not persuasion or argument. Look at the CV on the next page and answer the questions that follow.

Curriculum Vitae

PERSONAL DETAILS

Name: James Smith

Address: 3 Mill Street,
Tullabridge,
Co. Offaly.

Mobile no./e-mail: 083 88384493/jamessmith87@tinterweb.ie

Date of Birth: 7 June 1993

Nationality: Irish

Marital Status: Single

EDUCATION

1998–2005: Primary School:
Tullabridge National School, Tullabridge, Co. Offaly.

2005–Present: Secondary School:
Tullabridge Community School, Tullabridge, Co. Offaly.

Junior Certificate Results 2008: English (H) B, Irish (O) C, Maths (H) A, Geography (H) A, History (H) B, Science (H) A, French (O) B, Technical Graphics (H) B, Art (H) B, CSPE (H) C, Religion (H) B.

WORK EXPERIENCE

2009–2010: Sales Assistant: Bradley's Convenience Store, Main Street, Tullabridge.
Duties: Cashier, shelf stacking, general cleaning.

Achievements and Interests: I was captain of the school debating team that came second in the All-Ireland Debating Junior Competition in 2008. I won Best Original Design Award at Enterprise Ireland School Awards for my transition year enterprise project.

I participate in many sporting activities and like team sports in particular. I play hurling with Tullabridge Gaels. I am also a member of our school athletic club.

Referees: Jack Walsh, Principal, Tullabridge Community School, Tullabridge, Co. Offaly. Ph. 049 3383285.
Andrew Bradley, Bradley's Convenience Store, Main Street, Tullabridge. Ph. 049 3923423.

☝ SPOTLIGHT

1 How would you describe the language used in this CV? `OPINION` `REASON` `EVIDENCE`

2 Why do you think it is important that CVs are concise? `OPINION` `REASON`

3 What are your achievements and interests?

🎩 CENTRE STAGE

Your Course of Life

Using the above CV as a model, write out a mock CV for yourself.

Remember to be:
* polite;
* clear;
* factual;
* concise.

For a mock CV you can make up the details you don't have, such as your Junior Certificate results or work experience. Please note, however, that when you are drawing up a real CV, you have to be completely honest.

Review

A **review** is a guide to a product, event or service that has been tested by the author of the review. A review contains a mixture of facts and opinion. A review also **evaluates** a product. To evaluate is to judge the positive and negative values of something.

Normally the reviewer will first outline the facts about the item being reviewed and then give their subjective opinion and evaluation. We remember that subjective means based on your own perspective, including your thoughts and feelings.

Common reviews
* **Films.**
* **Restaurants.**

- Novels.
- Plays.
- Music.
- Games.
- Electronic products.
- Travel.
- Sports events.

It is possible to structure a review using different categories. You can also use stars and numbers, such as percentages. Below is a sample structure for a film review. Each category would be given its own paragraph.

- Introduction and background to film.
- Summary of plot.
- Performance of actors.
- Music, costume and special effects.
- Final evaluation and recommendation.

All reviews follow a similar format.

Here is a review of the animated film, WALL-E.

Robot Stars in Smart Space Drama

Introduction

I was pleasantly surprised when I took my young nephew to see the Pixar film *WALL-E* at the weekend. The cinema was busy with children excited at the chance to see an animated blockbuster, but what we saw was a mature film for all age groups. The animators at Pixar, the company that specialises in computer animation and special effects, have achieved a visually stunning masterpiece. They have been perfecting their computer graphic skills on other successful films, including *Finding Nemo* and *Toy Story*. In *WALL-E* they showcase everything they have learned.

Plot

So what is the film about? The film follows the fortunes of a small robot, WALL-E, as he goes about his daily routine of cleaning up waste on our planet. The difficulty for WALL-E is that humans have forgotten about him and have long left the earth because its environment is too toxic. WALL-E's world is suddenly changed when a more advanced robot, EVE, arrives on earth to look for any remaining plant samples for the humans who have left. WALL-E falls in love with her despite her hostile treatment of him. He manages to hitch a ride on her spaceship back to the human mothership. There he encounters, with surprising results, the humans who left him on earth so many years before.

Characters

As this is animation there are no live actors, but ironically, WALL-E the robot gives one of the most human performances I've seen in many years. The robot is unable to speak clearly and must communicate in mime and gesture. This adds humour to the film as he struggles to make himself understood. He is cleverly personified by such human traits as sentimentally collecting odds and ends, as well as watching old movies. His relationship with EVE shows positive human qualities, such as loyalty and affection.

Effects

An unusual feature of this film is the lack of dialogue. There is no talking for most of the film, but it makes you appreciate just how much drama can be created using mime and body language, even when the body is that of a robot! The sound effects are mostly of machines and robotic voices, but they manage to bring real life to the film. The animation effects are especially strong at the beginning, when we see the damage that humans have done to their planet.

Final recommendation

So now you can see why I am giving this film a five star review. It is surprisingly original for an animated film, yet it is entertaining in a way which appeals to everyone. It has an important message on how we should be looking after ourselves and our world, yet it manages to do it in a way that is humorous and fun. I won't give too much away by saying there is an exciting ending that gives our hero, WALL-E, a chance to save the day. All this and it also manages to fit in a love story! As you might have guessed by now, I am recommending that you watch this film.

SPECIALISES
to concentrate on

ADVANCED
more modern or capable

HOSTILE
aggressive towards

OPENING ACT

1 What information do you find out in the first paragraph of the review?

2 How is the robot EVE different from WALL-E?

3 How does WALL-E communicate?

4 Find an example of subjective opinion in the last paragraph of the review and explain why it is subjective. **EVIDENCE**

 # SPOTLIGHT

5 How would you best describe this review:

   i) informative;

   ii) entertaining;

   iii) positive?

   OPINION **REASON** **EVIDENCE**

6 Would you go to see this movie based on this review? **OPINION** **REASON**

7 From reading this review, what aspect of the film do you think would interest you the most? **REASON** **EVIDENCE**

8 What do you think the writer means by saying *'ironically, WALL-E the robot gives one of the most human performances I've seen in many years'*? **REASON** **EVIDENCE**

9 If possible, watch the first half an hour of *WALL-E* in class. Then answer the following questions.

   i) How do the animators personify WALL-E?

   ii) Identify two themes in the opening part of the film.

   iii) Based on what you have seen of the film, do you think the review is accurate?

   iv) How do the film-makers bring humour into the film?

 # CENTRE STAGE

Point of Review

Write your own review for one of the following.

i) A film.

ii) The last book you read.

iii) A day of the week.

iv) An album.

v) The last meal you had.

To begin, identify five categories that you are going to use to structure your answer. You can discuss suitable categories as a group beforehand, writing sample categories on the board. Try to write a similar amount for each category. Remember to give information as well as opinion.

Speech

Speeches are used for such purposes as to congratulate, express gratitude, welcome, inform or commemorate. To commemorate is to honour the memory of a person or event. The **correct register** of a speech is very important. It should be appropriate to the target audience and to the occasion.

The following speech uses the language of persuasion. This can include:

- **quotations;**
- **comparisons;**
- **superlatives;**
- **imperatives;**
- **repetition;**
- **rhetorical questions;**
- **historical references.**

Superlatives are adjectives that express the extreme of a quality, for example *the greatest* or *the most wonderful*. **Imperatives** are verbs or expressions that order us or make a plea with us, for example *you must* or *it is vital that we change*. Historical references make comparisons with the past in a positive or negative way.

Here is an extract from President Barack Obama's inauguration speech. This is a speech an incoming president gives when he is being sworn in for his term in office.

Era of Peace

Barack Obama

PATCHWORK
composed of a variety of parts

HERITAGE
tradition and history

SEGREGATION
keeping people or races apart

USHERING
guiding

MUTUAL
shared

DISSENT
to raise an objection

INDIFFERENCE
not to care

For we know that our patchwork heritage is a strength, not a weakness. We are a nation of Christians and Muslims, Jews and Hindus – and non-believers. We are shaped by every language and culture, drawn from every end of this earth; and because we have tasted the bitter pill of civil war and segregation, and emerged from that dark chapter stronger and more united, we cannot help but believe that the old hatreds shall someday pass; that the lines of tribe shall soon dissolve; that as the world grows smaller, our common humanity shall reveal itself; and that America must play its role in ushering in a new era of peace.

To the Muslim world, we seek a new way forward, based on mutual interest and mutual respect. To those leaders around the globe who seek to sow conflict, or blame their society's ills on the West – know that your people will judge you on what you can build, not what you destroy. To those who cling to power through corruption and deceit and the silencing of dissent, know that you are on the wrong side of history; but that we will extend a hand if you are willing to unclench your fist.

To the people of poor nations, we pledge to work alongside you to make your farms flourish and let clean waters flow; to nourish starved bodies and feed hungry minds. And to those nations like ours that enjoy relative plenty, we say we can no longer afford indifference to the suffering outside our borders; nor can we consume the world's resources without regard to effect. For the world has changed, and we must change with it.

OPENING ACT

1 What has shaped America, according to Obama? `EVIDENCE`

2 What message does Obama have for world leaders who cause harm? `EVIDENCE`

3 What pledge does Obama make to the poor nations of the world? `EVIDENCE`

4 What does Obama say we must do in a changed world? `EVIDENCE`

 # SPOTLIGHT

5 What do you think Obama means by 'the wrong side of history'?

6 What do you think is the purpose of this speech? `OPINION` `REASON` `EVIDENCE`

7 Would you like to have heard this speech? `OPINION` `REASON`

8 Do you think the register of this speech was appropriate to the target audience and occasion? `OPINION` `REASON` `EVIDENCE`

9 Do you find this speech inspirational? `OPINION` `REASON` `EVIDENCE`

 # CENTRE STAGE

Role Play

Write one of the following speeches and deliver it to your class. Use persuasion, argument or information, where appropriate. The class must help you by role-playing the audience.

i)   You have been elected youngest ever leader of this country and you are setting forth your vision for our future.

ii) You are a football team manager giving your team a talk before they play an important final.

iii) You are addressing a group of teachers about how they could improve school for students.

iv) You are giving a lifetime achievement award to a film or sports star of your choice.

Remember to plan and structure your speech.

Here is an example of paragraph headings for i) above.

What you will do for the future of the country ...
Opening paragraph.
Educational future.
Environmental future.
Economic future.

Sporting future.
Closing paragraph.

Use these features of speeches as a checklist to help you: quotations, comparisons, superlatives, imperatives, repetition, rhetorical questions, historical references.

IN YOUR OWN WORDS

SUPERLATIVES:

IMPERATIVES:

Debate

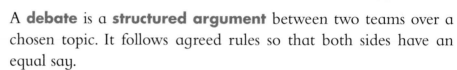

A **debate** is a **structured argument** between two teams over a chosen topic. It follows agreed rules so that both sides have an equal say.

How to Debate

Debates make effective use of all aspects of the language of information, argument and persuasion. You must **structure** your argument, **support** it with evidence, **convince** the audience of your position and **engage** their attention.

To structure: use a central argument, sub-arguments, paragraphs and a closing summation.
To support: use logic, statistics, anecdotes, quotations and facts.
To convince: use imperatives, comparisons, repetition and superlatives.
To engage: use irony, understatement, rhetorical questions and exaggeration.

Roles in a Formal Debate

Each team has **three members**, one of them being the **captain**. The teams take it in turns to speak. The captain must make the first speech for his side, followed by the captain of the other side. Each captain must also make a final speech for their team, short summaries called the closing argument.

The teams argue over one statement, called the **motion**. The team that agrees with the motion **proposes** it, while the team that disagrees with the motion **opposes** it.

INTERCLASS DEBATES
MOTION: HUNTING KEEPS THE COUNTRYSIDE ALIVE

TEAM A: PROPOSING THE MOTION   TEAM B: OPPOSING THE MOTION

LADIES AND GENTLEMEN, CHAIRPERSON, JUDGES, MEMBERS OF THE OPPOSITION, HUNTING TRULY DOES KEEP THE COUNTRYSIDE ALIVE...

CAPTAIN
THIRD SPEAKER
SECOND SPEAKER

CHAIRPERSON
JUDGES

AUDIENCE

TIME KEEPER

A **chairperson** adjudicates to see that the rules are kept and a **timekeeper** ensures that the debate speeches keep within time limits. A **panel of judges** may decide which team has won the debate. The **audience** watches and has a chance to contribute when the debate is opened to the floor at the end, meaning the audience can argue with the team members.

SPOTLIGHT

1 Write out three arguments for young people being allowed to vote.
2 Write out three arguments against complete freedom of speech.
3 Find a quotation, anecdote or statistic that supports one of your arguments above.

CENTRE STAGE

Statement / Rebuttal

A **rebuttal** is when you make a point arguing directly against another person's point.

This exercise is an informal class debate. It should take about ten minutes. The motion is: **Meat is murder.**

Note: The Importance of Good Manners

It is important to respect your opponents in a debate. You can lose points if you are rude or disrespectful. If you want to disagree with someone, you have to express yourself clearly in an appropriate register and tone.

Rules

- Remain seated in your chairs at all times.
- No one can talk over another person who is talking.
- When one person makes a point, anyone who wants to make a rebuttal must raise their hand at the end of the person's statement.
- You must be chosen to speak by your teacher.
- Each point must lead from the point that came before until you have exhausted the argument.

As a follow-up exercise, you can now write a one-page argument for or against this motion. To help you learn debating skills, you must now take the opposite side to how you really feel about the motion! Remember to use all the features you can of information, persuasion and argument.

IN YOUR OWN WORDS

MOTION:

PROPOSES:

OPPOSES:

curtain call

Now we will put together everything we have learned about functional writing. When you are answering the questions below and preparing to debate, use the following checklists to revise your writing skills and help you choose the appropriate register. You can also use it any time you are asked to write a review, letter or other functional writing task.

To inform:
- **serious;**
- **clear;**
- **factual;**
- **objective;**
- **concise.**

To persuade and argue:

- **tone of certainty;**
- **appeal directly to reader;**
- **support opinions with fact;**
- **quotations;**
- **rhetorical questions;**
- **imperatives;**
- **logic;**
- **comparisons;**
- **superlatives;**
- **repetition;**
- **historical reference.**

Always plan and structure your answers! Here is a motion that you can now debate. To prepare for the debate you can answer the Spotlight questions below.

Motion: English should be the language of the world.

 ## SPOTLIGHT

1 Write out three arguments proposing English as the language of the world.
2 Write out three arguments opposing English as the language of the world.
3 Choose one of your arguments above, on either side of the debate, and write out a short paragraph for your argument using the following features: rhetorical question, an imperative statement and a subjective opinion supported by an objective fact.

 ## CENTRE STAGE

Formal Debate
English should be the language of the world.

Have a class debate on this motion. This will take organisation and preparation. Divide the class into as many teams of three as possible. If there are extra students, they can join up with teams to give the closing argument in place of the captain.

If you don't like the above motion, there are more motions below that you can try out.

In class …
1 Each team must choose another team to debate against. This means that half the class will propose the motion and half the class will oppose it.
2 Each team must get together and divide the debate into different categories, with each member taking a sub-argument of the overall argument.

For homework …
3 Each member must then write a two-minute debate. Make sure team members don't repeat each other.

4 The captain must link the three sub-arguments together in his/her final summation. He/She can also include rebuttals to points already made.

In class …

You can now create a debate in the classroom between different teams. Set up tables for the two teams, facing the rest of the class. If possible, your teacher can photocopy the scorecard template so everyone can practise judging the debate.

Note: *it will take near to a full class to hold a proper debate. It might be best to start with a quicker informal first debate, without judges or time limits, so the class can get used to debating in action.*

5 Choose the chairperson, timekeeper and judges from other members of the class. The chairperson must sit in the middle along with a timekeeper. Photocopy the scorecard and let three students sit in as judges. They must read and understand the scorecard before the debate starts.

6 Each person is allowed to speak for a minimum of two minutes and a maximum of three. A timekeeper times the speeches and rings a bell when the speech reaches two minutes. Each speaker is encouraged to use some of their time to disagree with the other team's arguments.

7 You can apply a ten-point penalty for going more than thirty seconds over or under the time allowed.

8 At the end, as the judges are adding up the scores, you can open the debate to comments from the floor.

9 You can take a show of hands in the whole class to see who the class thinks has won. Then you can see what the judges' score is.

Note: *to help you understand the scorecard, here are some questions you can ask yourself for each category you are judging under.*

Purpose and preparation: has the speaker researched and prepared their argument properly, and does the speaker stick to the point, clearly outlining their side of the argument?

Persuasion: does the speaker convince by using logical argument and the features of persuasive language?

Delivery: is the speaker's body language and tone of voice confident, engaging and appropriate?

Rebuttal: is the speaker able to disagree with points made by the other team in a convincing way?

Here are some more motions for debating
• Women: The superior gender.
• School discipline needs to be tougher.
• Hunting is for animals.
• Irish identity is no more.
• Developing countries need a fair deal.

Scorecard template for Judging Class Debates

Motion: English should be the language of the world.

Proposing team names:	Opposing team names:
1 _____	1 _____
2 _____	2 _____
3 _____	3 _____

Proposing Team:

Mark (each out of 10):	Purpose and preparation	Persuasion	Delivery	Total
Captain				
Speaker 2				
Speaker 3				
Captain	Summation and rebuttal	The captain is given one overall mark out of 10 for his/her closing debate		
Total out of 100				

Opposing Team:

Mark (each out of 10):	Purpose and preparation	Persuasion	Delivery	Total
Captain				
Speaker 2				
Speaker 3				
Captain	Summation and rebuttal	The captain is given one overall mark out of 10 for his/her closing debate		
Total out of 100				

Grammar Station

Subject, verb, object

Basic sentences are structured with a subject, a verb and an object. Knowing this will help you to use the correct personal pronoun.

Here is a sentence: **The horse ate the fresh grass.**

Subject: this is the person or thing doing the action. In the above case, the **horse** is the subject.

Verb: this is the action. In the above case, **eating** is the action.

Object: this is what the action is done to. In the above case the fresh grass is being eaten, so the **fresh grass** is the object.

The subject, verb and object will usually be in this order, although there can be exceptions.

Homework *(object)* I *(subject)* love *(verb)*!
The dog (**object**) I (**subject**) patted (**verb**).
The man (**object**) that the police (**subject**) arrested (**verb**).

 ## OPENING ACT

Identify the subject, verb and object in the following sentences.

1 The player kicked the football.
2 I drank some juice.
3 The oranges that I picked.
4 I love tomatoes.
5 Anthony dances with his hips.
6 The train runs through the station.
7 Cyclists use the cycle path.
8 Rain annoys me.

9 I annoy my sister.

10 Rain I hate!

Personal Pronouns

1 When to use **I** or **me**?

We use the personal pronoun **I** for the subject of the sentence.
Example: **I** am sick of walking.
Who is sick of walking? I (subject).
You wouldn't say: Me am sick of walking.

We use the personal pronoun **me** for the object of the sentence.
Example: Jill is tired of **me.**
Who is Jill tired of? Me (object).
You wouldn't say: Jill is tired of I.

Remember: to find the object, ask who or what the action is being done to.

Subject pronouns	Object pronouns
I, you, he, she, it, they	Me, you, him, her, it, them

Here are some more examples of this rule.

1 I talked to him (object).

2 The dog jumped on me (object).

3 They were shouting at her (object).

4 It was him (object) I was talking to.

5 Francis and I (subject) are going to the shop.

6 The teacher gave out to Francis and me (object).

7 It was me (object) who he shouted at.

8 She can't speak for me (object).

9 It was me (object) they (subject) loved, not her (object).

10 She (subject) talked to me (object) but she (subject) ignored him (object).

It is good manners to leave your pronoun last in the list if there is more than yourself as the subject, or more than yourself as the object.

Subject: *Jane* and *I* are leaving soon.
Object: *The train will not wait for Jane and me.*

OPENING ACT

Use the correct pronoun in the following cases.

i) I talked to (they/them).
ii) (They/them) shouted at (I/me) to get off the fence.
iii) Jamie and (I/me) will be late for school.
iv) Pass the salt to Ann and (I/me).
v) You won't be as late as (they/them) were?
vi) It's you and (I/me) they were talking to.
vii) The ball hit (she/her) and (I/me).
viii) The heat of the Greek summer was too much for (they/them).
ix) Will you call (he/him) and then ring (I/me)?

Personal Pronouns

2 When to use **who** or **whom**?

Who is used for **subject**, the person or thing doing the action.

Examples:
Who is ringing me?
I am the student **who** ran in the corridor.

Whom is for **object**, the person or thing that the action is being done to.

Examples:
The boy **whom** the girl talked to.
The man **whom** the police arrested escaped.

We also use **whom** after prepositions: *to, by, for, under, from, over, beside, etc.*

Examples:
To whom it concerns.
The person **for whom** it was made.
The woman **under whom** I worked.

 # OPENING ACT

Use the correct pronoun in the following cases.

i) For (who/whom) the bells tolls.
ii) (Who/whom) fed the cat?
iii) The man (who/whom) I wrote to replied quickly.
iv) To (who/whom) were you talking?

v) (Who/whom) can say where we go from here?

vi) Here is the boy (who/whom) I talked of.

vii) She is the girl (who/whom) the president met.

viii) I won't talk about the boy (who/whom) broke my window.

ix) (Who/whom) can say why we should study grammar?

x) The people (who/whom) use language every day.

7

MEDIA STUDIES: NEWSPAPERS, ONLINE MEDIA AND MAGAZINES

I AM JASMINE WEBSTER, a journalist and reporter. In this unit we will focus on newspapers and print media as part of media studies. We will learn how it is possible to **communicate** on a **mass scale** with people, groups and society. Mass scale means of a very large size, with many people involved.

You will learn about the following:

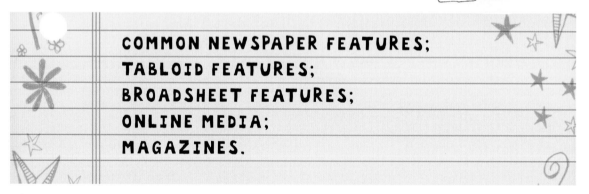

COMMON NEWSPAPER FEATURES;
TABLOID FEATURES;
BROADSHEET FEATURES;
ONLINE MEDIA;
MAGAZINES.

The **purpose** of newspapers and print media is to **inform, investigate, debate** and **entertain**. They can also persuade and argue through opinion-based articles and reporting. We will learn how to examine tone and evaluate the writer's use of information, persuasion and argument.

We will also learn about and revise **apostrophes** at the **Punctuation Station**.

common Newspaper Features

There are two common types of newspaper: **tabloid** and **broadsheet**. There are also other types of newspaper, such as local newspapers, specialty newspapers and foreign language newspapers. The **title** of the newspaper, the **masthead**, should be clearly recognisable across the top of the front page.

The people newspapers are aimed at are called the **target readership**. For example, a newspaper about fishing would be aimed at fishermen, and so fishermen would be the target readership.

 SPOTLIGHT

1 Who do you think the target readership of the following newspapers is?
  i) *Daily Star.*
  ii) *Irish Farmers Journal.*

iii) *USA Today.*

iv) *The Connacht Tribune.*

v) *The Racing Post.*

vi) *The Financial Times.*

vii) *Die Welt.*

viii) *Sydney Morning Herald.*

ix) *Galway Advertiser.*

x) *Sunday Independent.*

2 If you could start up a newspaper covering any type of news and aimed at any audience, what type of newspaper would you choose and what would you call it? Who would your target audience be?

3 Do you think young people should have their own newspaper?

IN YOUR OWN WORDS

MASTHEAD:

TARGET READERSHIP:

In this section we will learn about the most common features that newspapers share.

- **The front page.**
- **Newspaper sections.**
- **Staff roles.**

The Front Page

Below is the **front page** of a **broadsheet newspaper** with significant features labelled. Most newspapers share these features. Front pages can also have advertisements, free gifts and promotional offers.

Irish Independent

MASTHEAD

IRELAND'S BEST-SELLING DAILY NEWSPAPER — METRO EDITION 8 Jul 09

ROY KEANE'S **SPORT** IRISH DEBUT ENDS IN DEFEAT

POTTER MANIA **P2-3** WORLD PREMIERE

RECESSION IS NO EXCUSE FOR **P26** BAD HAIR

LIST OF CONTENTS

WEB ADDRESS — WWW.INDEPENDENT.IE Wednesday 8 July 2009 €1.80 (£1 IN N. IRELAND) — **DATE AND PRICE**

Electrician

BANNER HEADLINE

row sparks national strike fears

ICTU calls for all unions to vote on pay hike protests

●INSIDE

The men at
the coalface **P10**
How it came
to this **P11**
Why this could
cost us **P18**

Anne-Marie Walsh
Industry Correspondent

LEAD ARTICLE

THE threat of a national strik loom the electricians dispute took a sinister new turn.

ICTU, the unions' umbrella body, decided to ask its 600,000 members for the green light to effectively shut down the country.

The move came despite both sides in the electricians' dispute agreeing to enter fresh talks with the Labour Relations Commission today.

However, the TEEU, which represents electricians, insisted they would continue with a third day of crippling pickets at sites around the country.

The decision by ICTU to ballot its members was seen as a

serious development as a vote in favour of strike would hit every aspect of economic life and put tens of thousands of jobs in rdy.

ady last night there were ure orecasts of the implications of the first two days of the strike.

Business leaders claimed the action by electricians over a €2.49-an-hour pay rise has put the country's crucial €70bn export sector at "serious risk".

Major international manufacturers including Pfizer, Cadbury and Diageo, who have no involvement in the dispute "have been unfairly caught in the crossfire", they said.

Following a specially-convened meeting at its biennial conference in Kerry, ICTU announced that it had unanimously **Continued on page 10**

Tears and songs as children remember 'best dad' Jackson

IMAGE

MICHAEL Jackson's children Paris, Prince Michael II 'Blanket' and Prince Michael, bid an emotional farewell to their father at a public tribute

ceremony last night. Paris earlier broke down as she took the stage at LA's S' Centre with her brothe "Ever since I was born daddy has been the best

father you can ever imagine and I just want to say I love

SECOND ARTICLE

CE:
PAGES 24, 25

BARCODE

Recommended retail price of the Irish Independent compact edition is ROI is €1.80

Vol. 118 No. 161   Irish Independent

IN YOUR LIFESTYLE SECTION

SUPPLEMENT

●'I was only 31 when I got ovarian cancer' **P27**

●'The man who blinded me never apologised' **P29**

●MOTORS
All the latest news and reviews **P40**

🎩 CENTRE STAGE

Read All About It!

Let everyone bring in a newspaper. It can be tabloid, broadsheet, local or international.

Discuss and compare the differences between the newspapers.
• Who is the target audience of your paper?
• What difference is there between your front page and others?
• What are the three most striking features on the front page?
• Is there another newspaper you would prefer? Why?
• If you could improve your front page in one way, what would it be?

★ ⑦
★★

Newspaper Sections

A newspaper is divided into different sections. Below are different sections, with some examples.

National news section: this contains news events that happened in Ireland. The language is usually factual and informative. It is written in an objective tone with a formal register.

Regional news section: this contains a number of articles based in a particular region, for example Munster or the south-east. It often refers to local details and organisations. The writing is usually informative and formal.

Example of regional news section:

SHANNON AREA TO GET TOURISM BOOST

Towns along the Shannon are to get special funding from the government to upgrade tourist facilities and infrastructure. The importance of sustainable tourism and the responsible use of resources were highlighted in a report by a special task force on tourism.

"The Shannon is an internationally recognised tourist destination and we need to balance the protection of this resource with the fulfilment of its potential," a spokesperson for Athlone Tourism Board said, responding to the report.

World news section: this contains international news articles. It usually contains important global news events that are of interest or concern to us all. Larger, more powerful countries feature more than smaller ones. The writing is usually objective, formal and informative.

Sports section: this is reporting, commentary and coverage of recent sporting events. It contains action verbs and expressive adverbs as journalists give us a sense of the sporting action. The writing is usually sensational and informative.

Lifestyle and features section: this contains articles and information about aspects of people's lifestyles. For example, it could be about health, travel, shopping or celebrity. The register can be informal and the tone casual.

Example of lifestyle section:

HAVE YOU TRIED BOXERCISE CRAZE?

If you're like me you've probably tried every keep-fit craze going. I just can't seem to get enough of them. The problem is my interest wanes after a few weeks. Usually after I discover I am not going to become a yoga master or jiu-jitsu expert overnight.

This time it's going to be different, I told myself when I joined up for a ten-week course of boxercise at my local gym. I was fully committed to completing the course but I wondered if I could. Ten weeks later and I am still going strong.

Culture section: this contains articles and information about books, theatre, films, dance, music and art. It also contains reviews, where experts give their opinion on new books, plays, music and films. This can contain a variety of tones and can range from objective information to persuasion and subjective opinion.

Example of culture section:

COLFER OUR ANSWER TO TOLKIEN

Eoin Colfer is our answer to Tolkien, teenagers were told yesterday at a talk about the Wexford-born teacher and writer. He is internationally renowned for his Artemis Fowl series of fantasy novels.

He gave up teaching in 2001 after publishing the first Artemis Fowl book. It was a success, and since then he has enthralled readers with his vivid imagination and gripping plotlines.

Opinion articles: this is where different people give their opinions on different events that are happening in the news. These people could be journalists, politicians, sports people, writers or other people with specialist knowledge. Opinion articles can contain bias and use the language of persuasion and argument. **Bias** is when a person presents facts or opinions in a way that is influenced by their personal opinions and prejudices.

Example of opinion article:

ALL-IRELAND SOCCER TEAM NEEDED

No one would disagree that it's time for a soccer team that represents the whole nation. For too long Irish soccer has been divided into North and South, and now is the right time for change.

The success of our All-Ireland rugby team in recent years has shown how sport can create a unified spirit for the people of Ireland. Can we not see the same could be true for soccer?

Editorial: this is where the editor, who is the overall manager of the paper, gives an opinion on events that are happening in the news. You will find a detailed example of an editor's column later in the unit.

Business section: this section deals with daily events in the business and finance world.

Classifieds: these are advertisements. These range from small adverts for services and goods to established or large companies advertising their products. The larger and more complicated the advert, the more expensive it is.

 SPOTLIGHT

1 Which section of the newspaper would you read first? `OPINION` `REASON` `EVIDENCE`

2 Which section of the newspaper would you have least interest in? Why? `OPINION` `REASON` `EVIDENCE`

3 Of the sample articles above, which one do you think uses the most persuasive language? `OPINION` `REASON` `EVIDENCE`

4 Which of the articles uses the most informal or casual language, similar to language you would use in conversation? `OPINION` `REASON` `EVIDENCE`

5 If you could invent a new section for a newspaper, what would it be? `OPINION` `REASON`

6 In your opinion, which section of the newspaper plays the most important part in our society? `OPINION` `REASON` `EVIDENCE`

IN YOUR OWN WORDS

EDITORIAL:

CLASSIFIEDS:

BIAS:

Staff Roles

There are many different jobs in a newspaper. Here is a list of the most common roles.

The reporter: this is the journalist who finds stories and gathers information. They then file a report or article.

The photographer: this is the person who takes photo images. They will often work with the reporter so that the image matches the report.

The commentator: this person gives their opinion on current affairs. They are usually experts and have knowledge in a specialist area, such as sport or finance.

The foreign correspondent: this person reports from foreign regions, such as North Africa or South-East Asia. They must have knowledge of the language and cultures of the region, and they live there for an extended period of time.

The social diarist: diarists give a daily or weekly report on the events in their own life and in society. They usually mix gossip and celebrity news into their reporting. They can also report on cultural events, such as the opening of a film or play.

The reviewer: the reviewer evaluates a range of products, services or cultural events. These can include restaurants, films, plays, books, music and computer games.

The sub-editor: this person checks and edits the reports that journalists send into the paper. The sub-editor will also decide what stories a reporter should cover. Sub-editors manage different sections of the newspaper, such as sport or business.

The editor: the overall editor of the newspaper is responsible for managing the direction and content of the newspaper. They decide what issues the paper will cover.

🅾 SPOTLIGHT

1 Of the roles above, which one would you most like? Why? `OPINION` `REASON`

2 Which of the roles least appeals to you? `OPINION` `REASON`

3 Who do you think has the most important role? Why? `OPINION` `REASON`

Tabloid Features

The differences between tabloid and broadsheet newspapers aren't always clear and you need to be able to point to a number of features to prove that a newspaper is one type or the other. For example, a broadsheet, the *Irish Independent*, can be found in the same A3 size as tabloids.

Here are some common features of tabloid newspapers.

Appearance and layout of front page:

- small A3 size;
- red or colourful masthead;
- large headline font;
- capital letters for headlines;
- one or two news stories;
- shorter articles and less writing;
- reference to sports section at back;
- colourful and altered photographs and images;
- special offers;
- advertisement size and positioning often changes.

Content:
- emphasis on violent and sexual news content;
- focus on unusual news items;
- less global and financial news;
- star signs, fashion and 'agony aunt' columns;
- celebrity and TV entertainment;
- large sports section;
- quotations;
- 'agony aunt' column;
- gossip, rumour and scandal;
- brief news items;
- less factual information;
- less background information;
- regular supplements on TV/popular entertainment and soccer.

Language, style and tone:
- dramatic, sensational and humorous tone;
- bias is obvious;
- outrage and anger expressed;
- use of buzz words;
- use of imperatives;
- slang and casual register;
- puns and wordplay;
- purpose is to entertain.

We will now focus on four features of tabloids:
- masthead;
- tabloid headlines;
- sensational tone;
- bias.

Masthead

The mastheads of tabloid newspapers are sometimes called redtops, because of their bright red colour. They can be other colours apart from red though, for example green. The use of colour makes a newspaper more **eye-catching**.

Tabloid Headlines

The **purpose** of tabloid headlines is to **catch the reader's attention** and to amuse or express outrage. To do this, headlines use a large font and capital letters (sometimes called uppercase letters), often combined with images. The language used in the headlines has many features:

Clichés and idioms: headlines play with clichés and idioms.

Example: NICK OF TIME – watches stolen from jewellers.

Puns: puns play on words, meaning they make a joke about how words rhyme or what they mean.

Example: IT'S **SNOW** TIME TO PANIC – snowstorms hit country.

Alliteration: this is when the first letters of a series of words in a sentence sound the same.

Example: **F**URY **F**URNACE OF **F**IRE **F**ACTORY – fire burns down factory.

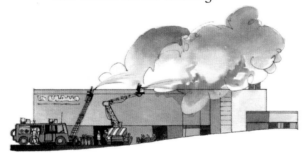

Buzz words: buzz words are clichéd and technical words often used for particular subjects. For example, a **target-man** is a buzz word used for a strong football player who plays in a striker's position. **Outlook** is a buzz word often used to describe the future, particularly in the economy.

Example: **Target-man** Tevez Is Up for Transfer – football player discusses move to another club.

Rhyme: words in the headline often rhyme.

Example: FROM G**OAL** TO D**OLE** – former footballer unemployed.

Sensation: this can be used to entertain or to express outrage and anger. The story could be real, exaggerated or very unusual.

Example: FANGS VERY MUCH! – man uses lotto win to get teeth like vampire.

Slang: slang language and an informal register are commonly found in tabloid headlines.

Example: WHAT'S THE **BUZZ**? – mystery disease harming bee populations.

CENTRE STAGE

Tabloid Headline Generator

Make your own tabloid headlines.

Tabloid headlines will always use a sensational or expressive word where possible.

Here is a word bank of tabloid-style words to help you think up tabloid headlines for the stories below.

Tabloid word bank:

gutted row stormy mad bovine bangers boom nelly crazy bling moo splash murder shock attack squashed bash explosive rfootie brekkie bust-up dosh loaded murder splat freezing blasted cash dough

Headlines

1 Ice stops Ireland football game.
2 Elephant tries to escape from zoo.
3 Minister caught accepting bribe in bag.
4 Robot car bomb detector bought by police.
5 Fireworks factory explodes.
6 Cows loose on motorway.
7 Most expensive house sold in Dublin.
8 Irish leaders argue with French leaders.
9 Toast is voted favourite breakfast.
10 Man is killed by falling piano.

Sensational Tone

Tabloids use a **sensational tone**. This means they exaggerate, use suggestion and choose words with a certain **connotation** to make an incident or event more exciting.

Connotation is the feeling or idea that a word or image gives us. For example, the word *sheep* has connotations of being foolish and easily led. The verb *claim* can have connotations of lying or dishonesty.

Here is a tabloid article:

FLAMES OF PASSION

Wife Burns Love Rat's Nest! A woman almost burned her husband's shed to the ground after accusing him of using it as a love nest. Angry Ann, wife of plumber John, found a bunch of flowers in her garden shed and went berserk. John, a local plumber, *claimed* they were a surprise for his wife.

"That rat never buys me flowers," his wife argued. "The surprise is that he expects me to believe him," she added furiously. Our expert psychologist Dr Cassandra Venus diagnosed the action as classic "*trigger-reaction behaviour*" and advised the couple to talk about their problems before turning to violence. The long-term outlook for their relationship wasn't good, she added.

Firemen called to the blazing inferno worked around the clock to get the flames under control. They were not amused. "The roof of the shed was damaged," said Fireman Mark. "It could have been so much worse." This is the third time this year emergency services have been called to the warring couple's house.

 ## SPOTLIGHT

1 What connotations does the word 'rat' have? `OPINION` `REASON` `EVIDENCE`

2 Do you think this article sides with Ann or John? `OPINION` `REASON` `EVIDENCE`

3 Why do you think the word 'claimed' is in italics? `OPINION` `REASON`

4 Identify five words that help to create the sensational tone of this article. `OPINION` `REASON` `EVIDENCE`

5 How reliable or truthful do you think this article is? `OPINION` `REASON` `EVIDENCE`

6 What do you think is the main purpose of this article? `OPINION` `REASON` `EVIDENCE`

 ## IN YOUR OWN WORDS

`CONNOTATION:`

Bias

Tabloid reporting often takes a one-sided and subjective point of view. Writers can mock or dismiss viewpoints that don't agree with their own. Tabloid journalists sometimes follow popular public opinion and stereotypes before fairness and fact.

Note: a **stereotype** is an opinion or idea held by many people that is accepted as fact, but is often wrong. Some stereotypes are harmless, for example it is a stereotype that young boys like the colour blue. Other stereotypes, particularly racial or nationality-based stereotypes, can be insulting to some people. For example, Irish people are often stereotyped as drinking too much alcohol!

We recognise bias by paying close attention to the tone, style and language of reporting.

Tabloids sometimes urge a course of action over an issue that concerns them. When they do this over a number of newspaper issues, it is called a **campaign**.

SPOTLIGHT

1 Discuss the language used in the following headlines. Can you find bias or sensation in them? Explain your conclusions.
- TIME-WASTING STUDENTS STRIKE AGAIN
- 'INNOCENT' MURDER-ACCUSED WALKS FREE ON BAIL
- MINISTER SPENDS YOUR DOSH BEING POSH
- WE'LL WIN WAR: ENGLAND TO PLAY GERMANY
- CLIMATE CHANGE HOAX: IT'S COLD, FOLKS!

2 Write three different headlines for different days of the week for a campaign you care about. Invent stories to suit the opinion you want to express. Use a tabloid bias to reflect your opinion.

For example, you could campaign about:
- sports facilities;
- school uniform;
- speeding.

CENTRE STAGE

Front Page Poseur

Make your own mock front page for your own tabloid newspaper.

Tips
- Make up news items about pets, family and friends.
- Create your own masthead to do with your school or community.
- Invent a sensational headline.
- Use photographs.
- Cut images out of magazines or newspapers to use.
- Make up a lead article and a second article.
- Have advertisements and promotional offers.

Warning: be careful not to write anything insensitive or inappropriate!

If you are reporting, focus on: **who, what, when, where, why and how!**

When you are finished, put labels on the different features and put the posters up on the wall of your classroom.

PECKING HELL ARNIE

Peek-a-boo

Peek-a-boo-parrot Arnie Carroll is driving owner, James Carroll, 14, crazy with constant chatter. The pecking parrot, 5, learned how to say "peek-a-boo" last year but the chat is wearing thin.

7

Broadsheet Features

Here are the features that are commonly found in broadsheet newspapers.

Appearance and layout of front page:
- **large A2 size;**
- **plain black banner headline;**
- **table of contents;**
- **photographic image;**
- **commentary cartoon;**
- **one lead article;**
- **one or two smaller articles;**
- **font is smaller than tabloid;**
- **advertisement in regular and distinct box.**

Content:
- **in-depth reporting;**
- **investigative journalism;**
- **smaller images;**
- **necessary background information provided;**
- **more information and facts;**
- **more articles;**
- **more sections;**
- **more world news, politics and business;**
- **editorial, opinion and letters page;**
- **regular supplements on employment, housing, culture, business and sports.**

Language, style and tone:
- **serious and reserved tone;**
- **formal register;**

MEDIA STUDIES: NEWSPAPERS, ONLINE MEDIA AND MAGAZINES

7

- **larger vocabulary;**
- **precise, clear and concise language;**
- **neutral perspective in news reporting;**
- **passive voice;**
- **purpose is to inform;**
- **objective reporting;**
- **persuasive and argumentative opinion columns;**
- **bias not as obvious as tabloid.**

We will now focus on four features of broadsheets:
- broadsheet headlines;
- photographic image;
- commentary cartoons;
- reporting.

Broadsheet Headlines

Here are some examples of broadsheet-style headlines:

World leaders meet in Davos
Hunt continues for man suspected of killing
Pope prays with crowds in Rome

The **purpose** of broadsheet headlines is to **inform**. They use a serious tone combined with a factual, formal register. The headlines will often contain more words, with a greater vocabulary range, than a tabloid headline. They typically present the news in an unbiased way. They only use uppercase letters where appropriate.

 SPOTLIGHT

It is not enough to be able to identify a broadsheet or tabloid headline. You must also be able to explain how you know what it is.

Contrast these headlines. Identify whether they are from a tabloid or broadsheet, and explain their defining features.

1 i) FARMER MILKED EU TO CREAM OFF PROFITS
   ii) Wicklow farmer found guilty of falsifying EU compensation forms
2 i) THE MICEST HOTEL IN IRELAND?
   ii) Cavan hotelier receives fine and warning over rodent infestation
3 i) Severe weather warning issued over bank holiday weekend
   ii) HURRICANE HOLIDAY
4 i) Record number of second-level students failing maths subjects
   ii) SUMS DON'T ADD UP

Photographic Images

Every photographic image tells a story and represents the world from a particular point of view. Features in the image are arranged and sometimes manipulated to capture this. The way a photograph is arranged is called the **composition**.

When looking at an image, you need to examine the image closely and identify what is happening in it.

These heading areas will help you identify content and see how it is composed.

Landscape: where was the image taken?

- Climate.
- Weather.
- Urban or rural.
- Indoors or outdoors.
- Evidence of human activity.
- Time of day.
- Occasion.

- Season.
- Era.
- Country.
- Region.
- Animals and wildlife.
- Plants and vegetation.

 OPENING ACT

1 Where and when do you think this image was taken?
2 What evidence in the image reveals where and when it was taken? EVIDENCE

People: who is in the image?

- Age.
- Gender.
- Ethnicity.
- Activity.
- Attitude.
- Facial expression.
- Gestures.
- Body language.
- Emotion.
- Interaction.
- Posture.
- Props.

 SPOTLIGHT

1 What profession do the people in this image belong to? OPINION REASON EVIDENCE

2 What do you think they are doing? OPINION REASON EVIDENCE

3 Is there anything surprising about this image? OPINION REASON

4 Are you curious about the story behind this image? OPINION REASON

7

Composition and purpose: how and why was the image taken?

- **Lighting.**
- **Colour.**
- **Shade.**
- **Time.**
- **Positioning.**
- **Angle.**
- **Perspective.**

- **Effects.**
- **Mood and atmosphere.**
- **Themes and issues.**
- **Pattern.**
- **Suggestion.**
- **Symbolism.**

 CENTRE STAGE

Editor's Choice: you are the editor of a photographic magazine and you must choose one of the above images to win the prize of Image of the Year.

You have to write a speech for an award night, explaining your choice of image.

Tips for Structure

- Praise the losing photograph first.
- Discuss the landscape in the winning photograph.
- Discuss the person in the winning photograph.
- Discuss the meaning, composition and purpose of the winning photograph.
- Write a closing paragraph.

Describing an Image

Here is how we label the different areas of an image. This will help you to refer to the different areas in the image:

Background Left	Background	Background Right
Centre Left	Centre	Centre Right
Foreground Left	Foreground	Foreground Right

When you are describing what is happening in an image, carefully and clearly discuss every significant part of it. You can use the checklists above to help you identify significant features.

 SPOTLIGHT

1 Describe what is happening in the image below. Structure your answer as follows:

i) Landscape:

ii) People:

iii) Composition and purpose:

Refer to different areas in the image when describing it.

2 The following image was chosen by the *Irish Independent* as one image of twelve to be used in a free calendar.

i)   What news story do you think this image represents? `OPINION` `REASON` `EVIDENCE`

ii) Why do you think this image was chosen over so many others? `OPINION` `REASON` `EVIDENCE`

iii) What month would you use this image for? `OPINION` `REASON` `EVIDENCE`

iv) Give a title to this image and explain your choice. `OPINION` `REASON` `EVIDENCE`

3 You have been asked to choose an image for a book of poems by the poet Seamus Heaney. Choose one of the images below and explain your choice.

If you aren't familiar with the poetry of Seamus Heaney, you can read three of his poems in Unit 8.

Refer to the different features of the images in your answer.

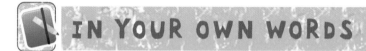
COMPOSITION:

Commentary Cartoons

Political and social commentary cartoons comment on events in politics or society. They often use satire to ridicule injustice, wrongdoing and incompetence. **Satire** is a xtype of comedy that mocks people's stupidity or bad behaviour, especially by observation and exaggeration of flaws. It is often used against powerful people, such as politicians. Commentary cartoons usually have one frame, the box in which the cartoon is drawn.

The cartoon below is a satirical cartoon by Martyn Turner, an award-winning cartoonist who draws for The Irish Times.

This cartoon exposes **hypocrisy**. *Hypocrisy is when you don't apply standards of behaviour equally. For example, if you expect people not to lie to you but then you lie yourself, you are being hypocritical. Someone who is hypocritical is said to have* **double standards**.

Commentary Cartoon Features

- **Social and political comment: the cartoon has a message for us.**
- **Exaggeration or hyperbole: the cartoon exaggerates behaviour or stupidity.**
- **Caricatures of people: the cartoon exaggerates peoples' looks and features.**
- **Satire: the cartoon mocks others' behaviour.**
- **Parody: the cartoon imitates others.**
- **Absurdity: the situations and actions are often unrealistic and odd.**

A caricature in a cartoon is the same as one in writing. It is an exaggerated sketch of a person, emphasising comical features. A parody is when a person or situation is made fun of by imitation.

Composition: cartoons can be in black and white or in colour. Colour is more eye-catching but more expensive to print. Speech bubbles and thought bubbles allow us to see what a character says or thinks. Cartoonists use different fonts to emphasise or highlight certain words. It can be normal, **bold** or *italicised*. Different fonts give us clues to the comment being made.

You will learn more about cartoons in Unit 9. Look at the Martyn Turner cartoon again and answer these questions.

OPENING ACT

1 Has the cartoonist drawn the characters in an attractive way? `EVIDENCE`

2 Why do you think he drew them the way he did?

3 What is the businessmen and government's attitude to the war against drugs? `EVIDENCE`

4 What is the government's attitude to the war against guns? `EVIDENCE`

5 What is the businessmen's attitude to the war against guns? `EVIDENCE`

SPOTLIGHT

6 i) What words are in bold in the text?

ii) What do you think the cartoonist is trying to highlight by using bold writing? `OPINION` `REASON`

7 How does the businessman's attitude to drugs contrast with his attitude to guns? `OPINION` `REASON` `EVIDENCE`

8 What do you think is the main comment being made in this cartoon? `OPINION` `REASON`

9 Can you think of any other examples of hypocrisy in our society? How does it make you feel? `OPINION` `REASON`

CENTRE STAGE

Your Comment

Draw your own cartoon to expose one of your examples of hypocrisy noted in question 9 above, or comment on another issue that concerns you.

It doesn't matter if you aren't a skilled artist – your comment is the most important thing!

Tips

* Plan your cartoon.
* Exaggerate the actions of your characters.
* Use thought bubbles.
* Use speech bubbles.

IN YOUR OWN WORDS

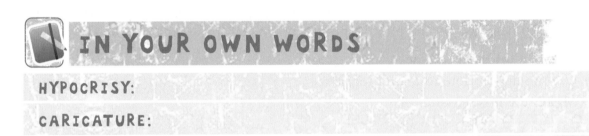

HYPOCRISY:

CARICATURE:

PARODY:

Reporting

Tabloid and broadsheet newspapers often report the same news item in different ways. A newspaper report focuses on certain aspects of the story, depending on its bias, and it can spin the facts to suit this. **Spin** is when you promote a particular view or version of an event by leaving out details and emphasising others.

All newspaper reporters ask the same questions:

- **Who?**
- **What?**
- **When?**
- **Where?**
- **Why?**
- **How?**

But they treat, present and analyse the facts according to their bias!

Investigative reporting is when journalists investigate news items. They often act on **tip-offs**, meaning someone tells them in secret about a newsworthy item. They then have to **research** the news item. This can include interviewing people, requesting and researching official documents, challenging people to tell the truth, observing people in secret and building documentary evidence.

 CENTRE STAGE

Sizzling Sensation!

It's important to be able to recognise the difference in tone between tabloid and broadsheet journalism, and this exercise is a fun way to learn.

You are a reporter for a tabloid newspaper and your editor has told you that your story isn't sensational enough.

Find a broadsheet story and rewrite it using all the tabloid tricks and features you have learned about. It can be fun to use a local paper. If possible, your teacher might be able to help you out by photocopying an article for the class.

- Create a tabloid headline.
- Use the appropriate tone and register.
- Make sure it is sensational!

 IN YOUR OWN WORDS

SPIN:

curtain call

Revise the different features of broadsheet and tabloid newspapers before answering the following questions. This includes:

- **appearance and layout;**
- **content;**
- **language, style and tone.**

Below are two front covers for you to contrast, taken from the same day and focusing on the same story.

Daily IRISH Mail

FRIDAY, JANUARY 9, 2009   www.dailymail.ie   IRELAND'S BEST VALUE NEWSPAPER €1

FROZEN OUT

Chill: The cold winds of economic reality blow through Limerick yesterday as the workers at Dell leave after being told 1,900 of them will be losing their jobs

As Dell boss tells the Mail another 1,500 jobs will go on top of the 1,900 that devastated Limerick yesterday, Tánaiste says she's too busy to visit city

EXCLUSIVE REPORTS AND ANALYSIS – PAGES 2, 8, 9, 10, 11, 12, 13

🔦 SPOTLIGHT

1 Contrast and comment on the headlines used by both papers.

2 Contrast and comment on the images used by both papers.

3 What differences are there in the way that both papers treat the same news item?
`OPINION` `REASON` `EVIDENCE`

4 Identify five major differences between each front page. `OPINION` `EVIDENCE`

5 Contrast the language, style and tone of the newspapers.

6 Which newspaper do you think is the most reliable news source? `OPINION`
`REASON` `EVIDENCE`

7 Identify one way in which a newspaper can manipulate a reader while still telling the truth. `OPINION` `REASON`

MEDIA STUDIES: NEWSPAPERS, ONLINE MEDIA AND MAGAZINES

7

Our Daily News

Create your own class newspaper. It can be five or six pages in length.

1 If possible, divide the class into two competing newspapers, a tabloid and a broadsheet.

2 Identify the same news items to report on, but treat and approach them differently.

3 Split each newspaper into three or four sections and have a small team working on each section. For example: front page, news, entertainment, sport.

4 Everyone must have at least one role.

5 The photographers don't have to actually take photographs. Use your imagination! Their job can be to find images from newspapers and magazines.

6 You must all work as a team.

online Media

Technology is changing mass media as we know it. The Internet is now one of the most important and popular news and media sources. It has brought radical changes to how we communicate and interact with the world.

Features of the Internet:
- **websites;**
- **e-mail;**
- **search engines;**
- **blogs;**
- **social networking;**
- **video sharing.**

Websites: websites are the Internet addresses where you can find an organisation or person's web pages, images, contact information and other details. Popular websites include the online encyclopaedia Wikipedia and newspaper websites, such as www.independent.ie and www.irishtimes.com.

E-mail: e-mail is electronic mail. It is a free and instantaneous way in which those with an Internet connection can send and receive messages.

Search engines: a search engine allows you to search for information on the Internet. How the engine displays results can influence what information you read and how you use it. For example, commercial sites can pay search engine operators to display their sites first so that you will buy their products. The most popular search engine is Google.

Blogs: a blog is a type of Internet diary that can cover a wide variety of subjects. The subjects can range from music criticism to debating human rights issues. Most blogs are free to set up and easy to use. The most popular ones are read by millions of people.

Social networking: social networking sites are interactive sites that allow people to share news, blogs, photos and comments. Facebook and Bebo are two popular ones.

Video sharing: video sharing allows users to upload and share video clips. These can then be watched by millions of people worldwide. The most popular video sharing site is YouTube.

WARNING: just as in real life, you need to follow a safe code of behaviour when on the Internet.

REMEMBER
- Never give out your name or personal details in public or to someone you don't personally know.
- Be polite: don't abuse or bully people.
- Stick to sites you know are safe.
- If you are unsure of anything, ask a parent or teacher for help.
- There are serious consequences for online behaviour.

There are many reasons why the Internet is so popular. It appeals to everyone, from casual social users to large companies and governments. It provides a vital role in international information access, communications and finance.

There are positive and negative points about the Internet. Here are some of the arguments.

Positive aspects	Negative aspects
It is relatively cheap and access is available to most people.	Governments and Internet agencies can influence and control access.
It is user friendly and allows people to get their voices heard quickly and cheaply.	It is difficult to police and people can abuse their anonymity.
A vast amount of information can be retrieved easily and cheaply.	It can be difficult to find the specific information you want.
It allows people freedom of speech.	People can abuse and be unfair to each other.

 SPOTLIGHT

1 What do you use the Internet for? Why? OPINION REASON
2 How important do you think the Internet is in the modern world? OPINION REASON
3 Identify one problem with the Internet. How do you think that problem could be solved? OPINION REASON
4 Contrast social networking on the Internet with socialising in the physical world. What are the main differences between them? OPINION REASON
5 Do you think traditional print media, such as newspapers, will continue to be as popular in the modern digital and Internet era? OPINION REASON

 CENTRE STAGE

Virtual Reality vs. Physical Reality

Have a class debate on the motion:

The virtual world is better than the physical world.

- Identify the different arguments beforehand by brainstorming.
- You can have a debate between two teams of three, or a point/counterpoint debate with the whole class.

Or

Write an article with the title:

For Better or Worse: How the Internet is Changing our World

Remember to:
- plan your article;
- structure your essay using paragraphs;
- use information, persuasion and argument where appropriate.

Magazines are a form of print media covering specialist areas, with specific target audiences. Magazines are typically A3 or smaller in size, and use a glossier print paper than newspapers. They contain a lot of advertisements and potential advertisers can reach a specific audience. They are usually published on a weekly or monthly basis.

Here are some common features of magazines:
- **glossy paper;**
- **many images;**
- **colourful graphics and effects;**
- **variety in font colour, size and style;**
- **free gifts and promotions;**
- **specialist and lifestyle features;**
- **advertisements;**
- **reviews and interviews;**
- **fashion and style pages;**
- **readers' letters;**
- **human interest articles;**
- **entertainment and TV listings.**

What features can you identify?

There is a huge variety of magazines available, covering every subject imaginable. Have a class competition to identify the most unusual magazine subject you can find.

 SPOTLIGHT

1 What is your favourite magazine? Why? `OPINION` `REASON`

2 Who do you think is the target audience of the following magazines? The first one is done for you. `OPINION` `REASON`

i) *Vogue:* women who are interested in fashion.

ii) *Surfer's Path:*

iii) *The Dubliner:*

iv) *Seventeen:*

v) *Newsweek:*

vi) *Tasmanian Rail News:*

vii) *Hello:*

viii) *BBC Wildlife:*

ix) *Ancient Egypt:*

x) *RTÉ Guide:*

3 If you wished to sell the following products, which magazine would you advertise in? Explain your answer `OPINION` `REASON`

i) Women's perfume.

ii) A Dublin restaurant.

iii) Tours of the Pyramids.

iv) Wetsuits.

v) Binoculars.

4 Give the following magazines their own titles. The target audience is identified for you.

A magazine for:

i) people interested in Mediterranean travel;

ii) Leaving Certificate students;

iii) fishermen visiting the west of Ireland;

iv) students interested in celebrity and gossip;

v) photographers.

5 Pretend you are the editor of one of the above titles. Identify a company that you would approach to advertise in your magazine.

Write a short note to the company explaining:

i) who your magazine is aimed at and why it will be successful;

ii) why they should advertise their product or service in your magazine.

Punctuation Station

Apostrophes

Apostrophes are used to show that someone or thing owns something. These are called **possessive apostrophes**. **Apostrophes** are also used when you remove letters from a word to shorten it.

We use an **apostrophe** when:

1 We want to say someone or something owns another thing. This is called the possessive apostrophe.

Examples:
The cat's mat.
The girl's house.
The school's library.

The cat is the owner and possesses the mat. These examples are all singular. This means there is only one cat, one girl and one school.

 ## OPENING ACT

Insert the correct **apostrophe** for the following singular nouns.

1 The boys jacket.
2 The farmers horses.
3 The prisons doctor.
4 Matthews schoolbag.
5 The childs pram.
6 The lions den.
7 The carpenters hammer.
8 The Frenchmans soup.
9 The days end.
10 The flowers head.

When the possessor (owner) is plural and ends in s, we leave out the last s. Think of how funny it would sound to say *dogs's* or *cats's*.

So the rule is simple: **If the noun is plural, ending in s, leave out the last s**.

Examples:
The cats' mat. (There are two or more cats.)
The girls' house. (There are two or more girls.)
The schools' library. (There are a number of schools sharing one library.)

 ## OPENING ACT

1 Insert the apostrophe in the correct place. All of these nouns are plural.
   i) The dogs bowl.
   ii) The snails grass.
   iii) The hairdressers shampoo.
   iv) The criminals tools.

v) The workers lunch.

vi) The cows feed.

vii) The students desks.

viii) The snakes cage.

ix) The lions den.

x) The preachers speeches.

2 Say whether the nouns are plural or singular in each case.

i) The goat's rope.

ii) The goats' rope.

iii) The stranger's bag.

iv) The oranges' skin.

v) The conductor's baton.

vi) The cows' feed.

vii) The bicycle's brakes.

viii) The bird's nest.

ix) The cow's shelter.

x) The chapels' graveyard.

There is one last rule for the possessive apostrophe.

If the plural possessor (the owners) does not end in an s, then we use the apostrophe as if the possessor was single.

Example:

The fishermen's boat.

The women's dresser.

The mice's cheese.

 ## OPENING ACT

1 Write the following in your copy and insert the apostrophe.

i) The girls coats. (There is one girl = singular.)

ii) The mens house.

iii) The horses field. (Plural)

iv) The boys shop. (Plural)

v) The womens shoes.

vi) The teachers room. (Plural)

vii) The devils tale. (Singular)

viii) The devils tale. (Plural)

ix) The geeses food.

x) The gooses beak.

xi) The firemens song.

xii) Angelas dog. (Singular)

2 We also use an **apostrophe** when we remove letters to shorten words. If we leave out numbers or letters, then we put the **apostrophe** in their place.

Examples:

It happened in the 1990s: It happened in the '90s.

Do not go there: Don't go there.

Could not: Couldn't.

It is good to see you: It's good to see you.

It has been wet lately: It's been wet lately.

She should have told you: She should've told you.

3 The last rule, *the exception:* the only time you use an apostrophe with 'its' is when you are shortening 'it is'; you never use it for possession.

Examples:

It's often the case. (It is often the case.)

It's too early to go out. (It is too early to go out.)

Its leg is broken. (Possession)

Its cover is over there. (Possession)

Its handle is in the garage. (Possession)

Note: *the shortening of words is called* **abbreviation**, *when letters are removed from the end. When letters are removed from the middle it is called* **contraction**.

POETRY: IN FOCUS

IN THIS POETRY UNIT WE WILL DEEPEN and develop our understanding of poetry and poetry-writing techniques. We will focus on one theme in detail and we will look at some classic poets from different eras. We will also focus on one poet, Seamus Heaney.

To do this, the unit is divided into three sections:

WAR POETRY;
CLASSIC POETS;
FOCUS ON SEAMUS HEANEY.

We will also learn about **suffixes** and **prefixes** at the **Grammar Station**.

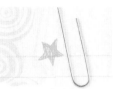

Lest We Forget

The themes of the following poems are war and conflict. Some of the poets fought in and lived through war. This brings the dimension of real experience to their poetry.

We will focus on:

* **satire;**
* **epitaph;**
* **detail;**
* **protest.**

Note: the words 'Lest We Forget' are written on tombs, war memorials and monuments around the globe as a reminder not to forget the suffering and harm caused by the great wars of mankind. These words remind us of the important purpose behind writing war poetry.

IN THE
GREAT WAR
1914–1919

"LEST WE FORGET"

Satire

We remember **satire** is comedy used to **ridicule people's stupidity** or **wrongdoing**. It is similar to normal comedy in the way that it entertains its audience with humour. It contrasts with normal comedy in that it educates the audience about the failings of its subject.

*The following poem is an anti-war poem that satirises the lifestyle and attitudes of high-ranking officers in the army who stayed far from the fighting during the war. It contains a **caricature** of a major. A caricature in words is a character sketch that exaggerates negative qualities through exaggerated description.*

Base Details

If I were fierce, and bald, and short of breath
I'd live with scarlet Majors at the Base,
And speed glum heroes up the line to death.
You'd see me with my puffy petulant face,
Guzzling and gulping in the best hotel,
Reading the Roll of Honour. "Poor young chap,"
I'd say – "I used to know his father well;
Yes, we've lost heavily in this last scrap."
And when the war is done and youth stone dead,
I'd toddle safely home and die – in bed.

Siegfried Sassoon

GLUM
sad and gloomy

PETULANT
childishly sulky

Note: we have already encountered alliteration. Now we will see how it is used in this poem to create character, tone and mood.

'**p**uffy **p**etulant face': the **p** sound is a spitting sound and creates a tone of anger and disgust.

'**g**uzzling and **g**ulping': the **g** sound is guttural, coming from the throat. It creates an image of the major scoffing food and it echoes the **g** words greed and gluttony.

Pay attention to the sound created by the consonant letters. Here are some common letter sounds and the qualities they can bring:

B/D/P: hard sounds. *These can give power, strength and force to a poem.*

F/H/S: soft sounds. *These can give gentleness, lightness and calm to a poem.*

 OPENING ACT

1 Make a list of all the adjectives used to describe the major. `EVIDENCE`
2 Make a list of all the verbs used to describe the major. `EVIDENCE`
3 How do the soldiers feel about being sent into battle? `EVIDENCE`
4 How does the major say he feels about the dead soldier? `EVIDENCE`
5 What will the major do when the war is over? `EVIDENCE`

 SPOTLIGHT

6 In your own words, describe the major that the poet uses to narrate this poem.
7 How do you think a major would feel after reading this poem? `OPINION`
`REASON` `EVIDENCE`

8 Try to identify and explain the following features of comedy in this poem:
   i) exaggeration;
   ii) comic irony;
   iii) sarcasm.

9 Identify another example of alliteration in the poem and explain what it brings to the poem. `OPINION` `REASON` `EVIDENCE`

10 Can you name another satirical text? You can include film and television. Why is it satirical? *It might be useful to have a class discussion. You could start by agreeing or disagreeing with this statement: Satire is cruel and should be banned.*

CENTRE STAGE

Poem Map

You can make a mind-map of a poem to help you remember its different features. This is a good way to learn and revise poetry. Keep the mind-map to help you study for your exams. You can even build up a folder of five or six maps.

Remember to include:
- The author and title of the poem.
- A quotation of your favourite line.
- Explanations and definitions for difficult words and lines.
- Examples of features such as similes and alliteration and explanations of what they bring to the poem.
- Visual features, such as drawings or images.
- Any context that might help in understanding the poem.

Epitaph

An **epitaph** is a poem or words **written to remember** someone who is **dead**. It can be words that person has chosen or words chosen by someone else.

These three short poems are taken from a series of poems called 'Epitaphs of the War'. Each poem in the series is an epitaph from the perspective of a different character killed in the war, ranging from innocent civilians to soldiers to political leaders. They are by the English poet Rudyard Kipling. Do you remember reading about him in the Drama unit?

Epitaphs of the War

The Beginner

On the first hour of my first day
   In the front trench I fell.
(Children in boxes at play
   Stand up to watch it well.)

Rudyard Kipling

 SPOTLIGHT

1 Who do you think the beginner is? EVIDENCE

2 Why do you think the poet tells the children to carefully watch what happens? OPINION REASON EVIDENCE

3 What is the tone of this poem? OPINION REASON EVIDENCE

Context: in the First World War a soldier could be court-martialled and executed for cowardice and desertion. Deserting soldiers were often executed in front of, and in some cases by, their fellow soldiers. Every soldier would have been aware of the consequences of their cowardice. Does knowing this context help your understanding of the next poem?

The Coward

I could not look on Death, which being known,
Men led me to him, blindfold and alone.

 SPOTLIGHT

1 What excuse does the coward give for his cowardice? `OPINION` `REASON` `EVIDENCE`

2 What do you think of the image of the coward in the line 'Men led me to him, blindfold and alone'? `OPINION` `REASON`

3 How do you feel about what happened to the coward? `OPINION` `REASON` `EVIDENCE`

4 What is the tone of this poem? `OPINION` `REASON` `EVIDENCE`

5 'It is ironic that the coward was motivated by his fear of death.' *Comment on this statement.* `OPINION` `REASON` `EVIDENCE`

Note: the **tone** of each epitaph in this series changes depending on the character being written about. The tones range from poignant to satirical. Does the tone reveal the different attitudes of the poet to his different subjects?

R.A.F. (Aged Eighteen)

MILK-TEETH
young teeth

SMOTE
to strike with a blow

Laughing through the clouds, his milk-teeth still unshed,
Cities and men he smote from overhead.
His deaths delivered, he returned to play
Childlike, with childish things not put away.

SPOTLIGHT

1 What aspects of the pilot's character does the poet highlight? `OPINION` `REASON` `EVIDENCE`

2 What is the tone of this poem? `OPINION` `REASON` `EVIDENCE`

3 What effect is created by the alliteration in the third line? `OPINION` `REASON` `EVIDENCE`

4 Can you find any examples of satire in this poem? `OPINION` `REASON` `EVIDENCE`

5 Name another poem that uses humour or satire. *Name the poem and poet, and explain how and to what effect the poet uses it. Try to structure your answer into at least two paragraphs.*

 CENTRE STAGE

Our Epitaphs of War

Create a character to write an epitaph for and write that epitaph.

For example, you could write from the perspective of:
• a crazy general;
• an old doctor;
• an innocent child;
• a brave soldier.

Imagine the background story of your character first:
• who they are;
• what they are like;
• what happened to them.

You could arrange them on your classroom wall when you are finished.

 IN YOUR OWN WORDS

EPITAPH:

Detail

Detail helps the reader to **clearly picture the scene** that is being described. This makes the point of view in the text more vivid and authentic for the reader. Detail can be expressed using the different features of descriptive writing and language.

- **Expressive words and action verbs.**
- **Imagery.**
- **Similes.**
- **Metaphors.**
- **Symbolism.**
- **Appealing to the senses.**
- **Personification.**
- **Alliteration.**
- **Repetition.**
- **Exaggeration.**
- **Caricature.**

Look for these features in the poem below. It is by a war poet who died in the First World War. The poem is perhaps the most famous of all anti-war poems and is known for its horrific imagery and vivid detail of a gas attack. It is addressed to those who argued that dying for your country was an honour. The Latin in the last two lines translates as 'It is sweet and proper to die for one's country'.

Dulce Et Decorum Est

Bent double, like old beggars under sacks,
Knock-kneed, coughing like hags, we cursed through sludge,
Till on the haunting flares we turned our backs
And towards our distant rest began to trudge.
Men marched asleep. Many had lost their boots
But limped on, blood-shod. All went lame; all blind;
Drunk with fatigue; deaf even to the hoots
Of tired, outstripped Five-Nines that dropped behind.

Gas! Gas! Quick, boys! — An ecstasy of fumbling,
Fitting the clumsy helmets just in time;
But someone still was yelling out and stumbling,
And flound'ring like a man in fire or lime. . .
Dim, through the misty panes and thick green light,
As under a green sea, I saw him drowning.
In all my dreams, before my helpless sight,
He plunges at me, guttering, choking, drowning.

FATIGUE
intense tiredness

FIVE-NINES
a type of artillery
shell

FLOUNDERING
struggling in mud
or water

If in some smothering dreams you too could pace
Behind the wagon that we flung him in,
And watch the white eyes writhing in his face,
His hanging face, like a devil's sick of sin;
If you could hear, at every jolt, the blood
Come gargling from the froth-corrupted lungs,
Obscene as cancer, bitter as the cud
Of vile, incurable sores on innocent tongues,—
My friend, you would not tell with such high zest
To children ardent for some desperate glory,
The old Lie: Dulce et Decorum est
Pro patria mori.

Wilfred Owen

CUD
partly digested
food

ZEST
energy and enthu-
siasm

ARDENT
passionate

 OPENING ACT

1 Make a list of ten action verbs from this poem. EVIDENCE
2 Find a simile in the poem. EVIDENCE
3 What did the men who lost their boots have to do? EVIDENCE
4 Did all the soldiers get their masks on during the attack? EVIDENCE
5 What happened to soldiers exposed to the gas? EVIDENCE

6 Identify three different features of descriptive writing in this poem and explain each feature. `OPINION` `REASON` `EVIDENCE`

7 In the second stanza, what metaphor does the poet use to describe the dying man? `OPINION` `REASON` `EVIDENCE`

8 What is the most vivid image in the poem for you? `OPINION` `REASON` `EVIDENCE`

9 How does the poet create a sense of urgency in the poem? `OPINION` `REASON` `EVIDENCE`

10 Does this poem present a good argument against war? `OPINION` `REASON`

11 Name another poem that you have studied that explores the theme of death. *Name the poem and poet, and explain how and why the poet explored the theme. Try to structure your answer into at least two paragraphs.*

Protest

Writers, musicians and artists create songs, poems, stories, films and artworks in **protest against war**. If the text or artwork becomes popular, then it raises awareness about what happened and it might help to prevent it happening again.

*The following poem is a protest poem that shows the **futility** of war. When something is futile, it is pointless and without benefit to anyone.*

The People of the Other Village

hate the people of this village
and would nail our hats
to our heads for refusing in their presence to remove them
or staple our hands to our foreheads
for refusing to salute them
if we did not hurt them first: mail them packages of rats,
mix their flour at night with broken glass.
We do this, they do that.
They peel the larynx from one of our brothers' throats.

We devein one of their sisters.
The quicksand pits they built were good.
Our amputation teams were better.
We trained some birds to steal their wheat.
They sent to us exploding ambassadors of peace.
They do this, we do that.
We cancelled our sheep imports.
They no longer bought our blankets.
We mocked their greatest poet
and when that had no effect
we parodied the way they dance
which did cause pain, so they, in turn, said our God
was leprous, hairless.
We do this, they do that.
Ten thousand (10,000) years, ten thousand
(10,000) brutal, beautiful years.

Thomas Lux

DEVEIN

to take out the intestines of shrimp

AMBASSADOR

a person sent to represent his or her people

PARODIED

to imitate someone so as to make fun of them

Note: it can sometimes help to think about the **intention** of the poet. The intention is what the poet is aiming to achieve. Ask yourself **why** the poet wrote the poem: to protest or to celebrate or to make the reader think?

OPENING ACT

1 How do the people from the narrator's village first hurt the people from the other village? EVIDENCE

2 What were birds trained to do? EVIDENCE

3 What happened to the 'ambassadors of peace'? EVIDENCE

4 Who did the narrator's village mock? EVIDENCE

5 For how long have the two villages been fighting? EVIDENCE

SPOTLIGHT

6 How different are the people from the two villages from each other? OPINION REASON EVIDENCE

7 How strong are their initial reasons for fighting with each other? OPINION REASON EVIDENCE

8 What do you think was the poet's intention in writing this poem? OPINION REASON EVIDENCE

8

9 Why do you think the poem describes the years as being 'beautiful' as well as 'brutal'? `OPINION` `REASON`

10 Do you think this poem is successful in protesting against war? Explain. `OPINION` `REASON`

11 Name another poem that you have studied that contains a message. *Name the poem and poet, and explain what the message was and how the poet gave that message. Try to structure your answer into at least two paragraphs.*

CENTRE STAGE

Guernica

Guernica is a famous painting by Pablo Picasso, a Spanish painter from the last century. It was painted to protest the bombing of the town of Guernica in the north of Spain during the Spanish civil war. The painting shows the pain and suffering of the many innocent people who were killed in the bombing and it has become a powerful anti-war symbol.

Research the story of this painting and write a short article about it.

• Who was Picasso?
• Why did he paint *Guernica?*
• What happened there?
• Where is the painting now?
• Describe the painting.
• What is your personal response to the painting?

You can include any other details you discover.

classic Poets

The following poems are all by poets who lived before the last century. Some of the language in these poems might seem strange to you, like another dialect of English, but the techniques and themes should be familiar.

The Shakespearean Sonnet

A sonnet is a poem consisting of fourteen lines that follows a particular rhyming scheme. A **Shakespearean sonnet** has three four-line stanzas, called **quatrains**, and a two-line **couplet** at the end. Notice how the final two lines of the poem rhyme on the last word. This is called a rhyming couplet.

Shakespeare wrote over 150 sonnets. They are known by their numbers, written in Roman numerals. The sonnet below is sonnet number 29. You can also use the first line of the sonnet as an alternative title.

XXIX

When, in disgrace with fortune and men's eyes,
I all alone beweep my outcast state
And trouble deaf heaven with my bootless cries
And look upon myself and curse my fate,
Wishing me like to one more rich in hope,
Featured like him, like him with friends possess'd,
Desiring this man's art and that man's scope,
With what I most enjoy contented least;
Yet in these thoughts myself almost despising,
Haply I think on thee, and then my state,
Like to the lark at break of day arising
From sullen earth, sings hymns at heaven's gate;

BEWEEP
to weep

OUTCAST
to be isolated

SCOPE
a range

STATE
condition and situation

SULLEN
sulky, moody

For thy sweet love remember'd such wealth brings
That then I scorn to change my state with kings.

William Shakespeare

 ## OPENING ACT

1 How does the poet describe heaven? `EVIDENCE`
2 What does the poet do when he looks at himself? `EVIDENCE`
3 Who does he wish to be when he considers his life? `EVIDENCE`
4 What changes the poet's mood? `EVIDENCE`
5 What does he compare his change in 'state' with? `EVIDENCE`
6 Who would he not swap his new 'state' with? `EVIDENCE`

 ## SPOTLIGHT

7 What do you think of the language used in this poem? *Try to structure your answer into at least two paragraphs.* `OPINION` `REASON` `EVIDENCE`
8 Do you think Shakespeare would have impressed the subject of this poem by writing this poem for her? `OPINION` `REASON`
9 Do you think poetry still has a role to play in modern love and romance? `OPINION` `REASON`
10 Do you think only money should be considered as wealth? `OPINION` `REASON`
11 Name another poem that you have studied on the theme of love or romance. *Name the poem and poet, and explain how the poet explored the theme. Try to structure your answer into at least two paragraphs.*

 ## CENTRE STAGE

Dear Shakespeare

Write a letter to Shakespeare, asking him to cease making romantic advances. You can write it in a comic or serious tone.

Use your imagination and choose to write from the perspective of one of the following.
i) The woman he was romancing.
ii) Her father.
iii) Her boyfriend.
iv) Her solicitor.

Create a story around the letter and refer to particular lines in the sonnet that you are unhappy with.

THE SHAKESPEAREAN SONNET:

QUATRAIN:

COUPLET:

The following poem is by Alfred Lord Tennyson, a famous English poet of the nineteenth century. He wrote it about a friend of his who died. Read the poem aloud a few times to get the sense of rhythm.

Break, Break, Break

Break, break, break,
　　On thy cold gray stones, O Sea!
And I would that my tongue could utter
　　The thoughts that arise in me.

O well for the fisherman's boy,
　　That he shouts with his sister at play!
O well for the sailor lad,
　　That he sings in his boat on the bay!

UTTER
to say

STATELY
majestic, splendid

HAVEN
a harbour

CRAGS
jagged rocks that stick out

GRACE
beauty, elegance

And the stately ships go on
  To their haven under the hill;
But O for the touch of a vanished hand,
  And the sound of a voice that is still!

Break, break, break,
  At the foot of thy crags, O Sea!
But the tender grace of a day that is dead
  Will never come back to me.

Alfred Lord Tennyson

OPENING ACT

1 What is the setting of this poem? **EVIDENCE**
2 How does the poet describe the stones in the first stanza? **EVIDENCE**
3 What sense is appealed to in the second stanza? **EVIDENCE**
4 What word is repeated most in this poem? **EVIDENCE**
5 What will never come back to the poet? **EVIDENCE**

SPOTLIGHT

6 Why do you think the poet repeats the word 'break'? **OPINION** **REASON**
7 What could be broken in the poet? Why? **OPINION** **REASON** **EVIDENCE**
8 What do you think is the mood of this poem? **OPINION** **REASON** **EVIDENCE**
9 How does the mood of the fisherman's boy and of the sailor lad contrast with the mood of the poet? *Try to structure your answer into at least two paragraphs.* **OPINION** **REASON** **EVIDENCE**
10 Try reading the poem in a few different tones of voice. What tone of voice is most suitable? **OPINION** **REASON**
11 Name another poem that you have studied that uses repetition. *Name the poem and poet, and explain how and why the poet used repetition. Try to structure your answer into at least two paragraphs.*

CENTRE STAGE

Sea Collage

The sea is often described by writers. It is also used as a metaphor for many things, such as sadness, love or life.

A **collage** is a collection of images and words pasted together to make a work of art.

You will need some glue, a scissors and some sheets of paper to do this exercise.

i) For homework, let everyone bring in a collection of images, words and photos related to the sea. Use your imagination. You could even bring in a sheet of blue-coloured paper or a holiday advertisement. *Get more than one thing!*

ii) In groups of three or four, arrange the different images onto a sheet, fitting them together and overlapping them. You could even make them into a shape, such as the figure of a man, a lighthouse or a boat. Glue them down.

iii) Photocopy or copy out Tennyson's poem and frame it in the middle of your collage.

iv) Put the poem up on the wall of your classroom.

v) You can do this for more than one poem!

The next poem is famous for its imagery of a tiger. The poem also contains imagery of a blacksmith at work, using this as a metaphor for God. In the poem the poet wonders how God made the fearsome tiger.

The writer, William Blake, was a famous painter as well as a poet. He was born in 1757 and lived to 1827. The poem uses alliteration to capture the power and force of the tiger, as well as to give pace and rhythm to the poem. This poem needs to be read aloud a number of times! You can also try different ways of reading it.

Note: a lamb is a symbol of Christianity, Jesus and God.

The Tyger

Tyger! Tyger! burning bright
In the forests of the night,
What immortal hand or eye
Could frame thy fearful symmetry?

In what distant deeps or skies
Burnt the fire of thine eyes?
On what wings dare he aspire?
What the hand dare seize the fire?

And what shoulder, and what art,
Could twist the sinews of thy heart?
And when thy heart began to beat,
What dread hand? And what dread feet?

What the hammer? what the chain?
In what furnace was thy brain?
What the anvil? what dread grasp
Dare its deadly terrors clasp?

When the stars threw down their spears,
And watered heaven with their tears,
Did he smile his work to see?
Did he who made the Lamb make thee?

Tyger! Tyger! burning bright
In the forests of the night,
What immortal hand or eye
Dare frame thy fearful symmetry?

William Blake

SYMMETRY
balance and
perfection

ASPIRE
to hope for and
work toward

SINEW
the tendon that
attaches muscle to
bone

ANVIL
a large metal
block used for
shaping hot metal

OPENING ACT

1 What words does the poet use to describe the 'tyger'? `EVIDENCE`

2 What words does the poet use that we associate with a blacksmith? `EVIDENCE`

3 Find two examples of alliteration. `EVIDENCE`

SPOTLIGHT

4 What qualities would you associate with a tiger? `OPINION` `REASON`

5 What is your favourite line in this poem? `OPINION` `REASON` `EVIDENCE`

6 Do you think the rhythm of this poem suits a poem about a tiger? `OPINION` `REASON`

7 What sort of mood does alliteration create in the last line of the fourth stanza? *Read the stanza out loud with force.* `OPINION` `REASON` `EVIDENCE`

8 Do you think a blacksmith is a good metaphor for God? *Try to structure your answer into at least two paragraphs.* `OPINION` `REASON` `EVIDENCE`

9 'Did he who made the Lamb make thee?'
Can you explain what the poet means by this rhetorical question? `OPINION` `REASON`

10 Name another poem that you have studied that uses different features of descriptive writing to create vivid imagery. *Name the poem and poet, and explain at least three of these features with examples. Try to structure your answer into at least two paragraphs.*

In the following poem the poet uses a metaphor of stepping from plank to plank. What could she mean? The poet, Emily Dickinson, didn't publish many poems in her lifetime (1830–66). It was only after she died that people discovered just how much poetry she had written and how important and skilled a poet she was. She has since come to be recognised as one of America's greatest poets.

I Stepped from Plank to Plank

I stepped from Plank to Plank
So slow and cautiously;
The Stars about my Head I felt,
About my Feet the Sea.

I knew not but the next
Would be my final inch,—
This gave me that precarious Gait
Some call Experience.

Emily Dickinson

PRECARIOUS
not secure, likely to fall

GAIT
the way a person walks

POETRY IN FOCUS

8

 # OPENING ACT

1 In what way did the poet step from 'Plank to Plank'? `EVIDENCE`

2 If the poet was walking along a plank, what could the 'final inch' be?

 # SPOTLIGHT

3 What do you think a plank would make a good metaphor for? *To help, think of the emotions you might feel if you were walking along a plank high in the air.* `OPINION` `REASON`

4 How could the poet feel the stars about her head and the sea about her feet? `EVIDENCE`

5 Why do you think the poet 'stepped from Plank to Plank' slowly and cautiously? `OPINION` `REASON`

6 Can you think of a metaphor for life? One example could be a tree. *Explain your metaphor.*

7 What do you think the central message of this poem is? `OPINION` `REASON` `EVIDENCE`

8 Name another poem that you have studied that uses metaphorical language. *Name the poem and poet, and explain the metaphor and its effect. Try to structure your answer into at least two paragraphs.*

CENTRE STAGE

Life Lines

Write your own poem about life using a metaphor for life. You can use the metaphor you answered with in question 6 if you wish.

You can use some of these tips if it helps:
• Use clear and vivid descriptive language.
• Create a setting of time and place.
• Describe an activity you like doing.
• Describe an incident that stands out in your mind.
• Describe your emotions.
• Use one simile.

Life is often puzzling. Can you end with a rhetorical question about life for the reader to think about?

Focus on Seamus Heaney

Seamus Heaney is one of Ireland's greatest poets. He was born in 1939 and would become the eldest member of a family of nine children. His family owned a small farm of 50 acres in County Derry. Seamus Heaney's poetry often uses the natural world as a theme, and his poetry links in to his early memories and sense of place on the farm he grew up on.

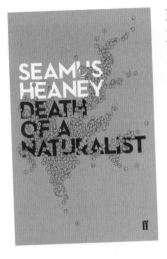

Heaney went to Queen's University, Belfast, in 1957 and studied English Language and Literature. After graduating from university he became a schoolteacher in Belfast and started to publish his poems. In 1966 he published his first major collection, *Death of Naturalist*. Since then he has published more than ten books of poems. He has won many awards for his work, including the Nobel Prize for Literature in 1995.

While reading the poetry of Seamus Heaney you will also learn about:

- **eulogy;**
- **the modern sonnet;**
- **nostalgia**.

Eulogy

A eulogy is a text or speech written in praise of someone else, often someone who has died. If you write or speak in praise of someone, it is said that you eulogise them.

'Digging' was the first poem in Death of a Naturalist. *In this poem Heaney remembers his father and grandfather, and considers his life in relation to theirs.*

Digging

Between my finger and my thumb
The squat pen rests; snug as a gun.

Under my window, a clean rasping sound
When the spade sinks into gravelly ground:
My father, digging. I look down

Till his straining rump among the flowerbeds
Bends low, comes up twenty years away
Stooping in rhythm through potato drills
Where he was digging.

The coarse boot nestled on the lug, the shaft
Against the inside knee was levered firmly.
He rooted out tall tops, buried the bright edge deep
To scatter new potatoes that we picked
Loving their cool hardness in our hands.

By God, the old man could handle a spade.
Just like his old man.

My grandfather cut more turf in a day
Than any other man on Toner's bog.
Once I carried him milk in a bottle
Corked sloppily with paper. He straightened up
To drink it, then fell to right away
Nicking and slicing neatly, heaving sods
Over his shoulder, going down and down
For the good turf. Digging.

The cold smell of potato mould, the squelch and slap
Of soggy peat, the curt cuts of an edge
Through living roots awaken in my head
But I've no spade to follow men like them.

Between my finger and my thumb
The squat pen rests.
I'll dig with it.

Seamus Heaney

OPENING ACT

1 What is the poet doing when he hears his father digging? **EVIDENCE**
2 How far back into the past does the poet remember when looking at his father?
3 Where did the poet's grandfather cut turf? **EVIDENCE**
4 Where was the best turf to be found? **EVIDENCE**
5 What senses are appealed to in the seventh stanza? **EVIDENCE**

SPOTLIGHT

6 Do you think this poem uses descriptive writing effectively? *Try to answer in at least two paragraphs with an example of descriptive writing in each.* **OPINION** **REASON** **EVIDENCE**
7 What qualities and talents does Seamus Heaney eulogise in his father and grandfather? *Try to structure your answer into at least two paragraphs.* **OPINION** **REASON** **EVIDENCE**
8 What talents does the poet have? **OPINION** **REASON** **EVIDENCE**
9 What senses are appealed to in this poem? **OPINION** **REASON** **EVIDENCE**
10 If you had to put this poem in a book categorised by theme, what theme would you put it under? *Try to structure your answer into at least two paragraphs.* **OPINION** **REASON** **EVIDENCE**
11 Name another poem that you have studied that explores the theme of family or generations. *Name the poem and poet, and explain how the writer explored the theme. Try to structure your answer into at least two paragraphs.*

CENTRE STAGE

How to Act?

How would you act out this poem or make a reading of it more dramatic? Discuss it as a group and act it out.

You might use:
- a narrator to read the poem slowly;
- three characters to mime the actions;
- people to do sound effects;
- props and positioning.

 ## IN YOUR OWN WORDS

EULOGY:

The Modern Sonnet

The next poem is a **modern sonnet**. You can recognise it as a sonnet because it has **fourteen lines**. This sonnet is divided in two, with the **first stanza** being the **eight-line octet**. It has **six lines** in the **last stanza**, called a sestet.

This sonnet is taken from a series of eight poems called 'Clearances', which the poet wrote in memory of his mother. They were published in his book The Haw Lantern.

When All the Others

When all the others were away at Mass
I was all hers as we peeled potatoes.
They broke the silence, let fall one by one
Like solder weeping off a soldering iron:
Cold comforts set between us, things to share
Gleaming in a bucket of cold water.
And again let fall. Little pleasant splashes
From each other's work would bring us to our senses.

So while the parish priest at her bedside
Went hammer and tongs at the prayers for the dying
And some were responding and some crying
I remembered her head bent towards my head,
Her breath in mine, our fluent dipping knives –
Never closer the whole rest of our lives.

Seamus Heaney

SOLDERING IRON

device for joining metal together

In a sonnet it is common for the sestet to have a different focus and tone from the octet. Reread the poem and see if you can notice a change in subject, theme, tone or setting in the sestet. Now reread the Shakespearean sonnet. Is there a similar change in focus and tone?

OPENING ACT

1 Find a simile in this poem. `EVIDENCE`
2 In the octet, what activity was the young poet doing with his mother? `EVIDENCE`
3 Where does the poet use the sense of touch in this poem? `EVIDENCE`
4 When the priest was saying the funeral mass and the people were responding and crying, what was the poet doing? `EVIDENCE`
5 When was the poet closest to his mother? `EVIDENCE`

SPOTLIGHT

6 Describe an activity you do where you are in harmony with someone. Explain why you are in harmony with that person.
7 Can you think of a time when you communicate with someone without talking? Explain how you communicate.
8 Do you think this would be a good poem to put in a book about families? *Try to structure your answer into two paragraphs.* `OPINION` `REASON` `EVIDENCE`
9 How and where does the poet's point of view change in the poem? `OPINION` `REASON` `EVIDENCE`
10 In your opinion, what is the most vivid image in this poem? `OPINION` `REASON` `EVIDENCE`
11 Name another poem that you have studied that was poignant. *Name the poem and poet, and explain why the poem was poignant. Try to structure your answer into at least two paragraphs.*

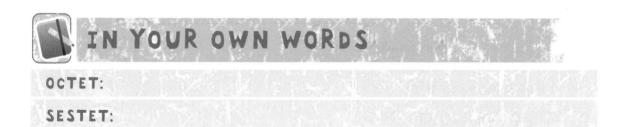

IN YOUR OWN WORDS

OCTET:

SESTET:

Nostalgia

Nostalgia is a **sentimental longing** or feeling for a time that has passed. The adjective of nostalgia is nostalgic. Have you ever heard older people being nostalgic?

This poem is set at a wedding. The poet imagines a mother and her feelings as her son is getting married.

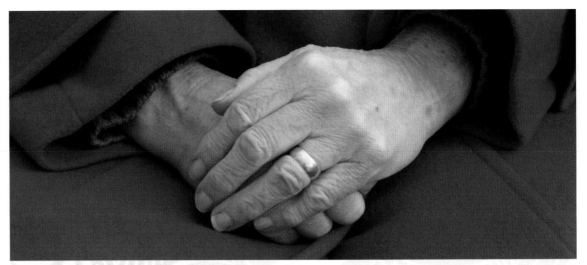

Mother of the Groom

What she remembers
Is his glistening back
In the bath, his small boots
In the ring of boots at her feet.

Hands in her voided lap,
She hears a daughter welcomed.
It's as if he kicked when lifted
And slipped her soapy hold.

Once soap would ease off
The wedding ring
That's bedded forever now
In her clapping hand.

Seamus Heaney

VOIDED

emptied

OPENING ACT

1 What does the mother remember of her son?

2 What simile is used in this poem and what does it describe?

3 Why does the mother of the groom start clapping?

4 What is the mother of the groom thinking of when she is clapping?

 # SPOTLIGHT

5 Apart from sight, what sense is appealed to most strongly in this poem? Why do you think this is? `OPINION` `REASON` `EVIDENCE`

6 Does this poem have a lesson to teach us about life? `OPINION` `REASON` `EVIDENCE`

7 'This poem contains both nostalgia and transience.'
Would you agree or disagree with this statement? Try to structure your answer into two paragraphs. `OPINION` `REASON` `EVIDENCE`

8 How does the subject of this poem contrast with the subject of the last two Heaney poems? `OPINION` `REASON` `EVIDENCE`

9 Name a poem you have studied that is about nostalgia or the past. *Name the poem and poet, and explain how the poem explored nostalgia or the past. Try to structure your answer into at least two paragraphs.*

 # CENTRE STAGE

An Introduction

You have been asked to write an introduction to a collection of poetry by Seamus Heaney.

Write a short introduction, using these headings to discuss his work. Try to refer to all the Seamus Heaney poems you know.

- **Background.**
- **Theme of family.**
- **Theme of nature.**
- **Skills and techniques as a poet.**
- **What we can learn from him.**
- **Your favourite Heaney poem.**

 ## IN YOUR OWN WORDS

NOSTALGIA:

Grammar Station

Many words in the English language are made using **prefixes** and **suffixes**. Learning how to use prefixes and suffixes will help you to increase your vocabulary and improve your spelling.

Prefixes

Some words are formed using **prefixes**. These are smaller words or letters that are joined to the front of root words to change their meaning.

Examples: **pro**active, **un**happy, **im**possible.

Common prefixes	Negative or opposite meanings:
	un–, dis–, im–, in–, mis–, anti– *Examples:* unhappy, dislike, improper, inability, misspell, disgrace, antitheft.
	Time meanings: pre–, post–, inter– (before, after, between) *Examples:* predate, postgraduate, intermission.
	Number meanings: mono–, bi–, tri–, dec–, cent– (one, two, three, ten, one hundred) *Examples:* monorail, bicycle, decade, centipede.
	Size meanings: micro–, mini–, semi– (small, half) *Examples:* microscope, miniskirt, semiconscious.
	Other specific meanings: Re- (again). Out- (out of). Over- (beyond a point, excessive). Ex- (in the past, or to do with motion). Trans- (to do with distance across). *Examples:* reopen, outcast, overdo, ex-principal, expedition, transport.

*Some words that have prefixes have no meaning or quite a different meaning if you take away the prefix. For example, the word **ex**pedition wouldn't mean anything without the **ex-**.*

Note: when you add a prefix, you rarely change the spelling of the root word. This includes joining two letters that are the same:
unnecessary, **mis**spell, **dis**service, **un**natural, **ir**responsible.

Suffixes

Some words are formed using **suffixes**. These are small words or letters that are joined to the end of longer words to change their meaning. In certain cases the spelling of the root word or the suffix changes.
Examples: care**ful**, happ**iness**, consider**able**.

Common suffixes	
	Turning nouns into adjectives: –ful, –free, –ous, –able, –less, –ly, –like, –y, –al *Examples:* hateful, carefree, courageous, lovable, friendless, lovely, childlike, cloudy, comical.
	Turning adjectives into nouns: –ness, –ship, –ity, –ist *Examples:* happiness, goodness, hardship, stupidity, loyalist.
	Turning verbs into adjectives: –able, –ing, –ive *Examples:* enjoyable, countable, laughing, falling, attractive.
	Turning adjectives into adverbs: –ly *Examples:* swiftly, cautiously.
	Turning nouns and adjectives into verbs: –ise, –en *Examples:* sympathise, terrorise, shorten, fallen.
	Turning verbs into nouns: –er, –or, –ment, –ation, –tion, –ing *Examples:* challenger, translator, statement, information, election, jogging.
	Changing verbs and tenses: –ing, –ed *Examples:* breaking, talking, walked, skipped.

Common spelling rules	Here are common spelling rules for using suffixes. These are general rules, so be careful – there are exceptions!
	1 If the root word ends in **y** and is preceded by a consonant, then you drop the **y** and add an **i** before the suffix.
	Examples:
	Cheery – cheeri**ness**.
	Happy – happi**ness**.
	Angry – angri**ly**.
	Satisfy – satisfi**ed**.
	2 If the root word ends in a silent **e**, you must drop the **e** before adding the suffix.
	Examples:
	Tone – ton**ing**.
	Space – spac**ing**.
	Care – car**ing**.
	3 If the root word ends in an **e** and the suffix begins with a consonant, then you *don't* drop the **e**.
	Examples:
	Care – care**ful**.
	State – state**ment**.
	4 The C-V-C rule: if the root word ends in a consonant, vowel, consonant, you must double the consonant before adding the suffix.
	Examples:
	Dig – digg**ing**.
	Control – controll**er**.
	Run – runn**er**.
	Fun – funn**y**.
	Label – labell**ed**.
	Swim – swimm**er**.
	Hot – hott**er**.
	This rule only applies to suffixes that start with a vowel (hotter/hotness). It also doesn't include root words ending in ther consonants c/h/w/y/x.

	5 The word full is **-ful** when used as a suffix. *Examples:* Mind – mind**ful**. Care – care**ful**. Faith – faith**ful**. **Note:** you can add both prefixes and suffixes to some words. *Examples:* **un**break**able**, **dis**satisfi**ed**, **mis**direc**tion**.

 ## OPENING ACT

1 Make as many words as you can with the following prefixes and suffixes.

i)	Anti-	vi)	–ship
ii)	Un-	vii)	–ment
iii)	Dis-	viii)	–able
iv)	Mis-	ix)	–like
v)	Uni-	x)	–ity

2 Add appropriate prefixes and/or suffixes to the following words to change their meaning.

i)	Appoint.	vi)	Depart.
ii)	Govern.	vii)	Patrol.
iii)	Commune.	viii)	Comprehend.
iv)	Emotion.	ix)	Suit.
v)	Economic.	x)	Spoil.

3 See how many different words you can get out of these root words by adding prefixes and suffixes.

i) Political.
ii) Fame.
iii) Similar.
iv) Spell.
v) Direct.

9 MEDIA STUDIES: ADVERTISEMENT, TELEVISION AND RADIO

JASMINE WEBSTER HERE, in my new role as advertising executive. This unit develops the vocabulary and knowledge you need to discuss and understand advertising, cartoons, television and radio.

Under Advertisement we will learn about:

BRAND, CAPTION AND COPY;
BODY LANGUAGE;
BRAND IMAGE;
COLOUR, FONT AND GRAPHICS.

We will also learn about:
• cartoons;
• television;
• radio.

There is also a spelling section with commonly misspelled words.

Advertisement

Advertisement is any way in which a company **encourages** people to use their product or service. Companies spend a lot of money on advertising and marketing, often spending more on **promoting the product** than they spend on making the product itself.

Advertisement can be obvious, such as a poster on an advertising billboard, or it can be subtle, such as product placement on a television show or in a film. **Product placement** is when actors use a product on a show in a casual way, without openly advertising the product.

Advertising has now reached into almost every aspect of our lives. Did you know that a lot of free services that you use, particularly services like social networking sites, are paid for by the companies who advertise to you while you are using the service?

Brand, caption and copy

Brand

The **brand** is the **name** of the **product** or **company**. When people recognise a brand name, it is called **brand recognition**. Advertisements are **aimed** at the **consumers** who are most likely to use the product, and these people are called the **target audience**.

A brand is usually represented by a **name**, a **logo** and a **slogan**.

A **logo** is a **symbol** that represents the brand, for example:

A **slogan** is a **catchy statement** or expression that we associate with a product, for example:
Enjoy Coca-Cola

The most successful slogans and logos are often those that are simple but stand out. They must be easy to remember. They are repeated often to increase brand recognition.

To catch your attention, slogans can use the following familiar features:

Rhyme: You **can** with a **Nissan**. (Nissan)

Alliteration: The low **f**ares **f**erry company. (Irish Ferries)

Suggestion: Get more. Get 3. (3 mobile)

Superlatives: The **best** built cars in the world. (Toyota)

Imperatives: **Make** the most of now. (Vodafone)

Slang and misspelling: Because change **happenz**. (Zurich Insurance)

They can also use questions, repetition, puns, clichés and other features you might recognise from other units. Have you ever thought about all the advertising work you do for free when you wear a branded clothing product?

SPOTLIGHT

1 Invent a new slogan for each of the following famous brands using any of the features above. To help, first write out who you think the target audience is.
- Coca-Cola.
- Ford cars.
- Brennan's Bread.
- Mars bars.
- Ryanair.

2 In the case of each new slogan above, explain why you think your new slogan will be successful with its target audience.

IN YOUR OWN WORDS

BRAND RECOGNITION:

LOGO:

SLOGAN:

CAPTIONS MAKE IT COOLER

Caption

The **caption** is the **group of words** that accompanies and **explains** the **image**. We recognise a caption because it often refers to the image, and the font is usually different in size and/or colour from the rest of the text.

The **brand** in this advertisement is **Gillette**.
The **slogan** in this advertisement is **The Best a Man Can Get**.
The **caption** in this advertisement is **He'll be smoother for it**.

A new caption is usually invented for an advertising campaign. A campaign is used to launch a new product or to promote a product over a period of time. It can include simultaneous print, radio, TV and online advertising to increase brand recognition during this time.

Note: *how do I tell the difference between a slogan and a caption?* The slogan is the recognisable statement that regularly accompanies the brand. The caption relates to the particular image or idea used in the advertisement.

Examine the advertisement above and answer the following questions.

OPENING ACT

1 How many times can you see the brand name in this advertisement?
2 What colour stands out most in this advertisement?
3 What does this product claim to 'give' the user?
4 Where can we find out more information about this product?

 # SPOTLIGHT

5 How does this advertisement increase brand recognition?
6 Who do you think the target audience for this advertisement is?
7 Identify other ways that Gillette could advertise and promote this product as part of a campaign.
8 Comment on the use of the footballer and celebrity David Beckham as a model in this advertisement.

 # CENTRE STAGE

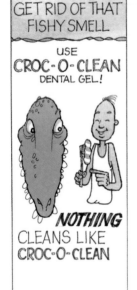

Pet Product

Invent an advertisement for a campaign to sell a product or service to pet-owners. You can use normal or exotic pets!

1 Draw or find a suitable image.
2 Include a brand and a slogan.
3 Create a caption to accompany your image.

 ## IN YOUR OWN WORDS

CAPTION:

ADVERTISEMENT CAMPAIGN:

Copy

The **copy** is the name given to the **main piece of text** in an advertisement. The copy gives us more **information**. Copy uses information, persuasion and argument to outline the advantages of a product for the consumer. Copy emphasises qualities of the product, such as speed, style, ease of use and value.

Copy can include:
- **specification;**
- **selling points;**
- **value;**
- **promotional offers;**
- **comparisons;**
- **rules and regulations;**
- **disclaimers.**

Specification is the **detailed information** of a product. **Selling points** are the **reasons** why you should **buy** the product. **Disclaimers** are **legal points** and **rules** that cover the product or company in case of problems. Disclaimers, rules and regulations are sometimes called **the small print**.

Here is an advertisement with copy.

Spot the difference.

For a limited time* the Golf Mark 5 Petrol is available from just €18,435, that's an incredible €2,750 saving.

And it comes loaded with value including: climatic air-conditioning, driver, passenger, side and head curtain airbags, ABS with ASR, CD player with MP3 connectivity, electrically heated door mirrors, remote central locking and front electric windows as standard.

Golf Mark 5 Petrol from just €18,435.
Available now at your local authorised Volkswagen dealer, or log on to www.volkswagen.ie

€18,435 €21,185

Golf Mark 5 Golf Mark 5

Das Auto.

*While stocks last. Car depicted is for illustrative purposes only. Volkswagen Golf Mark V 1.4l CO2 Emissions (g/Km) - 164 Combined Fuel Consumption (l/100km) 6.9

*When a product has a selling point that isn't available or present in a rival product, it is called a **unique selling point**, or USP. For example, a razor with six blades would have this as a USP!*

OPENING ACT

1 Looking at the advertisement above and reading the copy, identify:
  i) The brand:
  ii) Product specification:
  iii) Persuasive language:

9

iv) A slogan:

v) A caption:

vi) A disclaimer:

vii) Location information:

viii) Web address:

ix) The target audience:

SPOTLIGHT

2 What is the difference between the two cars? `OPINION` `REASON`

3 Do you think this is an effective advertisement? `OPINION` `REASON` `EVIDENCE`

4 What quality of this product is the advertisement emphasising? `OPINION` `REASON` `EVIDENCE`

5 Identify another quality of a car that you could emphasise in an advertisement. `OPINION` `REASON`

6 What do you think of the logo for this brand? `OPINION` `REASON`

CENTRE STAGE

Publicity Stunt

A publicity stunt is a carefully organised surprise stunt that promotes and creates interest in a brand or product. It could be a give away promotion, a celebrity endorsement or an actual stunt.

In pairs, create a publicity stunt for a Volkswagen Golf. Brainstorm together to help you come up with ideas.

Use your stunt to promote one or more selling points:
• value;
• safety;
• room and comfort;
• style.

Present your stunt to the class for evaluation.

Structure:
• outline the target audience;
• what is the purpose of the stunt?
• list of people involved;
• possible hazards of stunt;
• estimated cost of stunt;
• draw a diagram if necessary.

Think big! Be sensational!

IN YOUR OWN WORDS

Body Language

The **body language** of people in an advertisement is posed carefully to promote the product or service in a certain way, whether the advertisement is in print or on television.

Body language includes:
- **posture;**
- **gesture;**
- **facial expression;**
- **action;**
- **positioning;**
- **use of props;**
- **situation.**

Examine the following advertisement and answer the questions.

OPENING ACT

1 What product is being advertised? `EVIDENCE`
2 What is the brand behind the product? `EVIDENCE`
3 What is the facial expression of the person in the image?
4 How does the advertisement promote brand recognition? `EVIDENCE`
5 What is the main selling point of this advertisement? `EVIDENCE`

SPOTLIGHT

6 Who do you think the target audience of the product is? `OPINION` `REASON` `EVIDENCE`
7 Where would you expect to find this advertisement? `OPINION` `REASON`
8 Do you think the image used is appropriate for the purposes of the product being advertised? `OPINION` `REASON` `EVIDENCE`
9 'Advertisements exploit our fears.'
Exploit means to take advantage of. In light of this advertisement, would you agree or disagree with this statement? `OPINION` `REASON` `EVIDENCE`
10 Comment on the type of language used in the copy of this advertisement.

Brand image

Brand image is the image, style, ideas and activities that we are encouraged to associate with the brand.

Advertisement models promote the brand image by:

- **mood;**
- **appearance;**
- **age;**
- **gender;**
- **ethnicity;**
- **clothing;**
- **style.**

Examine the following advertisement and answer the questions.

OPENING ACT

1 What activity is the person in the advertisement engaged in?
2 What gender is the person?
3 How is repetition used in the slogan? **EVIDENCE**
4 Describe the dress of the person in the advertisement. **EVIDENCE**
5 Is the person's dress formal or informal? **EVIDENCE**

SPOTLIGHT

6 What activities would you normally associate with a bank? **OPINION REASON**
7 Why do you think a bank would wish to be associated with golf? **OPINION REASON**
8 'The posture of the person in this advertisement suggests strength, confidence and control.' *Would you agree with this statement?* **OPINION REASON EVIDENCE**

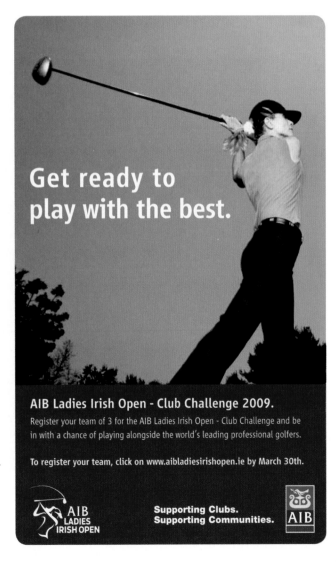

Get ready to play with the best.

AIB Ladies Irish Open - Club Challenge 2009.

Register your team of 3 for the AIB Ladies Irish Open - Club Challenge and be in with a chance of playing alongside the world's leading professional golfers.

To register your team, click on www.aibladiesirishopen.ie by March 30th.

Supporting Clubs.
Supporting Communities.

9 Why do you think the person is photographed from below? What qualities does the perspective emphasise? `OPINION` `REASON`

10 Do you think sponsoring a ladies golf open is a good use of sponsorship money for a bank? `OPINION` `REASON`

The **body language** of the person in the advertisement **promotes** the brand image by:

Demonstration: the person uses the product or service in a **positive way**, showing qualities such as ease of use or pleasure. For example, a person reversing a small car into a tight space without difficulty.

Association: the person in the advertisement is **successful** in some way, and so the product or service is **associated with** this **success**. This can include celebrity endorsement.

Suggestion: the person in the advertisement has a desirable quality or lifestyle, and it is **suggested** that the **product** is the **cause of this**. For example, a man in an aftershave advertisement could have a beautiful girlfriend.

Examine the following advertisement and answer the questions.

Note: when a company pays a celebrity to advertise their product, it is said that they **sponsor** the celebrity.

When a celebrity advertises or recommends a product, it is said that the celebrity **endorses** the product.

OPENING ACT

1 What clothing brand is being advertised in this advertisement? `EVIDENCE`

2 What is the logo of this brand? `EVIDENCE`

3 What colour is used most in this advertisement? `EVIDENCE`

4 What activities are the people in the advert involved in? `EVIDENCE`

SPOTLIGHT

5 Who do you think is the target audience for this advertisement? `OPINION` `REASON` `EVIDENCE`

6 What type of lifestyle is this advertisement trying to associate with the brand? `OPINION` `REASON` `EVIDENCE`

7 Describe the body language of the people in the advertisement and explain how it is used to create the brand image. `OPINION` `REASON` `EVIDENCE`

8 What do you think of the use of colour in this advertisement? `OPINION` `REASON` `EVIDENCE`

9 If you had to choose a celebrity to endorse this product, which celebrity would you choose? `OPINION` `REASON`

10 What body language and situation would you pose the celebrity in? `OPINION` `REASON`

CENTRE STAGE

Persuasive People Power

You have been asked by an advertising agency to come up with a plan for a new advertisement.

Draw an advertisement with a person in it to advertise one of the following products.

1 No-grief Anti-thief – an anti-theft device.

2 GloShow – glow-in-the-dark jacket for dogs.

3 Sprayhay – spray-on hay for farmers' clothes and hair.

The drawing doesn't have to be perfect! It is a plan for the agency to turn into an advertisement.

Include a logo, a slogan and a caption.

Under the advertisement, describe what the person is doing and explain why they are doing it. Include their mood, appearance and other relevant details.

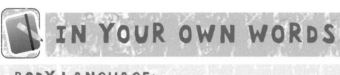

IN YOUR OWN WORDS

BODY LANGUAGE:

BRAND IMAGE:

SPONSOR:

ENDORSE:

colour, Font and Graphics

Colour

The colours used in an advertisement are chosen carefully. People make certain **associations** with different colours, and we say that **colours symbolise** certain **qualities** or **moods**.

For example:
Cleanliness is associated with the colour **white.**

The environment is associated with the colour green.

Femininity is associated with the colour **pink**.

Masculinity is associated with the colour blue or **navy**.

Wealth and luxury are associated with gold and silver.

Love and romance are associated with pink and **red**.

Sometimes you mightn't agree with an association, but it can still exist in people's minds!

Advertisers use colour to **reinforce the message** of their advertisement, to **appeal to the target audience**, to **associate** their product with certain **qualities or moods** and to **influence our perception** of their product and brand image. Our

MEDIA STUDIES: ADVERTISEMENT, TELEVISION AND RADIO

9

290 **WORDPLAY 7**

perception is what we see and think of something. Our perception of a product can be very different from how the product is in reality!

OPENING ACT

What colours would you associate with the following countries, products, services or businesses?

1 Holland.
2 Young boys' clothes.
3 A fire alarm.
4 Chocolate.
5 Recycling.
6 Italy.
7 Cheese.
8 Formal clothes.
9 Milkmen.
10 An Post.

Font

Font is the **lettering style**. Advertisements can use a **variety of lettering styles** for different **purposes**, for example the font used for the caption will often be different from that used for the copy. Font can be used to emphasise or highlight certain qualities of a product or service.

Font can be **bold**, *italics* or <u>underline</u>. It can be **in colour**, of **a completely different type**, or in a different size. It can be SERIOUS, c o o l, **FUN** or FUNKY!

Examine the following advertisement and answer the questions.

9

If it's
NOT in the
NEWSPAPER,
it's **not** in the **news.**

News, as the name indicates, is the essential component of newspapers.
At a time when there's so much important news, more than 86% of people*
now turn to newspapers each week for the coverage and analysis only newsprint can
deliver. Press is the one medium that never fails to actively engage information-seekers.
So if your advertising is in the newspaper, then it's also in the news.

Make the news today. With newspaper advertising.

NATIONAL
NEWSPAPERS
OF IRELAND

Irish Independent • Irish Examiner • The Irish Times • Irish Daily Star • Irish Daily Mirror • The Irish Sun • Irish Daily Mail • Evening Herald • Sunday Independent • Sunday World
The Sunday Business Post • The Sunday Tribune • Irish Mail on Sunday • Irish Daily Star Sunday • Irish News of the World • Irish Sunday Mirror • The Sunday Times • Irish Farmers Journal

* Source: JNRS 2007/08

 ## OPENING ACT

1 What word stands out in this advertisement? `EVIDENCE`

2 Why does it stand out?

3 Find an example of alliteration. `EVIDENCE`

4 What statistical information is used in this advertisement? `EVIDENCE`

 ## SPOTLIGHT

5 What do you think of the use of colour in this advertisement? `OPINION` `REASON` `EVIDENCE`

6 Do you think it is appropriate that this advertisement uses no images? `OPINION` `REASON`

7 Why do you think the advertiser varies the font size and style? `OPINION` `REASON`

8 Do you think this would be an effective newspaper advertisement? `OPINION` `REASON` `EVIDENCE`

Graphics

The **graphics** of an advertisement refer to the **visual** and **special effects** elements of the advertisement, which include the font, images, cartoons, design and style. Graphic artists are skilled at manipulating fonts and images and use them to create effects that appeal to a particular age group or audience.

Examine the following advertisement and answer the questions.

The delicate snack with a BITE

▲ OPENING ACT

1 What animal is represented in this advertisement?
2 What graphic effect is used to create this animal?
3 What colours are used in this advertisement?
4 What brand do you recognise in this advertisement? `EVIDENCE`
5 What is the animal in the advertisement doing?
6 Why is the word 'BITE' in uppercase letters?

📷 SPOTLIGHT

7 Do you think this is an effective advertisement? `OPINION` `REASON` `EVIDENCE`
8 Who do you think the target audience of this advertisement is? `OPINION` `REASON` `EVIDENCE`
9 This advertisement has very little copy. Do you think this is a strong or weak point in the case of this advertisement? `OPINION` `REASON` `EVIDENCE`
10 'This advertisement deserves an award for its striking visual pun.'
   Would you agree or disagree with this statement? `OPINION` `REASON` `EVIDENCE`

✏️ IN YOUR OWN WORDS

GRAPHICS:

Now we will revise the key features, vocabulary and terms we have learned.

- **Target audience: who is the advertisement aimed at?**
- **Brand and brand recognition: what is the logo and slogan, and how are they displayed?**
- **Caption: what words explain the image?**
- **Copy: what specification, selling points, offers, rules, regulations and contact details can I find in the main text?**

- **Body language:** what people are in the image, and what are their gestures, postures, facial expressions and positions?
- **Situation:** what situation are the people in, what are their actions and what props are they using?
- **Brand image:** what is the mood and appearance of people, how are they using the product and what lifestyle are they promoting?
- **Colour:** what colours are used, in what way and why?
- **Graphics:** what graphics are used and how do graphics contrast within the advertisement?
- **Font:** what font is used, and in what way?

Note: even if the product or service is very beneficial or good for people, such as what you'd find in a health or charity advertisement, the advertisement can still have many flaws or failings. Many people make the mistake of saying an advertisement is good because the product is one that they like or think is good. A good or positive product can have a bad advertisement!

The following advertisement is for a charity. Remember to only give your opinion on the advertisement's features and techniques, unless asked otherwise. So if you are asked if this is a good advertisement, discuss the **positive advertising features,** *not the fact that a charity is a good service to provide!*

OPENING ACT

1 What product or service is being advertised? `EVIDENCE`
2 Why is there an image of a paper coffee cup? `EVIDENCE`
3 How can you contact this charity? `EVIDENCE`
4 How does this advertisement use colour?

SPOTLIGHT

5 Do you think the caption of this advertisement is persuasive? `OPINION` `REASON` `EVIDENCE`

6 Do you think this is a good advertisement? *Remember, give your opinion on the effectiveness of the advertising features.* `OPINION` `REASON` `EVIDENCE`

7 Can you think of a way in which you could improve this advertisement? `OPINION` `REASON`

8 If you were advising World Vision on where to place this advertisement, where would you recommend? `OPINION` `REASON` `EVIDENCE`

9 'Simple advertisements are the most effective because people are so busy in modern times.'
   Agree or disagree with this statement, referring to the advertisement above. `OPINION` `REASON` `EVIDENCE`

10 Do you think advertisements do more harm than good? `OPINION` `REASON`

CENTRE STAGE

Agency Executives

You will have to first find an advertisement each.

Split up into pairs and choose one image per pair for this exercise.

Role-play as if you are both advertising executives who have been asked to create an advertisement for the product or service in your advertisement.

You have to do a five-minute presentation where you explain to representatives of the company why you made the advertisement as you did and why it will be effective.

Focus on:
• target audience;
• brand image and recognition;
• use of graphic features;
• copy and text.

Prepare this exercise for fifteen to twenty minutes and then present it. You can wait outside the 'boardroom' until you are called in!

Remember teamwork – plan your separate roles in the presentation!

cartoons

We've already learned about cartoons that make a comment on politics or society.

Now we will learn about:
- one-panel cartoons;
- comic strips;
- graphic novels.

JASMINE ALWAYS HAD TROUBLE WITH HOMOPHONES

One-panel Cartoons

The box in which a **cartoon** is **framed** is called a **panel** or frame. **One-panel cartoons** have the entire cartoon illustration inside one panel. It may have a **caption** underneath. Inside the panel there can be **thought** and **speech bubbles** as well as characters.

The following cartoon is from a panel series called 'The Flying McCoys' and is written and drawn by two brothers, Gary and Glenn McCoy.

Pay attention to all the features you've learned about in other units. You now know how to discuss such features as humour, puns, images, graphics, colour and font.

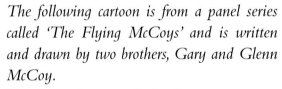 **OPENING ACT**

1 What is the setting of this cartoon?
EVIDENCE

2 What is the situation? **EVIDENCE**

3 What characters are in the cartoon?

4 What are they doing?

5 What is written in the speech bubble?
EVIDENCE

SPOTLIGHT

6 Explain the humour of this cartoon in your own words.

7 How important is the speech bubble to the humour of this cartoon? `OPINION` `REASON` `EVIDENCE`

8 Does the style in which the characters are drawn contribute to the humour? `OPINION` `REASON` `EVIDENCE`

9 Do you think the use of colour improves this cartoon? `OPINION` `REASON`

10 Do you think the unusual habits of animals are a good source of humour? *Explain.* `OPINION` `REASON`

11 'The humour of this cartoon partly comes from exaggeration.' *Would you agree or disagree with this statement?* `OPINION` `REASON` `EVIDENCE`

Look at the following one-panel cartoon and answer the questions that follow. It is by Martyn Turner.

 OPENING ACT

1 What is the setting of this cartoon?
2 What does the text in this cartoon tell us?
3 What is the main sign of human activity in the cartoon?

 SPOTLIGHT

4 Do you think this cartoon should be in black and white or colour? `OPINION` `REASON` `EVIDENCE`

5 How does the cartoonist portray Ireland? `OPINION` `REASON` `EVIDENCE`

6 What comment do you think this cartoon is making? `OPINION` `REASON` `EVIDENCE`

7 Do you think this would be a good cartoon to use in a Tourism Ireland brochure?
`OPINION` `REASON` `EVIDENCE`

8 How would you best describe the tone of this cartoon:
- humorous;
- sad;
- satirical?

`OPINION` `REASON` `EVIDENCE`

9 Would you agree or disagree with the social comment of this cartoon? `OPINION` `REASON`

 ## CENTRE STAGE

Ha-ha

Find a one-panel cartoon that you find funny and bring it into class.
- Where did you find it?
- Can you explain why it is humorous?
- Have a vote in the class to find the funniest cartoon.
- Could you make your own cartoon?

 ## IN YOUR OWN WORDS

ONE-PANEL CARTOON:

Comic Strips

Comic strips are stories told in a **number of panels**, called a **strip**. These form a **narrative** that can contain tension, conflict and humour, just like novels, short stories and plays. When the **cartoon** follows the **same characters** for a length of time, it is called a **series**.

Comic Strip features

Panels: panels, or frames, are the boxes joined in different shapes and sizes to form the strip that tells the story.

Characters: there are characters in the strip that we become familiar with, and we can sometimes predict their reaction to events.

Action: there is often exaggerated action taking place, with special graphics to express the action.

Humour: different features of humour, such as overstatement, sarcasm or irony, are used.

Situations: as with plays, films and stories, the characters often end up in dramatic situations.

Body language: humour often comes from the exaggerated body language of characters.

Here is a comic strip by Jim Davis, called 'Garfield', about the adventures of a cat called Garfield and his owner, Jon.

Now answer the following questions.

OPENING ACT

1 What action happens in the strip? `EVIDENCE`

2 Does the viewer know more about the action than the characters in the strip? `EVIDENCE`

3 Is there anything exaggerated about this comic strip? `EVIDENCE`

 ## SPOTLIGHT

4 What type of character do you think Garfield is? `OPINION` `REASON` `EVIDENCE`

5 What type of character do you think Jon is? `OPINION` `REASON` `EVIDENCE`

6 Can you explain why this cartoon is funny? `OPINION` `REASON` `EVIDENCE`

Here is another comic strip. This one is by Bill Watterson and is called 'Calvin and Hobbes'. It is about the adventures of a young boy, Calvin, and his stuffed animal, a tiger called Hobbes. When other people aren't present the tiger comes to life for Calvin.

OPENING ACT

1 What game are Calvin and Hobbes playing? `EVIDENCE`

2 How is the sound of the toy guns shown? `EVIDENCE`

3 How long does the game last? `EVIDENCE`

4 What frame contains the most action? `EVIDENCE`

5 What do facial expressions show in the third frame? `EVIDENCE`

 ## SPOTLIGHT

6 What comment do you think the cartoonist is making about war? `OPINION` `REASON` `EVIDENCE`

7 What does Calvin think of the game? `OPINION` `REASON` `EVIDENCE`

8 What age groups do you think this cartoon would be appropriate for? `OPINION` `REASON` `EVIDENCE`

9 Do you think cartoons are an effective way of exploring the theme of war? `OPINION` `REASON` `EVIDENCE`

 ## IN YOUR OWN WORDS

PANELS/FRAMES:

SITUATION:

Television

Television is a hugely **popular media** source around the world. Its primary use is as a source of entertainment, but it has many other important functions. It is a **quick** and **efficient way** of **communicating** important events and news on a **mass scale**. It is used to expose wrongdoing and injustice and to appeal for help in times of disaster or danger.

Content and categories of television:
• **news reporting and weather;**
• **entertainment;**

- drama;
- comedy;
- soaps;
- chat shows;
- sport;
- documentaries;
- film;
- cartoon;
- advertisements.

Television can be used for educational purposes. Programming content can cover a wide variety of subjects, including history, science, geography, the natural world and languages.

Why Do We Watch Television?

The reasons why we find television interesting are often similar to the reasons why we find stories, drama, poems and other texts interesting. Features of narrative, drama and storytelling, such as tension, suspense, conflict, characterisation, humour, music and sound effects, are all found in television.

OPENING ACT

1 What is your favourite television programme?
2 What is your favourite category of television programming?
3 What other functions does television have apart from to entertain us?
4 What type of programming would you like to see more of on television?
5 What type of programming would you like to see less of on television?

SPOTLIGHT

6 What do you think are the reasons behind television's popularity? OPINION REASON

7 How important do you think news programming is to society? OPINION REASON

8 What dramatic features can you find in sport programming? OPINION REASON

9 What programme do you find most humorous, and what features of humour make it funny? OPINION REASON EVIDENCE

10 What are the differences between television advertisements and print advertisements? OPINION REASON

CENTRE STAGE

Advertise This

This task can be done in small groups of three or four.

Write your own television advertisement script as part of a campaign. Choose one of the products or services that you have already used to make a print advertisement.

You can use:
- humour;
- music and sound effects;
- dramatic situations;
- celebrity endorsements;
- props.

Act out your advertisements when you are finished.

Radio

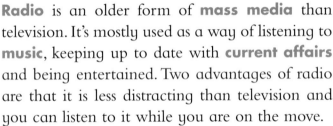

Radio is an older form of **mass media** than television. It's mostly used as a way of listening to **music**, keeping up to date with **current affairs** and being entertained. Two advantages of radio are that it is less distracting than television and you can listen to it while you are on the move.

Content and categories of radio:
- **news;**
- **documentary;**
- **music;**
- **current affairs;**
- **talk and call-in shows;**
- **drive-time show;**
- **drama;**
- **interview;**
- **light entertainment and humour;**
- **arts and culture show;**
- **advertisement;**
- **podcast.**

The drive-time show is what we call the morning or evening show that people listen to while driving to or from work. Podcasts are radio shows and audio extracts that are available on Internet websites.

Staff Roles

Radio show host: this is the star of the radio show, the person who regularly does all the talking.

Producer: this is the person who organises the show from behind the scenes, setting up interviews and deciding on topics to cover.

Researcher: this is the person who researches news items, topics and issues that the host will talk about.

Guest: this is the person who talks on the show about a particular subject that they are interested in. The guest can be a member of the public or a specialist commentator in an area such as politics.

Newscaster: this is the person who reads the regular news bulletins.

 # OPENING ACT

1 Have you ever listened to a radio show?

2 What do you dislike about radio?

3 Do you have a local radio station?

4 What radio stations can you name? `EVIDENCE`

 # SPOTLIGHT

5 Do you think local radio stations are important? `OPINION` `REASON`

6 What role would you most like to take in a radio station? `OPINION` `REASON`

7 What tasks could you do while listening to the radio that you couldn't do while watching television? `OPINION` `REASON`

8 If you could host your own radio show, what would your content be? `OPINION` `REASON`

9 If you could interview anyone for a radio show, who would it be? `OPINION` `REASON`

CENTRE STAGE

Very Special Guest

Now you can try role-playing a radio interview in pairs. Split into pairs. One of you can take the role of host and the other the role of guest. The guest can pretend to be a local person with a complaint, a politician who is in trouble or a celebrity or sports star.

Try to identify two or three issues that you will discuss.

1 Prepare your questions and answers. This should take ten or fifteen minutes in class, or you might prepare it for homework.

2 Arrange a 'studio' in your classroom.

3 Choose a pair of students from the class to have their interview.

4 Your teacher can be the 'producer' and help the show run smoothly.

5 If you want, your producer can take calls from the audience, but make sure to do the appropriate call sound effects!

6 Members of the class must put up their hands to 'call in' with comments, complaints or queries.

As with drama and storytelling, conflict can make the show more interesting. Let angry callers have their say!

IN YOUR OWN WORDS

RADIO SHOW HOST:

PRODUCER:

NEWSCASTER:

Spelling Section

Below is a list of thirty words that people commonly have difficulty spelling. If you have difficulty spelling a word, try to sound out the spelling by breaking up the word by syllable. You can also look words up in a dictionary if you feel you are close to the correct spelling.

Look over these spellings. Can you recognise any that you have had difficulty with before? Try to learn them. If possible, your teacher can test you on them.

MEDIA STUDIES: ADVERTISEMENT, TELEVISION AND RADIO

9

1 February.
2 Cough.
3 Assignment.
4 Because.
5 Occasion.
6 Fashion.
7 Automatic.
8 Could.
9 Different.
10 Majority.
11 Readily.
12 Famous.
13 Necessary.
14 Successful.
15 Exaggerate.
16 Surprise.
17 Suggestion.
18 Together.
19 Experience.
20 Friend.
21 Separate.
22 Official.
23 Height.
24 Knowledge.
25 Unusually.
26 Gradual.
27 Telephone.
28 Library.
29 Chimney.
30 Chose.

9

10

FICTION: IN FOCUS

I **N THE FIRST FICTION UNIT** we learned about the world of the text, characters, narrators, themes and relationships. In this unit we will continue learning about features found in novels and fiction writing. You will also be introduced to genre through three examples of genre. Genre is the category that a story fits into, for example horror or romance. In films you find genres such as the spy movie and the cowboy Western.

You will learn about:

> **KEY MOMENT;**
>
> **ISSUES;**
>
> **GENRE: ROMANCE;**
>
> **GENRE: COMEDY;**
>
> **GENRE: MYSTERY;**
>
> **GENRE: HORROR.**

There is also a **spelling section** with commonly misspelled words.

Key Moment

A **key moment** is an important moment in a novel, short story, drama or film. It could be when something unexpected happens, when a character changes, or it could be a thrilling climax or incident.

*The following extract describes a **key moment** in the relationship between the narrator, a young Afghan boy, Amir, and his friend, Hassan. Amir is from a wealthy background, while Hassan is poor and works as a servant. The narrator is feeling guilty because he didn't stand up for Hassan in a fight, when Hassan was protecting Amir's kite.*

The Kite Runner

Khaled Hosseini

One sluggish, hazy afternoon early that summer, I asked Hassan to go up the hill with me. Told him I wanted to read him a new story I had written. He was hanging clothes out to dry in the yard and I saw his eagerness in the harried way he finished the job.

We climbed the hill, making small talk. He asked about school, what I was learning, and I talked about my teachers, especially the mean math teacher who punished talkative students by sticking a metal rod between their fingers and then squeezing them together. Hassan winced at that, said he hoped I'd never have to experience it. I said I'd been lucky so far, knowing that luck had nothing to do with it. I had done my share of talking in class too. But my father was rich and everyone knew him, so I was spared the metal rod treatment.

We sat against the low cemetery wall under the shade thrown by the pomegranate tree. In another month or two, crops of scorched yellow weeds would blanket the hillside, but that year the spring showers had lasted longer than usual, nudging their way into early summer, and the grass was still green, peppered with tangles of wildflowers. Below us, Wazir Akbar Khan's white-walled, flat-topped houses gleamed in the sunshine, the laundry hanging on clotheslines in their yards stirred by the breeze to dance like butterflies.

SLUGGISH
lazy or slow

HARRIED
hassled and hurried

WINCED
to make a face in pain or disgust

We had picked a dozen pomegranates from the tree. I unfolded the story I'd brought along, turned to the first page, then put it down. I stood up and picked up an overripe pomegranate that had fallen to the ground.

"What would you do if I hit you with this?" I said, tossing the fruit up and down.

Hassan's smile wilted. He looked older than I'd remembered. No, not older, old. Was that possible? Lines had etched into his tanned face and creases framed his eyes, his mouth. I might as well have taken a knife and carved those lines myself.

"What would you do?" I repeated.

The colour fell from his face. Next to him, the stapled pages of the story I'd promised to read him fluttered in the breeze. I hurled the pomegranate at him. It struck him in the chest, exploding in a spray of red pulp. Hassan's cry was pregnant with surprise and pain.

"Hit me back!" I snapped. Hassan looked from the stain on his chest to me.

"Get up! Hit me!" I said. Hassan did get up, but he just stood there, looking dazed like a man dragged into the ocean by a riptide when, just a moment ago, he was enjoying a nice stroll on the beach.

I hit him with another pomegranate, in the shoulder this time. The juice splattered his face. "Hit me back!" I spat. "Hit me back, goddam you!" I wished he would. I wished he'd given me the punishment I craved, so maybe I'd finally sleep at night. Maybe then things could return to how they used to be between us. But Hassan did nothing as I pelted him again and again. "You're a coward!" I said. "Nothing but a goddam coward!"

I don't know how many times I hit him. All I know is that, when I finally stopped, exhausted and panting, Hassan was smeared in red like he'd been shot by a firing squad. I fell to my knees, tired, spent, frustrated.

Then Hassan did pick up a pomegranate. He walked toward me. He opened it and crushed it against his own forehead. "There," he croaked, red dripping down his face like blood. "Are you satisfied? Do you feel better?" He turned and started down the hill.

I let the tears break free, rocked back and forth on my knees. "What am I going to do with you, Hassan? What am I going to do with you?" But by the time the tears dried up and I trudged down the hill, I knew the answer to that question.

TRUDGED
walked wearily

This scene contains conflict between two characters. It also contains inner conflict. **Inner conflict** *is when characters are unhappy and struggling with their own decisions and behaviour. In this extract we see that Amir is really angry with himself, not Hassan.*

OPENING ACT

1 Why did Amir ask Hassan to go up the hill with him? `EVIDENCE`

2 What was the real reason why Amir was not punished by his teacher? `EVIDENCE`

3 Why was the grass still green on the hillside? `EVIDENCE`

4 Was Hassan expecting to be attacked? `EVIDENCE`

5 What did Amir call Hassan?

6 What did Hassan do when he picked up a pomegranate? `EVIDENCE`

SPOTLIGHT

7 Why do you think this is a key moment in the novel? `OPINION` `REASON` `EVIDENCE`

8 How does the writer create a peaceful mood and atmosphere at the beginning of this extract? *Try to structure your answer into two paragraphs.* `OPINION` `REASON` `EVIDENCE`

9 Do you think Amir planned to hit Hassan with the pomegranates? `OPINION` `REASON` `EVIDENCE`

10 Who do you think is the hero of this scene? *Try to structure your answer into two paragraphs.* `OPINION` `REASON` `EVIDENCE`

11 Why do you think Amir wanted Hassan to hit him back with the pomegranates? `OPINION` `REASON`

12 Can you think of a story or play you have read that featured a key moment where conflict occurred? *Name the text and author, and explain why there was conflict and why it was a key moment. Try to structure your answer into two paragraphs.*

CENTRE STAGE

Your Key Moment

1 What is the key moment of your year so far?
2 Explain why the moment stands out in your year.
3 What did you learn about yourself in this moment?
4 What did you learn about the world in this moment?

IN YOUR OWN WORDS

KEY MOMENT:

INNER CONFLICT:

Issues

Issues are **problems** and **concerns** that face people in **society**. Serious issues in society cause **discussion** and **debate**. You can read about these issues in newspaper reports and you can give your opinion by writing a letter to the editor of a newspaper. Characters in stories face issues, such as bullying or racism, in similar ways to people in real life.

Common issues include political, environmental, social, health, crime and educational issues.

By writing about issues and exploring them in stories, writers make us more aware of the problems that people and societies face. A writer can help us to see life from the perspective of another person. We can stand in their shoes and see how issues affect them. The following extract deals with the issue of bullying.

Tell Me No Lies

Malorie Blackman

'Give us a chip, Robyn,' Beth pleaded.

'Shush! Keep your voice down,' Robyn hissed. 'If Mrs Brewer catches us in here with chips, she'll go ballistic.'

'I'd rather be outside anyway. Why d'you want to stay in this grotty library?' Beth asked.

'Cos it's freezing outside. So much for sunny May! It's perishing and you might have anti-freeze flowing in your veins but I don't!' Robyn told her. 'So, is everyone all set for my party on Saturday?

'Of course.'

'You bet!'

'Can't wait.'

'Good.' Robyn smiled.

'So who's coming?' asked Livia.

'Everyone,' Robyn said with satisfaction. 'But hands off the new boy – OK? He's mine.'

'Who? Michael?' asked Livia.

'Listen to you. "Who? Michael?" Like you didn't know who I was talking about,' Robyn scoffed. 'You can't fool me. I've seen you looking him up and down.'

'That was just to see if he was labelled,' Livia laughed.

All around the table guffaws of disbelief sounded.

'I mean it, you lot,' Robyn stated. 'Mike is mine. OK?'

'How come you're going to get the most interesting boy we've had at this school in yonks?' Beth asked.

'Cos it's my party!' Robyn grinned.

'Have you already invited Mike?'

'Yep! And he's coming. I told you – everyone is.'

'You are lucky, having your birthday just after the hunkiest guy in the school arrives,' Livia said.

'It was fate.' Robyn gave a mock sigh.

'Is Gemma coming?' Beth lowered her voice just a fraction.

'You must be joking. When has she ever said more than five words to me at any one time?'

'Besides, she's so gloomy, she'd make it feel more like a funeral party than a birthday party,' Beth announced.

'So you didn't invite her?' said Livia.

'What d'you think?' said Robyn. 'As far as I know, she doesn't know a thing about it.'

'She's weird, isn't she?' Livia mused. 'I don't know what to make of her.'

'Does anyone?' asked Beth.

The others tittered, all agreeing with Beth.

Gemma closed her book and gathered up her belongings. She couldn't bear to hear any more. Piling everything into her bag, she slung it over her shoulder. How was she going to get out of the library without being seen by any of them? She was at the back of the library. They were seated at the table in the next aisle down, so unless she waited for all of them to leave or they all faced the wall as she walked past, there was no way they wouldn't know she had heard every syllable of their conversation. Gemma took a deep breath as she walked out of her aisle.

At Robyn's table, it suddenly went very quiet. Gemma couldn't help it. She knew she shouldn't look. She knew she should just keep walking, but she simply couldn't. She turned her head to look at them and her look became a scowl. Robyn, Beth, Livia and

Gillian – they all watched her. And of them all, only Robyn looked embarrassed. Gemma had to get out of there before she drowned in the stillness rippling from their table. She turned and headed for the door. It was only outside the library as she leaned against the wall panting for air, that Gemma realised she'd been holding her breath.

*In this extract the characters use **slang** when they are talking. Slang is a casual language that particular groups of people use when talking. Slang words are often adapted from other words. Examples of slang from this extract are 'yonks' and 'ballistic'.*

OPENING ACT

1 At what time of year is the story set? EVIDENCE
2 Where are the students eating their chips? EVIDENCE
3 Who is invited to Robyn's party?
4 What do the girls think of the new boy in the school? EVIDENCE
5 What action verbs are used to describe the students' chatting and behaviour? EVIDENCE

SPOTLIGHT

6 Why do you think Robyn was the only one who looked embarrassed when Gemma walked out? OPINION REASON
7 Is the world of the text familiar to you? *Explain why.* OPINION REASON
8 Do you think that Gemma is being bullied by the other students? OPINION REASON
9 i) Write out five slang words that you use. For each word give your own definition.
   ii) Do you know where any of these words might have come from?
10 What issues do you think the photographs below explore? OPINION REASON EVIDENCE

A

B

11 Can you think of a story or play you have read that explored an important issue? *Name the text and author, and explain what the issue was and how it was explored. Try to structure your answer into two paragraphs.*

 # CENTRE STAGE

Questionnaire

What issues affect young people today? A good way to find answers to such questions is to make out a questionnaire.

A good questionnaire asks questions in a clear way. The questions also need to be appropriate to the target group.

You also need to be sensitive to others' feelings and only ask questions that are appropriate.

The first thing you need to do is identify the correct questions to ask.

1 Make a list of three issues that concern young people today.
2 Write out three questions you would ask for each issue.

Now if you want to take it further, pair with someone and fill in each other's questionnaire. Afterwards you can **evaluate** your questionnaire. This means you check to see if it was useful and if it achieved what you wanted it to achieve.

• What did the person filling it out think of the questions?
• Were the questions appropriate?
• Could you have asked better questions?
• Did you get all the information you needed?

Could you write a report on what you found? Here are the five stages of writing a report. You can read more about them in Unit 12:
• **introduction;**
• **research;**
• **results;**
• **conclusions;**
• **recommendations.**

You could also make out a questionnaire for teachers to find out what issues affect them!

IN YOUR OWN WORDS

ISSUES:

SLANG:

EVALUATE:

Genre: Romance

Romance is a **popular genre** for lyrics, poems, stories and novels. It is a genre found in all cultures, from ancient to modern times. In this way it is a universal genre, meaning that it is common to everyone in all times and eras.

There is a romantic subplot in most stories and genre types. A **subplot** is a **smaller plot** within the main plot. For example, a hero might fall in love. Have you ever seen an action genre film with a romantic subplot?

Each genre has its own **conventions**. A **convention** is a feature or technique that is commonly found in a particular genre. A convention in romance stories is that there are often **obstacles** to a couple achieving their **goal**, which is usually forming a romantic relationship. A convention of a cowboy Western is a shoot-out at the climax.

*The extract below is a **key scene** in the romance between the central character, Jess, an English girl with Indian parents, and Joe, the coach of her football team. Their different cultural backgrounds become an obstacle to their relationship. Do you know of any other romantic tale where a couple have to overcome an obstacle?*

Bend It Like Beckham

Narinder Dhami

SARI

an Indian dress made of light, colourful fabric

'Joe! Joe!' I raced across the pitch, holding my sari up with one hand. He was out under the floodlights on his own, juggling a football to his knees. 'I'm going! They said I could go!'

At first he looked stunned, then he beamed as I threw myself into his arms and we hugged each other to bits. 'That's brilliant, Jess.'

There were some wolf whistles from some guys on the neighbouring pitch, and I pulled away from him, embarrassed.

'Sorry, I forgot.'

'It's OK now, Jess,' Joe said quickly. 'I'm not your coach any more. We can do what we want.'

He reached out to pull me to him again, but I backed away. This was one of the hardest things I'd ever had to do. But I'd thought things through, and it was the only way.

'Joe,' I began uncomfortably.

Joe looked behind him, an expression of alarm on his face. 'Your dad's not here, is he?'

I shook my head. 'I'm sorry, Joe. I can't…'

Joe looked confused and I almost melted, but I forced myself to harden my heart again.

'Jess, I thought you wanted—'

'Letting me go is a really big step for my mum and dad.' I couldn't look at him. Instead, I reached out and fiddled with the zip of his trackie top. 'I don't know how they'd survive if I told them about you too.'

There was silence for a moment.

'Well, I guess with you going to America, there's not much point anyway,' Joe said bravely. 'Is there?'

He was giving me a way out without making it hard for me. I shook my head, and we hugged each other goodbye. It might be the right decision, but it still hurt. Why couldn't life just be simple and straightforward?

*In this scene Jess has just made a difficult choice, choosing to move to America to play football over staying with her family in England. A difficult choice between two options is called a **dilemma**. This dilemma is complicated for Jess because in going to America, she will also leave Joe.*

OPENING ACT

1 Why did Jess have difficulty running across the field? `EVIDENCE`

2 What was Joe's initial reaction to the news that Jess was allowed to go to America? `EVIDENCE`

3 Why did the boys wolf-whistle at Jess and Joe? `EVIDENCE`

4 Why was Joe suddenly alarmed when Jess backed away from him? `EVIDENCE`

5 How did Jess feel about leaving Joe? `EVIDENCE`

SPOTLIGHT

6 What obstacles were there to the romantic relationship of Jess and Joe? `OPINION` `REASON` `EVIDENCE`

7 What impression do you get of the character of Joe in this extract? *Try to structure your answer into two paragraphs.* `OPINION` `REASON` `EVIDENCE`

8 Do you agree with Jess that life is not 'simple and straightforward'? `OPINION` `REASON`

9 Would you rather have a life that is simple and straightforward or complicated? `OPINION` `REASON`

10 Here are three film genres. Name one convention you can think of for each and give a movie as an example:

i) horror movie;

ii) spy movie;

iii) romantic comedy.

11 Can you think of a story or play you have read where obstacles existed in people's relationships? *Name the text and author, and describe the relationship, explaining what the obstacle was. Try to structure your answer into two paragraphs.*

CENTRE STAGE

Perfume Potion

You have to invent a perfume with a special ingredient that makes people fall in love with the wearer. Make an advertisement for that perfume.

Here are some tips …

1 Give your perfume a catchy name.
2 Invent a good slogan for your perfume. Try to use alliteration.
3 Make a scientific claim for the powers of your perfume.
4 Include a promotional offer.
5 Make a list of advantages to your product.

 IN YOUR OWN WORDS

UNIVERSAL:

SUBPLOT:

CONVENTION:

OBSTACLE:

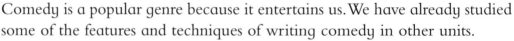
Genre: comedy

Comedy is a popular genre because it entertains us. We have already studied some of the features and techniques of writing comedy in other units.

Here are four popular styles within the genre of comedy.

Parody: when a comedy imitates another story and its characters as a source of entertainment.

Farce: this is a comedy that has some basis in reality but gets more and more absurd and unbelievable as the story develops.

Slapstick: a comedy containing much physical humour, typically where characters hurt themselves in unusual ways.

Romantic comedy: when a comedy contains a romantic element.

The following extract is from a comic novel. In it a young boy, Joe Jefferson, is mysteriously transported to a strange land. What book do you think it parodies?

Muddle Earth

Paul Stuart

'Are you sure I can't tempt you with any more?' said Randalf, ten minutes later.

'No, thanks,' said Joe.

'You'll need to keep your strength up,' Randalf persisted.

'Such as it is,' added Veronica unkindly.

Joe looked at the ladle of slop hovering above his bowl. 'I'm really full,' he lied.

Without any doubt, Norbert had produced the strangest breakfast Joe had ever eaten in his life – lumpy, green porridge that tasted of gooseberries, a small cake iced with love-hearts and a mug of foaming stiltmouse milk.

'But you haven't touched your snuggle-muffin,' said Norbert, looking hurt.

'I'm saving it for later,' said Joe. 'It looks lovely, though.'

The ogre sighed. 'Dear Quentin taught me everything I know. He was an artistic genius with icing sugar.'

'Right, then,' said Randalf, clapping his hands together. He stood up and grabbed his staff. 'Let's get this show on the road.'

Relieved, Joe jumped up from the table, grabbed Henry by his lead and followed Randalf downstairs. Norbert stomped down after them.

'Eager to get started, eh, Joe?' said Randalf warmly. 'An excellent sign for a warrior-hero. We've summoned a good'un this time, Veronica.'

'You said that about Quentin,' the budgie was not slow in reminding him. 'And look how that turned out.'

'We must not look to the past,' said Randalf as he opened the door. 'But to the future.'

He stepped outside. Joe followed him, still none the wiser about what exactly was going on. He seemed to be on the lower deck of a houseboat, but it was difficult to know for certain.

Underneath the vessel, fat fish swam round and round in the crystal clear water. They reminded him of the goldfish at home and, for a moment, he thought that perhaps it wasn't so crazy here after all.

High above him, small fluffy purple clouds scudded across the sky. Below him – and attached to the side by a rope – was a small boat. At least that's what Joe thought at first. It was only as he stepped across from the rope ladder to the bobbing vessel that he realized it was not a boat at all, but a bathtub. Joe clapped his hand to his forehead.

'What was I expecting?' he said to himself. 'Of course it's not a boat. After all, this is Muddle Earth.'

The bathtub gave a wild lurch as Joe stepped into it. Henry jumped in beside him.

'Not there,' said Veronica. 'You sit at the other end where the taps are.'

'If you don't mind,' said Randalf, climbing in and sitting down. 'Just watch your head on the shower attachment if it gets a little bit…errm…choppy.'

'It always gets choppy with Norbert in charge,' said Veronica. 'You've sunk two boats, one wardrobe and an inflatable mattress. Now we're using our last bathtub. It'll be the kitchen sink next!'

'Shut up, Veronica!' said Randalf. 'Come on, Norbert. We're all waiting.'

The ogre climbed into the bathtub, which wobbled about dangerously on the water. Kneeling down, Norbert seized two objects from the bottom of the bath. One was an old tennis racquet, the other was a frying pan. He leaned forwards and began paddling furiously.

The bathtub reared up in a great swell of spray and froth, and sped across the surface of the lake. Norbert's arms were like pistons; up down, up down, up down they went. The edge of the lake came closer. Joe gasped.

PISTON

a pressurised cylindrical pump

'We're going to fall off!' he shouted.

'Trust me, I'm a wizard,' said Randalf. 'A little further left, Norbert,' he told the ogre. 'That's it.'

Joe looked up. He saw that they were heading for a waterfall.

'Hold on tight and watch out for that shower attachment,' the ogre smiled, and paddled faster than ever.

Closer and closer the waterfall came, louder and louder grew the sound of the raging torrent spilling over the edge.

'This is crazy!' Joe yelled.

'True,' said Randalf. 'But it's the only way down. Trust me, I'm a…'

'I know,' Joe muttered as he gripped the sides of the bathtub with white-knuckled ferocity, 'you're a wizard.'

OPENING ACT

1 What breakfast did Norbert produce? `EVIDENCE`
2 Where did Joe 'seem' to be?
3 What reminded Joe of home?
4 What vessel did the characters climb into from the houseboat?
5 How did they paddle the vessel? `EVIDENCE`
6 What is Randalf? `EVIDENCE`

 # SPOTLIGHT

7 Do you think comedy is a universal genre? `OPINION` `REASON`
8 What type of comic writing is this? *It can be a combination of different styles.* `OPINION` `REASON` `EVIDENCE`
9 What features of comic writing can you identify? *Try to structure your answer into two paragraphs.* `OPINION` `REASON` `EVIDENCE`
10 What do you think of the names of the characters? `OPINION` `REASON`
11 Can you identify two comedy films or TV programmes made in any of the comic styles listed above? `OPINION` `REASON`
12 Do you think this novel would make a good film?
Identify dramatic features in the text that also work in film: action, suspense, tension, humour. Try to structure your answer into at least two paragraphs. `OPINION` `REASON` `EVIDENCE`

 # CENTRE STAGE

Reloaded

Retell a text that you are familiar with, turning it into a parody. Try to use exaggeration, name changing and other comic techniques. You can use:

* a poem – *for example, you could rewrite a Shakespearean sonnet in modern language and with a modern twist;*
* a fairytale;
* a novel or film;
* a news story from your locality;
* a sports story such as a football transfer;
* a historical text.

 ## IN YOUR OWN WORDS

PARODY:

SLAPSTICK:

Genre: Mystery

Mystery is a genre that creates a puzzle for the reader to solve. A character in the story is often set the puzzle, and as readers we see the same clues as the character and attempt to figure out the solutions as the plot unfolds. This creates suspense.

Crime, detective and adventure stories often feature a mystery plot. The following extract is from a work of fiction that poses the reader an unusual puzzle to solve. The mystery at the centre of this novel is one that has puzzled philosophers since the dawn of humankind!

Sophie's World

Jostein Gaarder

Sophie Amundsen was on her way home from school. She had walked the first part of the way with Joanna. They had been discussing robots. Joanna thought that the human brain was like an advanced computer. Sophie was not certain she agreed. Surely a person was more than a piece of hardware?

When they got to the supermarket they went their separate ways. Sophie lived on the outskirts of a sprawling suburb and had almost twice as far to school as Joanna. There were no other houses beyond her garden, which made it seem as if her house lay at the end of the world. This was where the woods began.

She turned the corner into Clover Close. At the end of the road there was a sharp bend, known as Captain's Bend. People seldom went that way except on the weekend.

It was early May. In some of the gardens the fruit trees were encircled with dense clusters of daffodils. The birches were already in pale green leaf.

It was extraordinary how everything burst forth at this time of year! What made this great mass of green vegetation come welling up from the dead earth as soon as it got warm and the last traces of snow disappeared?

As Sophie opened her garden gate, she looked in the mailbox. There was usually a lot of junk mail and a few big envelopes for her mother, a pile to dump on the kitchen table before she went up to her room to start her homework.

From time to time there would be a few letters from the bank for her father, but then he was not a normal father. Sophie's father was the captain of a big oil tanker, and was away for most of the year. During the few weeks at a time when he was at home, he would shuffle around the house making it nice and cosy for Sophie and her mother. But when he was at sea he could seem very distant.

There was only one letter in the mailbox – and it was for Sophie. The white envelope read: 'Sophie Amundsen, 5 Clover Close.' That was all; it did not say who it was from. There was no stamp on it either.

As soon as Sophie had closed the gate behind her she opened the envelope. It contained only a slip of paper no bigger than the envelope. It read: Who are you?

Nothing else, only the three words, written by hand, and followed by a large question mark.

She looked at the envelope again. The letter was definitely for her. Who could have dropped it in the mailbox?

Sophie let herself quickly into the red house. As always, her cat Sherekan managed to slink out of the bushes, jump onto the front step, and slip in through the door before she closed it behind her.

*We sometimes recognise that characters have lives that are similar to our own in many ways. When this happens it is said that we **identify with** the character. When we identify with a character we care about what happens to them, and this increases our interest in the outcome of the plot.*

OPENING ACT

1 What did Joanna think of the human brain?
2 Where was Sophie's house? `EVIDENCE`
3 What time of year was it? `EVIDENCE`
4 What job did Sophie's father do?
5 Describe the envelope Sophie received.
6 What was in the envelope?
7 Identify the rhetorical questions that are asked in this extract. `EVIDENCE`

SPOTLIGHT

8 Based on this extract, who do you think is the hero of this novel? `OPINION` `REASON` `EVIDENCE`

9 Is there any way in which you identify with Sophie Amundsen? `OPINION` `REASON` `EVIDENCE`

10 Do you think this is a good opening for a novel? *Try to structure your answer into two paragraphs.* `OPINION` `REASON` `EVIDENCE`

11 Would you like to read more of this novel? Why? *Try to structure your answer into two paragraphs.* `OPINION` `REASON` `EVIDENCE`

12 Do you think it is difficult or easy to answer the question, *'Who are you?'* `OPINION` `REASON`

13 Can you think of a story or play you have read where you identified with a character? *Name the text and author, describe the character and explain why you identified with him or her. Try to structure your answer into two paragraphs.*

Who Are You?

If you had to answer the question 'Who are you?', what would you say first? Are you a boy or a girl? Are you Irish or are you from somewhere else?

i) Write ten statements answering and explaining who you are.

ii) When you are finished, read over the statements. Is it easy to see what is important to you?

iii) Do you think a friend would know that it was you who wrote it from reading the statements that you gave?

iv) If you are comfortable with what you have revealed, share your results with those around you. Having looked at what is important to others, is there anything you would change?

 IN YOUR OWN WORDS

IDENTIFY WITH:

Genre: Horror

Horror is a genre that thrills people with **suspense**. Writers use **descriptive writing** to create a scary **atmosphere** and to slow down the action. This **escalates suspense** as we become excited to know the outcome of the scene.

Relief is when tension and suspense are brought down or relaxed. Writers use **relief** to create **contrast** with the **horror** that is to come, and relief is always followed by an escalation of tension. Relief can be comic, romantic or simply a peaceful scene. Have you ever seen a young romantic couple on a date by a calm lake in a horror film? Do you know what happens next?

This diagram shows the escalation and relief of tension as a line diagram, rising and falling from the beginning of the story to the climax.

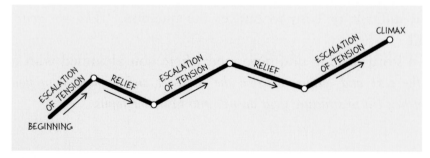

The following extract is from a popular series of books about vampires. In this scene a man, Stanley Collins, is walking down a quiet country lane. Pay attention to how the writer appeals to different senses in this scene to escalate the suspense.

The Vampire's Assistant

Darren Shan

He started walking again.

Crunch. Crunch. Crunch.

There. Back to the familiar sounds. There was nobody else about. He would have heard more than a single branch snapping if there was. Nobody could creep up on Stanley J. Collins. He was a trained Scout Master. His ears were as sharp as a fox's.

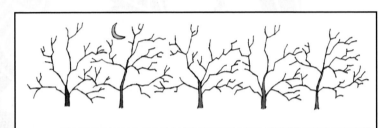

Crunch. Crunch. Crunch. Crunch. Cru—

Snap.

He stopped again, the fingers of fear tightening around his beating heart.

That hadn't been his imagination. He'd heard it, clear as a bell. A twig snapping, somewhere overhead. And before it snapped: had there been the slightest rustling sound, as if something was moving?

Stanley gazed up at the trees but it was too dark to see. There could have been a monster the size of a car up there and he wouldn't have been able to spot it. Ten monsters. A hundred! a thou—

Oh, that was silly. There were no monsters in the trees. Monsters didn't exist. Monsters weren't real. It was a squirrel or an owl, something ordinary like that.

Stanley raised a foot and began to bring it down.

Snap.

His foot hung in the air and his heart pounded quickly. That was no squirrel! The sound was too sharp. Something big was up there. Something that shouldn't be up there. Something that had never been there before. Something that—

Snap!

The sound was closer this time, lower down, and all of a sudden Stanley could stand it no longer. He ran.

Stanley was a large man, but fairly fit for his age. Still, it had been a long time since he'd run this fast, and after a hundred metres he was out of breath and had a stitch in his side.

He slowed to a halt and bent over, gasping for air.

Crunch.

His head shot up.

Crunch. Crunch. Crunch.

There were footsteps coming towards him! Slow, heavy footsteps. He listened, terrified, as they came closer and closer. Had the monster leapt ahead of him through the trees? Had it climbed down? Was it coming to finish him off? Was...

Crunch. Crunch.

The footsteps stopped and Stanley was able to make out a figure. It was smaller than he'd expected, no bigger than a boy. He straightened up, gathered his courage about him like a cloak and stepped forward for a better look.

It was a boy! A small, frightened-looking boy, dressed in a dirty suit.

Stanley smiled and shook his head. What a fool he'd been! The wife would have a field day when he told her about this.

"Are you OK, lad?" Stanley asked.

The boy didn't answer.

Stanley didn't recognise the youngster, but a lot of new families had moved into the area recently. He no longer knew every child in the neighbourhood.

"Can I help you?" he asked. "Are you lost?"

The boy shook his head slowly. There was something strange about him, something that made Stanley feel uneasy. It might have been the effect of the darkness and shadows, but the boy looked very pale, very thin, very...hungry.

"Are you all right?" Stanley asked, stepping closer. "Can I—"

SNAP!

The sound came from directly overhead, loud and menacing.

The boy leapt back quickly, out of the way.

Stanley just had time to glance up and spot a huge red shape which might have been a bat, slashing its way down through the branches of the trees.

And then the red monster was on him. Stanley opened his mouth to scream, but before he could, the monster's hands – claws? – clamped over his mouth. There was a brief struggle, then Stanley was sliding to the floor, unconscious, unseeing, unknowing.

Above him, the two creatures of the night moved in for the feed.

OPENING ACT

1 What had Stanley Collins trained as?

2 Find a line that appeals to the sense of sound. **EVIDENCE**

3 What did Stanley initially think was making the noise? **EVIDENCE**

4 What made him change his mind? **EVIDENCE**

5 Who was following Stanley?

6 What did Stanley see when he looked up?

SPOTLIGHT

7 Is horror a genre that you like? `OPINION` `REASON` `EVIDENCE`

8 Do you think there is good descriptive writing in this extract? *Structure your answer into two paragraphs, giving two clear reasons.* `OPINION` `REASON` `EVIDENCE`

9 How is suspense created in this extract? `OPINION` `REASON` `EVIDENCE`

10 Do you think this would make a good film? *Structure your answer into two paragraphs, giving two clear reasons.* `OPINION` `REASON` `EVIDENCE`

11 Identify three conventions often used in horror. Why do you think they are used?

12 Can you think of a story or play you have read with tension in it? *Name the text and author, describing the tension and explaining how it was created. Try to structure your answer into two paragraphs.*

 ## CENTRE STAGE

Spooky Story

Write your own spooky story.

Here are some titles:
• The Old Factory.
• From Dusk to Dawn.
• The Endless Forest.
• An Unusual Taste.

Remember to follow the rules of essay-writing:
• plan;
• paragraph;
• descriptive writing;
• plot.

IN YOUR OWN WORDS

RELIEF:

curtain call

When you are reading a play, novel or short story, it is important that you keep **notes** on the plot and any significant features of the story. You can use these to **revise** before an exam. On the next page there is a **template** for reviewing chapters, scenes or sections. Fill in the template or make your own. Do this in your copybook or photocopy this page if you can.

Hold onto the copybook or pages after you have finished filling them in!

When you have finished reading your novel, you can do a number of exercises to help you remember it, such as:

- write a book report on the novel;
- give a speech awarding a prize to the novel;
- write the author a letter telling him or her why you liked their novel;
- write a review of the novel for a newspaper;
- write a letter to a film director explaining why you think the novel would make a good film;
- write a blurb or back-cover review of the novel so that people will be persuaded to buy it;
- imagine and write out an interview you would like to have with the writer of the novel;
- turn a key moment or scene from the novel into a first person diary entry;
- write a letter from one fictional character in the novel to another one;
- make a poster advertisement for the novel;
- change a key moment or scene from the novel into a short drama and act it out.

Use the chapter reviews that you have made to help you do these exercises. There is also a short review of narrative terms in the last unit, The Short Story.

Main characters and their traits	
Development of main character	
Summary of main events	
Key moments	
Themes	
Development of relationships	
Personal response	

Spelling Section

Below is a list of thirty words that people commonly have difficulty spelling. If you have difficulty spelling a word, try to sound out the spelling by breaking up the word by syllable. You can also look words up in a dictionary if you feel you are close to the correct spelling.

Look over these spellings. Can you recognise any that you have had difficulty with before? Try to learn them. If possible, your teacher can test you on them.

1 Government.
2 Environment.
3 Careful.
4 Believe.
5 Fatigue.
6 Wednesday.
7 Beautiful.
8 Especially.
9 Imagination.
10 Opposite.
11 Tomorrow.
12 Sandwich.
13 Whether.
14 Stationary.
15 Neighbour.
16 Handkerchief.
17 Beginning.
18 Business.
19 Vegetable.
20 Busy.
21 Calendar.
22 Bread.
23 December.
24 Children.
25 Committee.
26 Conceal.
27 Region.
28 Patient.
29 Suppose.
30 Examination.

DRAMA: IN FOCUS

Shakespearean Texts

WILLIAM SHAKESPEARE IS THE MOST famous and popular playwright of all time. He is known to have written thirty-seven plays, but some people argue that he wrote even more. He wrote tragedies, historical dramas and comedies. His plays are still enjoyed today, exactly as they were in his time, and they are also the source of many modern adaptations in theatre and film.

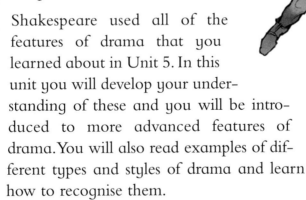

Shakespeare used all of the features of drama that you learned about in Unit 5. In this unit you will develop your understanding of these and you will be introduced to more advanced features of drama. You will also read examples of different types and styles of drama and learn how to recognise them.

You will learn about:

TRAGEDY;
HISTORICAL DRAMA;
COMEDY.

Tragedy

A **tragedy** is a play where a character's circumstances become more difficult as the plot develops, eventually leading to the destruction of that character. We say that the character suffers **escalating misfortune** during the play, ending in downfall or death. Downfall is the ruin of a character, for example in loss of money, friends or family. We usually identify with and have sympathy for a tragic character.

It is often the case that the **tragic character** seems destined for greatness, but **fails because of poor choices** or decisions. A tragic character normally has obvious **negative qualities** as well as **positive qualities**. Negative qualities are called flaws, for example the character could be too passionate or too trusting. A character may also suffer tragedy because of **events outside of their control**. It often happens, however, that a character's **poor judgment** and behaviour contribute most to their own downfall.

Shakespeare wrote many tragedies, including *Romeo and Juliet* and *Hamlet*.

The following extract is from the beginning of Romeo and Juliet. *Romeo is a Montague and Juliet is a Capulet, and the two families are in conflict with each other. This play is a tragedy as both characters die at the end. In this scene we see the conflict between the two families for the first time. From the beginning of the play we realise that the two families hate each other and therefore won't accept Romeo and Juliet's relationship.*

Romeo and Juliet

William Shakespeare

(Gregory, Sampson and Benvolio are Montagues. Abraham, Balthasar and Tybalt are Capulets. The Prince is trying to keep the peace between the two warring families.)

GREGORY: Draw thy tool; here comes two of the house of the Montagues.

Enter Abraham and Balthasar

SAMPSON: My naked weapon is out; quarrel, I will back thee.

GREGORY: How! turn thy back and run?

SAMPSON: Fear me not.

GREGORY: No, marry; I fear thee!

SAMPSON: Let us take the law of our sides, let them begin.[1]

GREGORY: I will frown as I pass by, and let them take it as they list.

SAMPSON: Nay, as they dare. I will bite my thumb at them; which is a disgrace to them, if they bare it.[2]

ABRAHAM: Do you bite your thumb at us, sir?

SAMPSON (*Aside to* **GREGORY**): Is the law of our side if I say ay?[3]

GREGORY (*Aside to* **SAMPSON**): No.

SAMPSON: No, sir, I do not bite my thumb at you, sir; but I bite my thumb, sir.

GREGORY: Do you quarrel, sir?

ABRAHAM: Quarrel, sir! no, sir.

SAMPSON: If you do, sir, I am for you[4]: I serve as good a man as you.

ABRAHAM: No better.

SAMPSON: Well, sir.

GREGORY: (*Aside to* **SAMPSON**): Say, 'better;' here comes one of my master's kinsmen.

SAMPSON: Yes, better, sir.

ABRAHAM: You lie.

SAMPSON: Draw, if you be men. Gregory, remember thy swashing blow.[5]

They fight. Enter Benvolio.

BENVOLIO: Part, fools! Put up your swords; you know not what you do.

[1] Let us obey the law.

[2] It was a grave insult to bite your thumb at someone.

[3] Is the law on our side if I say yes?

[4] I will fight you.

[5] Thrust or slash of sword.

Beats down their swords. Enter **TYBALT**.

[6] A hind is a peasant.

TYBALT: What! Art thou drawn among these heartless hinds?[6]
Turn thee, Benvolio, look upon thy death.

BENVOLIO: I do but keep the peace: put up thy sword.
Or manage it to part these men with me.

TYBALT: What! Drawn, and talk of peace? I hate the word,
As I hate hell, all Montagues, and thee.
Have at thee, coward!

They fight.

Enter several persons of both houses, who join the fray; then enter Citizens, with clubs and partisans.[7]

[7] A partisan is a pike-like weapon.

CITIZENS: Clubs, bills, and partisans! strike! beat them down!
Down with the Capulets! down with the Montagues!

Enter Capulet in his gown, and Lady Capulet.

CAPULET: What noise is this? Give me my long sword, ho!

LADY CAPULET: A crutch, a crutch![8] Why call you for a sword?

[8] A crutch is more suitable in his old age.

CAPULET: My sword, I say! Old Montague is come,
And flourishes his blade in spite of me.

Enter Montague and Lady Montague.

MONTAGUE: Thou villain Capulet! Hold me not; let me go.

LADY MONTAGUE: Thou shalt not stir one foot to seek a foe.

Enter Prince with his Train.[9]

[9] His soldiers and companions.

PRINCE: Rebellious subjects, enemies to peace,
Profaners of this neighbour-stained steel,[10]
Will they not hear? What ho! you men, you beasts,
That quench the fire of your pernicious rage
With purple fountains issuing from your veins,
On pain of torture, from those bloody hands
Throw your mis-temper'd weapons to the ground,[11]
And hear the sentence of your moved prince.
Three civil brawls, bred of an airy word,[12]
By thee, old Capulet, and Montague,
Have thrice disturb'd the quiet of our streets,
And made Verona's ancient citizens
Cast by their grave beseeming ornaments,
To wield old partisans, in hands as old,
Canker'd with peace, to part your canker'd hate.[13]

[10] Their only use for their swords is to kill their neighbours, and so they misuse their swords.

[11] To temper is part of the process of making a sword. This is a pun as the families have angry tempers.

[12] All the fighting came first from a small verbal insult.

[13] Canker is a pun with two meanings, one for the weapons, meaning rusted, and secondly for the people, meaning corrupted by evil.

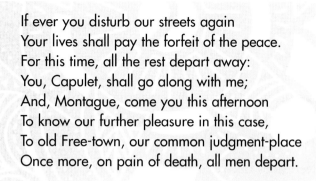

If ever you disturb our streets again
Your lives shall pay the forfeit of the peace.
For this time, all the rest depart away:
You, Capulet, shall go along with me;
And, Montague, come you this afternoon
To know our further pleasure in this case,
To old Free-town, our common judgment-place
Once more, on pain of death, all men depart.

The audience is aware that Romeo and Juliet are going to die from the beginning of the play, and this makes Romeo and Juliet's love and plans for the future more poignant. When the audience is aware of something that the characters in the play are not aware of, it is called **dramatic irony**.

🎬 OPENING ACT

1 How does Tybalt respond when asked to stop fighting by Benvolio?
2 What evidence can you find to show how much the families hate each other?
   EVIDENCE
3 How do the citizens respond to the two families fighting?
4 Does Lady Montague want her husband to fight? **EVIDENCE**
5 What is the penalty for any more fighting according to the Prince? **EVIDENCE**

📷 SPOTLIGHT

6 If you had to play the part of the Prince, how would you play it with regard to:
   i) costume;
   ii) tone of voice;
   iii) body language;
   iv) positioning?
7 Do you think it is effective to have an opening scene with conflict and tension in it? **OPINION** **REASON** **EVIDENCE**
8 What is your impression of Tybalt based on this scene? **OPINION** **REASON** **EVIDENCE**
9 'The hatred between the two families is too great. Romeo and Juliet are doomed to tragedy from the beginning.' *Based on what you have read in the extract, would you agree with this statement?* **OPINION** **REASON** **EVIDENCE**
10 Have you ever read a play that contains conflict and tension between characters? *Name the play and playwright, and explain why there was conflict and tension between the characters. Try to structure your answer into at least two paragraphs.*

CENTRE STAGE

Romeo and Juliet – The Film

If possible, get a copy of the film *Romeo and Juliet* by the Australian director Baz Luhrmann. It is adapted from Shakespeare's play. Watch the opening scene of the film up to the end of the Prince's speech. Make notes for the first three questions below while you watch the film.

1 Find five differences between the film and the play.

2 Which do you think is easier to follow? Why?

3 Do you think the director made a good adaptation of the play for modern audiences?

4 From watching the film and reading the extract from the play, do you think it is fair to say that Shakespearean plays are still relevant to modern audiences?

Now reread the extract from the play and answer these questions.

5 i) Do you know of any modern place where there is a conflict similar to the one in *Romeo and Juliet*, where two communities who are very alike find it difficult to get on?

 ii) If you were to make a film adaptation of *Romeo and Juliet*, how would you set it there?

6 What set, scenery, costumes and style of music would you use for the film?

IN YOUR OWN WORDS

TRAGEDY:

DOWNFALL:

FLAW:

DRAMATIC IRONY:

Historical Drama

A historical drama is a drama based on real events from the past. Shakespeare wrote a number of historical dramas, including *Julius Caesar*, a tragedy based in Ancient Rome. In this way Shakespeare was inspired by events and stories from the past, just as we are now inspired by his plays. The themes Shakespeare saw in historical events, such as love, greed, loyalty and deception, are still relevant to us today. This shows how human nature hasn't changed since those times, and why audiences will continue to enjoy Shakespeare's plays long into the future.

For this extract we will focus on an important feature of Shakespearean drama: the key speech. A **key speech** can change or complicate events, alter the fortune of characters or reveal characters' intentions. In Shakespearean times speeches were as important to the audience as a twist in the plot or a dramatic climax.

In the following scene Marc Antony is making a speech after the murder of his friend and ruler, Julius Caesar. Brutus and a number of other men have killed Caesar to seize power over Rome, and initially they win the support of its citizens. Brutus allows Marc Antony to make a speech, not realising Marc Antony's intention.

Julius Caesar

William Shakespeare

FIRST CITIZEN:	Stay, ho! and let us hear Marc Antony.
THIRD CITIZEN:	Let him go up into the public chair; We'll hear him. Noble Antony, go up.
ANTONY:	For Brutus' sake, I am beholding to you.[1]
Goes into pulpit	
FOURTH CITIZEN:	What does he say of Brutus?

[1] Antony is claiming that he is speaking as a favour to Brutus and as a duty to the crowd.

THIRD CITIZEN:	He says, for Brutus' sake, He finds himself beholding to us all.
FOURTH CITIZEN:	'Twere best he speak no harm of Brutus here.
FIRST CITIZEN:	This Caesar was a tyrant.
THIRD CITIZEN:	Nay, that's certain: We are blest that Rome is rid of him.
SECOND CITIZEN:	Peace! let us hear what Antony can say.
ANTONY:	You gentle Romans,—
CITIZENS:	Peace, ho! let us hear him.
ANTONY:	Friends, Romans, countrymen, lend me your ears. I come to bury Caesar, not to praise him. The evil that men do lives after them; The good is oft interred with their bones [2]; So let it be with Caesar. The noble Brutus Hath told you Caesar was ambitious: If it were so, it was a grievous fault, And grievously hath Caesar answer'd it. [3] Here, under leave of Brutus and the rest— For Brutus is an honourable man; So are they all, all honourable men [4] Come I to speak in Caesar's funeral. He was my friend, faithful and just to me: But Brutus says he was ambitious; And Brutus is an honourable man. He hath brought many captives home to Rome, Whose ransoms did the general coffers fill [5]: Did this in Caesar seem ambitious? When that the poor have cried, Caesar hath wept: Ambition should be made of sterner stuff [6]: Yet Brutus says he was ambitious; And Brutus is an honourable man. You all did see that on the Lupercal I thrice presented him a kingly crown, Which he did thrice refuse: was this ambition? [7] Yet Brutus says he was ambitious; And, sure, he is an honourable man. I speak not to disprove what Brutus spoke, But here I am to speak what I do know. You all did love him once, not without cause:

[2] The good men achieve is forgotten when they are dead.

[3] Caesar has died because of his ambition.

[4] 'They' are the other conspirators.

[5] Antony is listing Caesar's achievements on behalf of his citizens.

[6] Antony is criticising Caesar for crying over the city's poorer citizens.

[7] In a display of modesty Caesar refused to be crowned ruler three times.

What cause withholds you then, to mourn for him?
O judgement! thou art fled to brutish beasts,
And men have lost their reason. [8] Bear with me;
My heart is in the coffin there with Caesar,
And I must pause till it comes back to me.

FIRST CITIZEN: Methinks there is much reason in his sayings.

SECOND CITIZEN: If thou consider rightly of the matter, Caesar has had great wrong.

THIRD CITIZEN: Has he not, masters?
I fear there will a worse come in his place.

FOURTH CITIZEN: Mark'd ye his words? He would not take the crown;
Therefore 'tis certain he was not ambitious.

FIRST CITIZEN: If it be found so, some will dear abide it.

SECOND CITIZEN: Poor soul! his eyes are red as fire with weeping.

THIRD CITIZEN: There's not a nobler man in Rome than Antony.

[8] If there's no logic then there can be no justice, and without justice people become like beasts.

The speech: in this famous speech, Marc Antony makes intelligent use of flattery to win the crowd over. **Flattery** is when you praise someone so that they think favourably of you or your opinions. Antony also **hides his true intention**, uses repetition, manipulates his audience with **logic and reason** and **stirs their emotions** by constantly referring to the death of Caesar. Now read the speech again and look for these features.

 ## OPENING ACT

1 What do the crowd initially think of Caesar? `EVIDENCE`
2 How does Marc Antony address the citizens of Rome? `EVIDENCE`
3 What kind of a friend was Caesar to Marc Antony? `EVIDENCE`
4 What kind of person is Brutus, according to Marc Antony's speech?
5 Where does Marc Antony claim his heart is?
6 What do the citizens think of Marc Antony at the end of this speech?

 ## SPOTLIGHT

7 How does Marc Antony use flattery in his speech? `OPINION` `REASON` `EVIDENCE`
8 Why does Marc Antony use flattery in his speech? `OPINION` `REASON`
9 Do you think this is an effective speech? Why? *Try to structure your answer into at least two paragraphs with clear reasons in each one.* `OPINION` `REASON` `EVIDENCE`

10 What is your impression of the citizens of Rome? `OPINION` `REASON` `EVIDENCE`

11 Why do you think speeches play such an important part in Shakespearean dramas? `OPINION` `REASON`

12 Would you like Marc Antony to represent you in a court case? `OPINION` `REASON` `EVIDENCE`

13 Have you ever read a play where you admired or were disgusted by the behaviour of a main character? *Name the play and playwright, and give your opinion, explaining why you felt as you did. Try to structure your answer into at least two paragraphs.*

CENTRE STAGE

Speech! Speech! Speech!

This scene needs to be acted out. Drama involves a lot of practice and preparation. When you act out a scene, it also makes it easier to remember important lines.

Written work for homework

1 Identify how you would adapt a stage or your classroom for this scene.

2 Where would Marc Antony stand and would his position on the stage change during the speech?

3 What body language, tone and props would he use?

Audition work for the start of the next class

4 Audition for the parts of Marc Antony and the citizens by reading part of the scene.

Stage work in class

5 Act out the scene, paying close attention to stage positioning and physical movement.

6 The class can watch the scene without comment.

7 Now act it out again. This time the class can take notes on how to improve the scene. Look for improvements in these categories:
- body language, including physical movement and facial expressions;
- positioning;
- tone, volume and pace of voice;
- use of props.

8 Get feedback from the group.

For homework

9 Practise the scene at home by learning lines and, if possible, getting the group of actors together to rehearse.

10 Act it out one last time the next day in school.

Remember, actors rehearse a play for weeks and months! Can you appreciate how much work goes into staging a play?

IN YOUR OWN WORDS

comedy

Shakespeare wrote comedies as well as tragedies. Audiences like to be entertained by humour as well as action. Shakespeare used comedy and romance to provide **relief** for conflict, excitement, tension and suspense. When the action begins again, the tension is increased because it contrasts with the relief.

Advanced features of climax

Escalating tension and suspense: as we reach the climax, our excitement to see the outcome grows. Action intensifies as characters react to the quickening pace of events.

Crisis for a character: a misfortune or unexpected event happens to a character.

Revelation: a revelation is when an important or outcome – changing fact is revealed to characters in the play or to the audience. This can lead to a turning point in the fortune of the characters.

Reversal: a reversal is when the fortune or circumstances of a character change completely, to the opposite of what it was. For example, a prisoner is found innocent and set free.

Anticlimax: this is the moment of relief after the climax is over, or if there is a false climax.

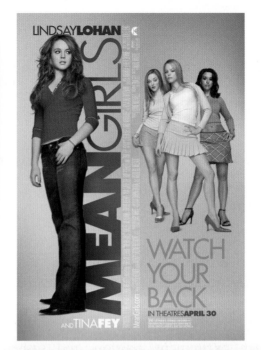

Do you know of any films that feature a climax? Could you identify any of the above features of climax in the film?

The following scene contains both comedy and tragedy. Some people call it a tragi-comic play! This extract is taken from the climax of the play. Complicated and tense climaxes are a common feature of Shakespearean drama. That is why there is a long introduction to the scene, in italics below.

The following extract is taken from the court scene in The Merchant of Venice. *Antonio has borrowed money for his friend, Bassanio, from a Jewish moneylender, Shylock, but can't repay it. The terms of the loan are such that if Antonio can't repay it, he must give Shylock a pound of flesh from near to his heart. Shylock is now collecting that debt.*

The other characters are Portia, the bride-to-be of Bassanio. She is in disguise as the judge. Nerissa is her waiting-woman, and she is in disguise as a clerk of the court. Nerissa is to be married to Gratiano, another friend of Antonio. Only the audience members are aware that the judge and the clerk are in fact Portia and Nerissa, and this creates dramatic irony and is a source of comedy in this scene.

The Merchant of Venice

William Shakespeare

ANTONIO: Most heartily I do beseech the court[1]
To give the judgement.

PORTIA: Why then, thus it is:
You must prepare your bosom for this knife.

SHYLOCK: O noble judge! O excellent young man!

PORTIA: For the intent and purpose of the law
Hath full relation to the penalty,
Which here appeared due upon the bond. [2]

SHYLOCK: 'Tis very true. O wise and upright judge!
How much more elder art thou than thy looks!

PORTIA: Therefore lay bare your bosom.

SHYLOCK: Ay, his breast,
So says the bond, doth it not, noble judge?
'Nearest his heart', those are the very words.

PORTIA: It is so. Are there balance here to weight
The flesh?

SHYLOCK: I have them ready.

PORTIA: Have by some surgeon, Shylock, on your charge,
To stop his wounds, lest he do bleed to death.

SHYLOCK: Is it so nominated in the bond?[3]

PORTIA: It is not so expressed, but what of that?
'Twere good you do so much for charity.

SHYLOCK: I cannot find it; 'tis not in the bond.

PORTIA: You, merchant, have you anything to say?

ANTONIO: But little. I am armed and well prepared.
Give me your hand, Bassanio, fare you well.
Grieve not that I am fallen to this for you,
For herein Fortune shows herself more kind
Than is her custom; it is still her use
To let the wretched man outlive his wealth
To view with hollow eye and wrinkled brow
An age of poverty, from which lingering penance

[1] To beseech is to beg.

[2] The bond is the legal agreement for the debt.

[3] It is not written in the bond that Shylock has to provide a surgeon.

Of such misery doth she cut me off. [4]
Commend me to your honourable wife,
Tell her the process of Antonio's end,
Say how I loved you, speak me fair in death,
And when the tale is told, bid her be judge
Whether Bassanio had not once a love.
Repent but you that shall lose your friend,
And he repents not that he pays your debt,
For if the Jew do cut but deep enough,
I'll pay it instantly with all my heart.

BASSANIO: Antonio, I am married to a wife
Which is as dear to me as life itself,
But life itself, my wife, and all the world
Are not with me esteemed above thy life. [5]
I would lose all, ay sacrifice them all
Here to this devil, to deliver you.

[5] His own life, his wife and his world.

PORTIA: Your wife would give you little thanks for that
If she were by to hear you make the offer.

GRATIANO: I have a wife who I protest I love;
I would she were in heaven, so she could
Entreat some power to change this currish Jew. [6]

[6] He wishes his wife were dead in heaven so she could ask God for help.

NERISSA: 'Tis well you offer it behind her back;
The wish would make else an unquiet house.

SHYLOCK: These be the Christian husband! I have a daughter;
Would any of the stock of Barabbas
Had been her husband, rather than a Christian. [7]
We trifle time. [8] I pray thee pursue sentence.

[7] Barabbas was a Jew and the criminal freed instead of Jesus before the crucifixion.

[8] We waste time.

PORTIA: A pound of that same merchant's flesh is thine,
The court awards it, and the law doth give it.

SHYLOCK: Most rightful judge!

PORTIA: And you must cut this flesh from off his breast,
The law allows it, and the court awards it.

SHYLOCK: Most learned judge! A sentence! Come, prepare!

OPENING ACT

1 Is Antonio willing to accept the consequences of his bad debt? `EVIDENCE`

2 How does Shylock praise Portia? `EVIDENCE`

3 What does Antonio think of Bassanio? `EVIDENCE`

4 How does Portia react when Bassanio says he would sacrifice his wife and his own life to save Antonio? `EVIDENCE`

5 Where does Gratiano wish his wife were?

SPOTLIGHT

6 How is the tension escalated in this scene? `OPINION` `REASON` `EVIDENCE`

7 Do you think this is an exciting climax to a play? `OPINION` `REASON` `EVIDENCE`

8 What part does dramatic irony play in the comedy of this scene? *Remember: dramatic irony is when the audience is aware of something that some or all of the characters on stage aren't aware of.* `OPINION` `REASON` `EVIDENCE`

9 What features of a climax can you find in this scene? *Find at least two features and write a paragraph for each.* `OPINION` `REASON` `EVIDENCE`

10 If you had to play the part of Portia, how would you play it with regard to:
  i) costume;
  ii) tone of voice;
  iii) body language?
  Make reference to both the serious and comic parts of her role.

11 Have you ever read a play with an exciting climax or moment in it? *Name the play and playwright, and explain how the excitement was created and what the outcome of the moment was. Try to structure your answer into at least two paragraphs.*

CENTRE STAGE

Groom's Speech

Write the speech that Bassanio might give at his wedding. Antonio has survived to be his best man.

Remember to:
• praise your wife-to-be;
• praise Antonio and describe what he means to you;
• describe serious events at the court hearing;
• describe humorous events at the court hearing;
• use a quotation from the play;
• imagine other details.

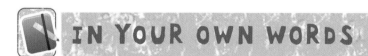
IN YOUR OWN WORDS

REVELATION:

REVERSAL:

12

FUNCTIONAL WRITING: IN FOCUS

WE HAVE ALREADY LEARNED about writing letters, reviews and speeches, as well as practising our debating skills. In this unit we will learn how to identify more features of information, persuasion and argument. We will learn and practise using those features in functional texts.

We will learn about more functional writing tasks:

```
BROCHURE;
INSTRUCTIONS;
REPORT;
INTERVIEW.
```

Brochure

A brochure is a **leaflet**, usually with **text** and **corresponding images**, which contains **information** about a particular **subject**. Brochures are often used in advertisement, but can also be used to promote education and awareness about issues such as the environment or health. Brochures can use **information**, **persuasion** or **argument**, depending on their **purpose**. Images can be photographic or cartoon

FUNCTIONAL WRITING IN FOCUS

images, which are often used in advertisements, or they can be map or diagram images, often used to give information.

Structure is very important in brochure writing. The purpose of the brochure should be stated clearly and concisely in the title or heading. The text is then broken down into **sections**, with each section clearly marked with a **subheading**. A **subheading summarises** or captures the **main point** of the section that follows it. The text in a brochure can be longer than in a typical print advertisement or information notice because there is more room.

Read the following advertising brochure. It uses both information and persuasion. Note how each section covers a different part of the subject, giving the brochure a clear structure. This structure is identified in blue as: introduction, culture, entertainment, sport, closing paragraph.

Discover New York!

THE BIG APPLE
Introduction
All your life you've heard of Central Park, the Manhattan skyline, the Statue of Liberty and the Empire State Building. You've dreamt about seeing a show on Broadway or taking a famous subway downtown. You recognise the yellow cabs and neon billboards even though you haven't been there in the flesh. When I ask you to visit the city that never sleeps, the Big Apple, the greatest town in the whole wide world, you know exactly where I'm talking about. But have you been to the world's most famous city? There's never been a better time to visit New York than now.

THE CAPITAL OF THE WORLD
Culture
For centuries New York has been the first port of call for arriving immigrants to the United States, and people of all races and cultures have made it their home. If Washington, DC is the capital of America, then New York is the capital of the world. Why fly all that way to China when you can visit Chinatown in New York, and have pizza in Little Italy in the afternoon? Want to watch the All-Ireland final? Why not take a train out to Woodlawn?

12

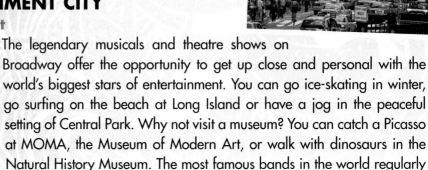

Choose the comfort of a local bar or brave foreign and exotic new experiences. New York is world culture in the palm of your hand.

ENTERTAINMENT CITY
Entertainment

The legendary musicals and theatre shows on Broadway offer the opportunity to get up close and personal with the world's biggest stars of entertainment. You can go ice-skating in winter, go surfing on the beach at Long Island or have a jog in the peaceful setting of Central Park. Why not visit a museum? You can catch a Picasso at MOMA, the Museum of Modern Art, or walk with dinosaurs in the Natural History Museum. The most famous bands in the world regularly visit and play to electric crowds, and lovers of classical music can experience the best orchestras in the world on their doorstep.

WORK HARD, PLAY HARD
Sport

New York is not just a city that works, it's also a city that plays. New Yorkers love sport and the city is home to some of the most famous teams in the world.

If you're looking for an authentic New York experience, go see a baseball game, and don't forget to order a soda and hot dog. If you want to experience atmosphere and tension, dare to see the New York Yankees take on the New York Mets, their fiercest rivals. You could also watch the New York Knicks play a game of basketball or take in the Giants playing a game of American football. If you're feeling fit enough you might want to sign up with the many visitors who take part in the New York City Marathon every year.

VISIT SOON!
Closing paragraph

Do you want to let the opportunity to visit the greatest city in the world pass you by? You can visit in winter and watch the snow fall, do some Christmas shopping and marvel at the lights and decorations of the festive season. In spring you'll see the trees coming into bloom and you can take your time visiting parks and museums. In summer you can roll your towel out at the beach or sit out late into the evening on a restaurant terrace. Watch the leaves turn red in the fall and take in an outdoor concert. Whether you are an old friend or a new beginner, New York City has its doors open to the world and welcomes you with a big smile.

OPENING ACT

1 What does the writer mean by 'the city that never sleeps'?

2 Identify a feature of persuasive writing in the text and explain why it is used. `EVIDENCE`

3 Find three persuasive adjectives in the text that are used to make places or experiences sound more exciting or attractive. `EVIDENCE`

4 What are the most repeated words in the text and why do you think they are repeated? `EVIDENCE`

 # SPOTLIGHT

5 Do you think the title of this brochure is appropriate? `OPINION` `REASON`

6 From your own perspective, which section of the brochure do you find most convincing? Explain. `OPINION` `REASON` `EVIDENCE`

7 Comment on the use of rhetorical questions in the brochure. `OPINION` `REASON` `EVIDENCE`

8 Describe one image – a photograph, cartoon, diagram or map – which you would add to this brochure. Explain why you would add it. `OPINION` `REASON`

9 Do you think this brochure uses information well? `OPINION` `REASON` `EVIDENCE`

 # CENTRE STAGE

Here are five photographic images of Ireland. Write a tourism brochure advertising Ireland, using these images to accompany your text.

Remember:
- give your brochure an appropriate title;
- use subheadings for each paragraph or section;
- use persuasive language techniques;
- give information in a clear, factual way.

Instructions

Instructions use information. Instructions could be directions to get to a certain place, a recipe for a meal or a manual to explain how a product functions. As with all information, instructions must be **clear, factual** and **concise**. They must also be very **precise**, so that the person who is following them will know exactly what to do every step of the way. When instructions are clear and easy to follow, we say they are **user friendly**.

Here are some safety instructions for cycling a bicycle on the road.

1 Make sure your bike is roadworthy
Only use a bicycle that is in good working order. This means you need to regularly check important features, such as the brakes and tyres. You should have lights and a bell for your bicycle. Mudguards and wet gear will stop the distraction of mud and water in the rain.

2 Cycle where you are allowed to cycle
Cycling on the footpath is not safer than the road—it endangers you and pedestrians. It is also illegal! If you aren't able to cycle on the road, then dismount from your bicycle and walk on the footpath until you get an opportunity to cycle again.

3 Be safe, be seen
Most accidents happen to cyclists because motorists cannot see them. Always use lights at night, both in front and behind. Wearing a high-visibility vest will help you to be seen both at night and during the day.

4 Use clear road signals
Communicate with other road-users by using your arms to signal your intentions with advance warning. If possible, make eye contact with other road-users, as this makes communication easier and helps to connect you with other people.

5 Look around you

Be aware of what is happening around you. Look over your shoulder every few moments and watch the road ahead of you as you go. Turn off distractions, such as a mobile phone or MP3 player.

6 Be aware of junctions and roundabouts

If you come to a complicated junction or roundabout, remember to use clear signals and follow the rules of the road. If you think it is going to be difficult or dangerous, dismount safely from your bicycle and use the footpath.

7 Watch the weather

Be aware that wet weather makes it more difficult for motorists to see you. Cold and wet weather can also make a vehicle more difficult to control and stop. It is important to equip your bicycle for different weather conditions and to dress accordingly.

8 Get on your bike

It's a proven fact that the more cyclists there are on the roads, the safer roads become. Motorists become more used to looking out for cyclists and their awareness of cycle safety grows. The countries with the best cycle safety records in Europe are also the countries with the highest numbers of cyclists. It's time to make Ireland one of them!

 OPENING ACT

1 Why is it important to only cycle where you are allowed to cycle?

2 What distractions does a cyclist need to be aware of?

3 What are the dangers of wet weather?

4 What countries in Europe have the best cycle safety records?

 SPOTLIGHT

5 Do you think this text achieves its purpose? `OPINION` `REASON` `EVIDENCE`

6 Do you think the numbering of the steps is a good idea? Why? `OPINION` `REASON`

7 What is your opinion on instruction number 8? `OPINION` `REASON` `EVIDENCE`

8 Which step would you find most difficult to follow? Why? `OPINION` `REASON`

9 Do you think these instructions are user friendly? `OPINION` `REASON` `EVIDENCE`

 CENTRE STAGE

How To

Here is another instruction text on safety. It is written in a different tone and style of language from the list of instructions on safe cycling. Read the text and change it into a numbered list of safety instructions about barbecuing. You can use the safe cycling instructions as a model. Include any other barbecue safety instructions you think might be suitable.

Take care this summer!

We all know how good it is to have a barbecue on a hot summer afternoon. Sizzling sausages, hot hamburgers and satisfying steaks all go down a treat. It's rare that we get to eat outdoors in Ireland, so it's important when we get the chance to do it safely. There are a few things you should think about before you begin.

You should make sure you start with a clean area around the barbecue. This is important so that no one trips over any objects. Needless to say, you should use proper barbecue lighter fluid to start your barbecue, and keep the fuel away from the barbecue once it's lit. I once had a friend who used petrol to light the coals, and he ended up in hospital getting treatment for some nasty burns on his hands.

Be careful of animals such as pets when you're barbecuing, or you could end up with a real hot dog! Keep a close eye on children too. They mightn't realise how hot the barbecue is, and they love to stretch for out-of-reach objects. When I barbecue I don't allow anyone else to come near the grill. I say that it's for safety reasons, but some people think I want to be the first to try all the food. It's also important to extinguish the barbecue or cover it safely until it cools, even if you feel like relaxing on the lawn with a full stomach.

Remember:
• be clear, factual, concise and precise;
• structure your answer;
• use subheadings.

Or

You can write your own instructions on how to do a favourite activity. This could be instructions such as a recipe for a meal you like to cook or how to prepare for sporting activity, or a fun set of instructions, such as how to find success in love. Remember to follow the rules above.

IN YOUR OWN WORDS

USER FRIENDLY:

Report

> **REPORT:**
> FOR A GREENER PRINTING PRESS
>
> **CONCLUSIONS:**
> OUR PRINTING USES TOO MUCH
> ENERGY AND COULD BE GREENER
>
> **RECOMMENDATION:**
> MORE RECYCLED PAPER, SMARTER
> ENERGY USE, ONLINE PUBLICATION

The purpose of a report is to **investigate, measure** and **record** information about an issue or topic. The report **presents** the **information** found and can then make **conclusions** based upon that information. After this it is possible to make a **recommendation** for action or change based upon the conclusion.

There are five steps used to write a report:
• **introduction;**
• **research;**
• **results;**
• **conclusions;**
• **recommendations.**

Information for reports is collected through polls, surveys and censuses. Large amounts of information can be turned into statistics by statisticians and presented through percentages, graphs, bar charts and pie charts. This collected information can then reveal the habits, patterns and trends of large groups of people.

Large amounts of information presented in numbers can be difficult to understand. By converting information into percentages, graphs and charts, statistics help us to quickly understand large amounts of information. Statistics can then be used to reinforce an argument or to persuade us of a point.

Example:

Fact: one in four (27%) of all students surveyed were currently smokers, smoking an average of seven cigarettes a day.

Conclusion: smoking is a serious health risk taken by a large number of Irish students.

Recommendation: students need better education about the dangers of smoking and need more support to help them to stop smoking.

The following extract is from a larger report on the health of students in Ireland. This section of the report shows the results of the research.

Dietary Habits
Health Promotion Unit of Ireland

One in five of all students were on a special diet, with females more than twice as likely to report such a practice. Weight-reduction diet was the most common, where 15% of females compared to 2% of males reported such a practice. These figures were similar to a comparative group in the national lifestyle survey. One-third of students reported using food supplements on a regular basis.

The most common foods consumed on a daily basis among students were: bread (80%), meat (56%), cooked vegetables (50%), fruit (42%) and sweets (39%). More male students had bread, meat and milk at least daily and more female students ate fruit and salads. Salads and cooked vegetables were more popular among third year students.

Among the less healthy foods, sweets (39%) and fizzy drinks (27%) were the most popular on a daily basis. A higher number of males used fizzy drinks, cakes/biscuits, crisps and fast foods in comparison to females. These foods were more popular among first year students. Fizzy drinks (40%) and crisps (26%) were most popular among first year male students.

Males drank more milk than females in all years, and consumption declined over the three years for both genders. Just 6% of students did not drink milk at all. Females were nearly twice as likely to use low-fat or skimmed milk in comparison to males.

There are many different types of report. As a student, you will be well aware of school exam reports. The report begins with measuring what you have learned through an exam. Then this exam is corrected and the data organised into percentage and grade statistics for the report. The report is then sent home, often with conclusions and recommendations included.

 ## OPENING ACT

1 What was the most common form of diet?

2 What types of food were popular among third year students?

3 What types of food were more popular with first year students?

4 Who drank more milk, males or females? `EVIDENCE`

 ## SPOTLIGHT

5 How would you describe the language used in this report? `OPINION` `REASON` `EVIDENCE`

6 Make three reasonable conclusions about student health based on the information provided in this report. `OPINION` `REASON` `EVIDENCE`

7 Make three recommendations based on your conclusions. `OPINION` `REASON`

8 Are there any statistics that surprised you in this extract? `OPINION` `REASON` `EVIDENCE`

9 What conclusions can you make about how male and female dietary habits contrast? `OPINION` `REASON` `EVIDENCE`

 ## CENTRE STAGE

Your Report

Here is some factual and statistical data concerning road safety. You can use it to write your own report.

Students using a seatbelt in the front seat of a car: 82%.

Students wearing a helmet when riding a motorbike: 86%.

Students always wearing seatbelts in back of car: 25%.

Students using bicycles, by gender: male: 71%, female: 45%.

Students wearing cycle helmets: 10%.

Students rarely using cycle helmets, by gender: male: 83%, female: 75%.

First year students are less inclined to wear front seatbelt than third-year students.

Third year students were more compliant with helmet use than first or second year students.

Female students were more compliant with road-safety measures in comparison to male students.

Here are some tips to help you:
• Give your report a title.
• Write a short introduction explaining what the report is about.
• Present your research by explaining what you found.
• Draw a conclusion based on your findings and show how the evidence proves it.
• Make a recommendation based on your conclusions.

Interview

Interviews follow a particular **format**. The format is the way in which information is arranged and presented. The common format of an interview is question and answer. When you are using functional writing, it is very important to use the appropriate format.

The format of instructions is usually a step-by-step numbered format. The format of a report usually makes an investigation, measures and records findings, presents information, draws conclusions and makes recommendations.

This is an interview with J.K. Rowling, the writer of the Harry Potter series of novels. Snape is a character from that series.

An Interview with J.K. Rowling

Lindsey Fraser and J.K. Rowling

Where did you come in the family?

I was the older of two girls. My earliest memory is of my sister being born – she's just under two years younger than me. My dad gave me playdough the day she arrived, to keep me occupied while he ran in and out of the bedroom. I have no memory of seeing the new baby, but I do remember eating the playdough.

Were books important in your family?

Another early memory is of having the measles – I must have been about four – and Dad reading *The Wind in the Willows*. I don't remember feeling ill at all – just lying there listening to those stories. Both my parents loved reading. My mother was a huge reader – she was quite bookish – and never happier than when she was curled up, reading. That was a big influence on me. She came from a family of teachers and I think my dad followed her example.

BOOKISH

to like reading
and books

Did you have any pets?

When I was very, very tiny we had a dog called Thumper, named after the rabbit in the Disney film, *Bambi*. I was very sad when he was put down. We had two guinea pigs later on, but they were eaten by a fox. I remember the scene of carnage on the back lawn – it not pleasant…And we had another dog, Misty, who was around until after I went to university.

   As a teenager I had tropical fish. That was a big hobby and I still love them.

Did you like all your teachers?

No, not all of them. My least favourite teacher was just a bully. I've met quite a few teachers now, both when I was teaching and when I've been visiting schools, and the bullies really do stand out. I understand from the teacher's point of view that it's very easy to be a bully, but it's also the worst, shabbiest thing you can do. We're back to Snape here.

Was there anything else you didn't like?

My least favourite subject was metalwork. I was the worst in my class – just terrible. I am not a practical person … It seemed to me to be all about hammering stuff until I broke it. I did try, but I just could not do it. Mum always kept a ridiculous flat teaspoon I made which was useless, completely hopeless. I was terrible at woodwork too – I remember arriving home with a photograph frame composed mainly of glue.

I was also dreadful at sport, although I vaguely liked gym. I especially hated hockey. But I did like swimming and dancing.

And I loathed the uniform. It was brown and yellow, two colours I will now never, ever wear on principle.

Do you think your teachers thought you would become a writer?

I think Miss Shepherd might have believed I could be a writer but I don't think she expected it of me. I always, always wanted to be a writer but I never shared my burning ambition with anyone.

When I was about six I wrote a book – just a little story – and when I finished it I remember thinking, well now we can publish this. I wanted the complete experience, even then. I was a lot less arrogant by the time I was 26. By then, I didn't think I had any chance whatsoever.

ARROGANT

over confident in an unpleasant way

OPENING ACT

1 What is J.K. Rowling's earliest memory?

2 What was a big influence on her? **EVIDENCE**

3 What did she think metalwork was 'all about'? **EVIDENCE**

4 What activities did she like in school?

SPOTLIGHT

5 Do you think that you learned much about J.K. Rowling from reading this interview? **OPINION** **REASON** **EVIDENCE**

6 Based on this interview, what sort of experience did J.K. Rowling have in school? **OPINION** **REASON** **EVIDENCE**

7 What do you think of the questions asked in this interview? **OPINION** **REASON** **EVIDENCE**

8 Write out two other questions you would ask J.K. Rowling and explain why you chose them. `OPINION` `REASON`

9 If you could interview anyone, who would you interview and why? `OPINION` `REASON`

 **CENTRE STAGE**

Say What?

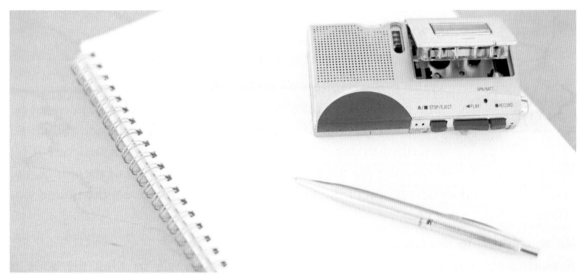

Conduct your own interview in one of the following topic areas:

* sporting achievements;
* issues (e.g. crime/bullying/racism);
* school life.

You can interview someone you know, such as a sports player, your parents or even a teacher in your school, or you can imagine an interview with someone you haven't met.

To prepare:

1 Write out four categories you are going to use in your interview. If you are interviewing a sports person, for example, you could use background, inspiration, achievements and hopes for the future.

2 Write out two or three questions per category.

Now conduct your interview! You can ask the questions in person or give the person a sheet with the questions on it.

 **IN YOUR OWN WORDS**

FORMAT:

FUNCTIONAL WRITING: IN FOCUS

curtain call

There are many different functional writing tasks you could be asked to do in an exam situation. Remember to always use the **appropriate language, tone** and **register**. To help you with this, you must decide what the **main purpose** of the task is: to **inform, persuade** or **argue**. You also need to **structure** and **plan** your answer, using the **correct format**.

Here are some other tasks you could be asked to do.

Write a description of an image

The purpose is to inform. The language for this task needs to be clear, precise, concise, factual and serious. The image should be described in five or six short paragraphs. You can structure it by using a paragraph to describe the people in the image, the location of the image, the activity in the image, the mood of the image and the reason you feel the image was taken.

Write a blurb to describe a book

A blurb is the writing on the back cover of a book that tells us what the book is about. The purpose is to inform the reader what the book is about and to persuade the reader to buy it. The language for this task must be colourful, persuasive and enthusiastic. You should highlight five or six positive aspects about the book in short paragraphs. A brief outline of the plot and characters should be given, but don't reveal the ending.

Write an application

You could be asked to write an application for a job, for a competition or even to apply for a position on a space station! The purpose is to introduce yourself, inform the reader of your good qualities and persuade the reader of your ability. The language should be informative and persuasive. The structure should divide your positive qualities into five areas and clearly develop each one in short paragraphs.

Write a nomination for an award

To nominate a group or person for an award, you need to inform the reader of the reasons why you feel the award should be given. The language should be informative and persuasive. The structure should clearly develop each reason and you should include an opening and closing paragraph.

PERSONAL WRITING

IN YOUR JUNIOR CERTIFICATE ENGLISH EXAM you will have to write an essay in the Personal Writing section. We will use three categories to explore your options.

ONCE UPON A TIME, A LONG TIME AGO...

1 Autobiographical writing: you can write an essay based on your own life and personal experiences.

2 Fiction writing: you can write a narrative essay based in a fictional world.

3 Discursive writing: you can write your own response to topics, issues and ideas from society and the world.

You must decide on the **form** that best suits your writing. For example, your form could be narrative, descriptive, dramatic, discursive or functional, depending on the choice you make.

You must decide on the **style** that best suits your writing. For example, your style could be comic, argumentative, informative, persuasive, formal, casual or realistic.

You must decide on the **content** that you will use. For example, you can use statistics and statements, or concentrate on descriptive features such as similes and appealing to the senses.

PERSONAL WRITING

13

PERSONAL WRITING **361**

Autobiographical Writing

Your own life is a fertile source of ideas and inspiration for writing.

- **Experience.**
- **Biography.**
- **Anecdote.**

Experience

Learning to **value** and **write about** your own life experience is important for your **creative** and **personal writing** skills.

Diary

Keeping a **diary** of your own life will help you to learn about the **basic elements** of **story telling**. Your day begins in the morning, is at the middle in the afternoon and ends in the evening.

A diary will help you learn the importance of:

- **background;**
- **describing everyday settings;**

- **discussing thoughts;**
- **reflecting on emotions;**
- **identifying key moments.**

CENTRE STAGE

Keep a Diary

Keep a diary every night for a week or on alternate nights over the course of a few weeks.

Tips

- Imagine you are addressing it to someone in a different country or time than your own.
- Describe the different settings of your life.
- Use similes, personification, metaphors and appeal to the senses.
- Balance your diary between description, incident, emotion and reflection.

Letters

Writing **personal letters** will help you to **structure thoughts, express emotion, identify key incidents** and become familiar with **appropriate register**.

CENTRE STAGE

Keep a Correspondence

A **correspondence** is an exchange of letters. Write a personal letter to a family member or friend you would like to keep in contact with.

- Try to start a regular correspondence with them.
- Try to use descriptive writing.
- Make a copy of the letters you send.
- Keep the letters you receive.

If you're sometimes feeling lazy, send a card or postcard instead. You can even make and personalise the postcard to give the person an extra surprise!

Biography

Life can be written down as a story or captured in images. So far you might only have enough material for a few chapters, but you are already on the way!

Photographs

Photographs tell a **story** of their own and hold the **key to stories** inside us. Look through old photographs at home and see if you know the story behind the moments they capture. Get a camera and start taking your own photographs.

Narrative features of photographs:
- **background;**
- **freeze frame;**
- **character;**
- **incident and anecdote.**

A **freeze frame** is a moment in time that is captured forever. It is sometimes called a snapshot. **Imagery** and **descriptive writing** help to **freeze frame** in writing.

 CENTRE STAGE

1 Find one photograph from your life that sums up what is important to you.
- Give the image a title.
- Explain the background of the image.
- Describe the image.
- Explain your choice.

Or

2 Make a photo journal of your world. Take ten photographs that explain who you are. Put them together in a copybook or album.
You will need to:
- give the journal a title;
- put them in a sequence;
- write out captions.

Or

3 Find an image from any source that you think expresses the statement, 'Life for me today'.
- Explain what you were looking for in the image.
- Explain your choice.
- Describe your image.

Family History

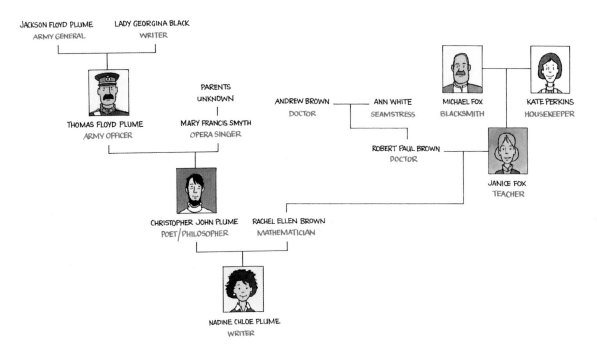

Your family history is a rich source of stories and incidents. If you think about it, your family stretches back to the very dawn of time! How far back can you trace your family tree? Has your family lived through any remarkable moments in history?

It is not just your family that has a remarkable history. It could be neighbours, friends or the teachers in your school. For the following exercises you can use any of these people.

CENTRE STAGE

1 Interview a family member about the most remarkable moment of history they lived through or experienced first hand. Remember to be careful about asking sensitive questions.
• Write out the questions beforehand.
• Find out the background to the moment.
• Ask about emotions and feelings.
• What stood out?

- How did the experience affect the person?
- Find and include any documentary evidence.

Don't forget to include what you learned from the project!

Or

2 Find a photograph of your family from before you were born and write a composition based on what you see in it. Describe what is happening in the image and explain the background to the image.

You will need to:
- research;
- interview;
- structure into paragraphs;
- identify key incident or story;
- how has life changed?

Or

3 Find a family member or member of your community who has a sporting achievement. This achievement can be big or small! Tell the story of their achievement in the first person, from their point of view.
- Interview the person.
- Explain the background.
- Structure into paragraphs.
- Build up tension.
- Include documentary evidence.

Stay in first person by using first person pronouns!

Anecdote

In our everyday life we already turn incidents and experiences into stories. You need to use them!

Humour

Lots of us have humorous stories to tell based on our own life or on stories that friends or family members have told us.
The difficult part is turning these oral stories into written stories. You can use plot types to help you and remember to use the features of comic writing:
- **observation;**
- **comparison and simile;**
- **exaggeration;**

- **understatement and hyperbole;**
- **comic irony;**
- **suggestion.**

CENTRE STAGE

Funny Ha-ha

Retell an anecdote you heard or an experience of your own that was funny.
Remember:
• use comic features;
• set the scene;
• structure your story;
• build up tension.

Interest and Adventure

We all know at least one interesting anecdote. It could relate to such things as achievement, adventure, discovery, accident, incident or coincidence. Your task is to turn it into a suitable story with a beginning, middle and end.

CENTRE STAGE

Stranger than Fiction

Retell an anecdote:
• Use first or third person.
• Set the scene.
• Fill in background.
• Use descriptive writing.
• Beginning, middle, end.

Now read them out in class!

13

Fiction Writing

We have already learned a lot about writing fiction in Unit 3. You can revise what we learned in that unit. Here we will look further at:

- modelling;
- inspiration.

Modelling

In Centre Stage, below, you are given the bare details of a plot on which to model a story. Even though everyone is given the same plot, you will be surprised at how different the final stories will be.

You need to add:

- **first or third person narrator;**
- **descriptive setting;**
- **character;**
- **mood and atmosphere;**
- **tension;**
- **conflict;**
- **structure.**

 CENTRE STAGE

Just Add Story

Here is the basic plot for the title: **A Light Between the Trees**.

You will have to give all the characters names, including Character A!

1 Character A goes on camping trip to the woods with other characters.
2 Character A goes with another character to collect wood.
3 Characters see a light between trees in the distance while collecting wood.
4 Characters return to camp, discuss light and decide to go in search of it.
5 One character remembers background story of house that was burned down and something ghoulish that happened there.
6 Characters get lost in the woods.
7 One character trips over old piece of wood and discovers it is scorched from fire.
8 Characters make their way back to campsite.

9 Fire is now put out and their firewood stolen.

10 Characters spend sleepless night in the woods.

You can add or take away details depending on what you need. Do you think the story would be scarier in first person or in third person? Why? Whose point of view will you tell it from?

Inspiration

Inspiration for a character or story can come from a variety of places. It could be from real life, another book, a film or pure imagination. Don't ever copy directly, but always look out for a story or character that inspires you.

Here are some sources of inspiration:

- **Your own real-life situations.**
- **Family stories.**
- **Friends' stories.**
- **Films, books, poems and plays.**
- **Characters you meet or see.**
- **Holidays.**
- **Sports and pastimes.**
- **Incidents from the newspaper.**
- **Other people's culture, such as food, music and customs.**
- **Props from long ago, such as an antique clock or an old map.**
- **Photographs and images.**
- **The natural world.**
- **An injustice — this is something that you think is wrong.**

Below is an exercise that will hopefully inspire you!

Read the questions in Spotlight, below, and then choose one of the images and answer the questions using that image.

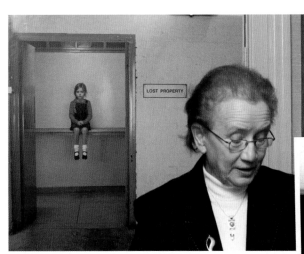

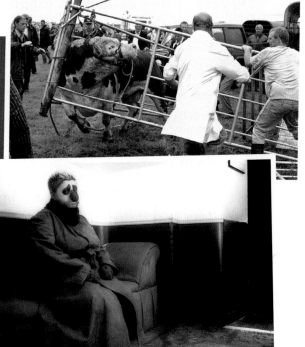

📷 SPOTLIGHT

1 Can you think of a story or character inspired by your image? *It can be fantasy, if you want.*

2 Can you think of a narrator who might be able to tell your story?

3 What is the setting of your story? Where and when does it take place?

4 Can you think of a goal that a character in the story wants to achieve? What does your character want?

5 Can you think of obstacles for that character? Who is trying to stop the character and why?

6 What will be the outcome of your story? Will the character achieve what he or she set out to do?

🎩 CENTRE STAGE

1 Using the image and the answers you have written out above, write a story.

2 Give your story a title.

3 Mind-map and plan your story.

4 Use your details from Spotlight and invent more details.

5 Use descriptive writing.

Remember:
- **Paragraphs.**
- **Similes.**
- **Appeal to the senses.**
- **Expressive and descriptive language.**

Discursive Writing

In Unit 6 and Unit 12 you learned how to express your opinions and respond to issues and ideas in society. Now you need to learn how to structure these opinions and responses into an essay. We will revise and learn more about:

- **mind-map and planning;**
- **personal response;**
- **development.**

Mind-map and Planning

It is important that you plan and structure all of your essays. To get started you can draw a quick mind-map.

In Your Neighbourhood

1 Mind-map

Write this sentence at the centre of your mind-map:

Improvements to My Local Area

Now you can plan these sections leading from the central statement:
- introduction;
- sport and leisure;
- infrastructure;
- education;
- culture and entertainment;
- tourism;
- closing paragraph.

In the case of each one, explain:
- the present situation;
- problems;
- solutions;
- hopes for the future.

2 Planning

Plan your essay in a column plan. You can copy this template. There are some suggestions for areas to cover under the **introduction** heading.

Introduction	Sport and Leisure	Infrastructure	Education	Culture and Entertainment	Tourism	Closing Paragraph
Personal interest. Background. Town history. Problems. Potential. Public opinion. Politics.						

3 Now write the following essay: *My Town: A Plan for Change*
You can write it in the form of:
• a composition;
• a speech;
• a news article.

Personal Response

If you are asked for **your own response** or opinion, don't be afraid to give it. You need to be able to relate your own **ideas** and **views** clearly and with confidence.

Tips for personal response:
• **Be consistent.**
• **Think about how you feel.**
• **Plan your response.**
• **Give examples from your own life.**
• **Support your opinions with evidence.**
• **Avoid stereotypes and clichés.**
• **Suggest solutions to problems.**
• **Speak for your generation.**
• **Avoid slang language.**

1 If you could change one thing about each of the following, what would it be and why?
i) Your life.
ii) Ireland.
iii) Celebrities.

2 Write three paragraphs giving your personal opinion on one of the following topics.
• The positive effects of sport.
• Manners are important.
• Men should do more housework.
• Dublin, capital city.
• Celebrities.

Structure your answer!

Development

Development in a discursive essay is the **logical linking** of **arguments** together to form one **overall argument.** You need to build up your argument, line by line, always aiming to prove your **central statement** by the end.

In this section we will look at:
* **logic;**
* **reference;**
* **alternative argument.**

Developing an argument is like building a fence: you must link each part together so that the overall fence is strong. If one link is missing, then it doesn't matter how strong the rest of it is!

Logic

Logic asks us to **agree** with a statement that **seems reasonable** or **true.** It then asks us to agree with further statements that lead from the first one. **Logic** leads us **step by step** to a specific **conclusion.**

Sometimes logic is used to lead us to conclusions that we disagree with!

Hunting encourages respect for the natural world.

We begin with an opening statement:

1 If you don't experience something, you can't put a value on it.
2 Hunting gives you experience of the natural world, and hunters value this experience.
3 Therefore hunting encourages people to value the natural world.

You don't have to agree. Can you think of any flaws in the logic of the arguments above?

SPOTLIGHT

1 Use logic to argue for or against two of the following statements. You must use at least three steps for each argument.
  i) Ireland should remain neutral.
  ii) Hunting should be banned.
  iii) Transport is more important than the environment.
  iv) Crime is only solved through punishment.
  v) Mobile phones should be forbidden in school.

2 Take one of the statements above and write out four clear arguments for or against it, using logic for each argument.

Reference

A **reference** is what we call a point of evidence used to support an argument or to show that a statement is true. A reference can be taken from research, something that happened in the greater world or another person or text.

Types of reference:
- **statistics;**
- **fact;**
- **example;**
- **quotation;**
- **law;**
- **morality;**
- **public opinion.**

Morality is our sense of what is right and wrong. Public opinion is often used to support arguments, but you can find many examples in history where public opinion has been proved very wrong!

SPOTLIGHT

Make an argument that the following references can be used to support.

Here is an example:

Oil is running out and we have no similar energy source to replace it. *Clearly, then, we must cap the amount of oil people are allowed to use.*

1 Twenty-five per cent of students say that increasing the price of cigarettes would help them to stop smoking.

PERSONAL WRITING

13

2 Male students are more physically active than female students.

3 My friend was attacked and his mobile phone was stolen.

4 'A nation that forgets its history is condemned to repeat it.'

5 It is illegal to litter.

6 The United Nations was founded so that governments in the world would work closer together.

7 Our Taoiseach is paid one of the highest salaries of any leader in Europe.

 CENTRE STAGE

Supporting Cast

Write a one-minute speech for or against one of the following statements. Use at least three different types of reference to support your argument.

1 Cigarettes should be banned.

2 Rock 'n' roll will save your soul.

3 Celebrities are famous for being famous.

4 Sport should be compulsory for young people.

5 Ireland is more interested in America than Europe.

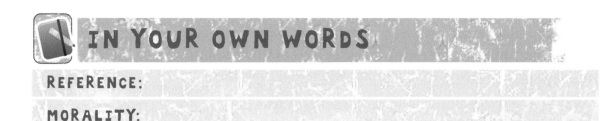 IN YOUR OWN WORDS

REFERENCE:

MORALITY:

Alternative Argument

Sometimes the easiest way to deal with another person's argument is to make the same argument yourself first and then dismiss it.

It is true that longer prison sentences will keep criminals off the street …
but it is then harder for criminals to rejoin society when they are eventually released.

I couldn't agree more with people who say that we need to support industry above the environment …
but if the temperature of the globe rises too much, there will be no people left to work in industry.

If you can think of a reason to disagree with your own argument, don't ignore it, deal with it! You can use certain opening statements to help you recognise the alternative argument.

Examples:

- **Some people will say that ...**
- **It might appear logical to argue that ...**
- **Without thinking properly one might assume ...**
- **I'm sure you will have heard ...**
- **It is true that some people are persuaded by ...**

 ## SPOTLIGHT

Begin by agreeing or disagreeing with the following arguments, but finish by taking the opposite view.

1 Students should wear school uniforms.

2 Air travel causes global warming.

3 Eating meat is wrong.

4 Students should be allowed to choose their teachers.

5 Nuclear power is the future.

 ## CENTRE STAGE

Write out a short speech for or against one of the following motions. Use logic to build up your argument, use reference to support it and recognise alternative arguments. You should also try to use features of persuasion and argument, such as imperatives and rhetorical questions, where appropriate!

- We need to make our cities more pedestrian friendly.
- All schools should be mixed gender.
- Ireland is better off out of the EU.
- Three months for summer holidays is too long.

curtain call

The best way to learn how to write an essay is by doing it! **Practice really does make perfect.** When you are writing your essay, you will be applying what you have learned in all areas of English.

It is also a very good exercise to rewrite essays you have already done, paying close attention to comments and criticisms that have been made of them. It is also a good idea to read other students' essays and to let them read yours, but make sure you have all agreed to it first. You can then share advice and comments.

Here are some past titles from the Personal Writing section of the Junior Certificate.

Write a prose composition on any one of the following.

- A summer's evening.
- It's a weird and wonderful world.
- My greatest fear.
- The motion for your next debate is: 'The Irish are the litter louts of Europe.' Write the speech you would make for or against the motion.
- Heroes.
- Write a composition beginning, 'Finally the smoke cleared and I could see ...'
- Memories of childhood.
- You awake one night to find a small but friendly alien sitting at the foot of your bed.
- Movie magic.

Remember:
- Plan and structure your essay.
- Use the different features of narrative writing, such as character, setting, conflict, mood and atmosphere, where appropriate.
- Use the different features of the language of information, persuasion and argument where appropriate.
- Use descriptive writing and expressive language.

14

THE SHORT STORY

THE SHORT STORY USES the same narrative features as a novel, but will often only use a selection of those features. We will now revise those features.

CONFLICT, TENSION, SUSPENSE, DILEMMA, REVELATION, REVERSAL, HUMOUR, CLIMAX.

Common narrative features

- **Setting: what type of society or place does the story happen in and when does it happen? What is the world of the text like?**
- **Background: where do the characters come from and what sort of things happened to them in the past?**
- **Descriptive writing: how are the details and images created?**
- **Character: what are the characters in the story like and how do they change and develop?**
- **Relationships: how do different characters in the story interact with each other?**
- **Dialogue: when do characters speak and what do they say to each other?**
- **Conflict: are any of the characters unhappy with each other or themselves?**
- **Goals and obstacles: do the characters have everything they want and is there anything stopping them from getting what they want?**
- **Tension and suspense: do we expect something exciting will happen?**
- **Relief: is the tension relaxed at any point?**
- **Themes and issues: what is the story about on a deeper level?**
- **Key moments: when are the important moments that cause change in the characters or plot?**
- **Dilemma: do the characters have to make any difficult decisions?**

- **Revelation:** are important facts or events hidden from characters or the reader and when are these revealed?
- **Reversal:** do any of the characters end up in a different situation at the end from the one they were in at the start?
- **Humour:** does the writer use any feature of humour?
- **Climax:** at what moment does the action or drama reach its highest point?
- **Resolution:** at the end, what is the outcome of everything that happens?

A short story will not normally have space for a subplot or detailed descriptions of setting or character.

Revelation

We remember that a revelation is when an **important detail** or fact is **revealed** to the reader. It can also be revealed to a character in the story. A revelation usually causes a **turning point** in the plot of the story and can change the outcome or **resolution** of the plot. A **turning point** is a moment that causes significant change in the central character or plot.

Writers use revelations in short stories to create surprise. When readers begin a story, they are curious to see what will happen. They look for clues and try to guess what twists the plot will take and how the plot will be resolved.

A skilful writer carefully reveals details that the reader did not expect. **Timing** and **suspense** are used to reveal details at the **climax** or at crucial moments.

Roald Dahl is famous and much loved for his children's stories, but older readers also delight in the unexpected twists and turns of the short stories he wrote. When you read the following short story, look out for its narrative features, particularly the revelation.

The Umbrella Man

Roald Dahl

I'm going to tell you about a funny thing that happened to my mother and me yesterday evening. I am twelve years old and I'm a girl. My mother is thirty-four but I am nearly as tall as her already.

Yesterday afternoon, my mother took me up to London to see the dentist. He found one hole. It was in a back tooth and he filled it without hurting me too much. After that, we went to a café. I had a banana split and my mother had a cup of coffee. By the time we got up to leave, it was about six o'clock.

When we came out of the café it had started to rain. 'We must get a taxi,' my mother said. We were wearing ordinary hats and coats, and it was raining quite hard.

'Why don't we go back into the café and wait for it to stop?' I said. I wanted another of those banana splits. They were gorgeous.

'It isn't going to stop,' my mother said. 'We must get home.'

We stood on the pavement in the rain, looking for a taxi. Lots of them came by but all had passengers inside them. 'I wish we had a car with a chauffeur,' my mother said.

Just then, a man came up to us. He was a small man and he was pretty old, probably seventy or more. He raised his hat politely and said to my mother, 'Excuse me. I do hope you will excuse me...' He had a fine white moustache and bushy white eyebrows and a wrinkly pink face. He was sheltering under an umbrella which he held high over his head.

'Yes?' my mother said, very cool and distant.

'I wonder if I could ask a small favour of you,' he said. 'It is only a very small favour.'

I saw my mother looking at him suspiciously. She is a suspicious person, my mother. She is especially suspicious of two things – strange men and boiled eggs. When she cuts the top off a boiled egg, she pokes around inside it with her spoon as though expecting to find a mouse or something. With strange men, she has a golden rule which says, 'The nicer the man seems to be, the more suspicious you must become.' This little old man was particularly nice. He was polite. He was well-spoken. He was well-dressed. He was a real gentleman. The reason I knew he was a gentleman was because of his shoes. 'You can always spot a gentleman by the shoes he wears,' was another of my mother's favourite sayings. This man had beautiful brown shoes.

'The truth of the matter is,' the little man was saying, 'I've got myself into a bit of a scrape. I need some help. Not much, I assure you. It's almost nothing, in fact, but I do need it. You see, madam, old people like me often become terribly forgetful...'

My mother's chin was up and she was staring down at him along the full length of her nose. It is a fearsome thing, this frosty-nosed stare of my mother's. Most people go to pieces completely when she gives it them. I once saw my own headmistress begin to stammer and simper like an idiot when my mother gave her a really foul frosty-noser. But the little man on the pavement with the umbrella over his head didn't bat an eyelid. He gave a gentle smile and said, 'I beg you to believe, madam, that I am not in the habit of stopping ladies in the street and telling them my troubles.'

'I should hope not,' my mother said.

I felt quite embarrassed by my mother's sharpness. I wanted to say to her, 'Oh, Mummy, for heaven's sake, he's a very very old man, and he's sweet and polite, and he's in some sort of trouble, so don't be so beastly to him.' But I didn't say anything.

The little man shifted his umbrella from one hand to the other. 'I've never forgotten it before,' he said.

'You've never forgotten what?' my mother asked sternly.

'My wallet,' he said. 'I must have left it in my other jacket. Isn't that the silliest thing to do?'

'Are you asking me to give you money?' my mother said.

'Oh, good gracious me, no!' he cried. 'Heaven forbid I should ever do that!'

'Then what are you asking?' my mother said. 'Do hurry up. We're getting soaked to the skin standing here.'

'I know you are,' he said. 'And that is why I'm offering you this umbrella of mine to protect you, and to keep forever, if ... if only...'

'If only what?' my mother said.

'If only you would give me in return a pound for my taxi-fare just to get me home.'

My mother was still suspicious. 'If you had no money in the first place,' she said, 'then how did you get here?'

'I walked,' he answered. 'Every day I go for a lovely long walk and then I summon a taxi to take me home. I do it every day of the year.'

'Why don't you walk home now?' my mother asked.

'Oh, I wish I could,' he said. 'I do wish I could. But I don't think I could manage it on these silly old legs of mine. I've gone too far already.'

My mother stood there chewing on her lower lip. She was beginning to melt a bit, I could see that. And the idea of getting an umbrella to shelter under must have tempted her a good deal.

'It's a lovely umbrella,' the little man said.

'So I've noticed,' my mother said.

'It's silk,' he said.

'I can see that.'

'Then why don't you take it, madam,' he said. 'It cost me over twenty pounds, I promise you. But that's of no importance so long as I can get home and rest these old legs of mine.'

I saw my mother's hand feeling for the clasp on her purse. She saw me watching her. I was giving her one of my *own* frosty-nosed looks this time and she knew exactly what

SIMPER
to smile awkwardly

THE SHORT STORY

THE SHORT STORY **381**

I was telling her. Now listen, Mummy, I was telling her, you simply *mustn't* take advantage of a tired old man in this way. It's a rotten thing to do. My mother paused and looked back at me. Then she said to the little man, 'I don't think it's quite right that I should take a silk umbrella from you worth twenty pounds. I think I'd just better *give* you the taxi-fare and be done with it.'

'No, no, no!' he cried. 'It's out of the question! I wouldn't dream of it! Not in a million years! I would never accept money from you like that! Take the umbrella, dear lady, and keep the rain off your shoulders!'

My mother gave me at triumphant sideways look. There you are, she was telling me. You're wrong. He *wants* me to have it.

She fished into her purse and took out a pound note. She held it out to the little man. He took it and handed her the umbrella. He pocketed the pound, raised his hat, gave a quick bow from the waist, and said, 'Thank you, madam, thank you.' Then he was gone.

'Come under here and keep dry, darling,' my mother said. 'Aren't we lucky. I've never had a silk umbrella before. I couldn't afford it.'

'Why were you so horrid to him in the beginning?' I asked.

'I wanted to satisfy myself that he wasn't a trickster,' she said. 'And I did. He was a gentleman. I'm very pleased I was able to help him.'

'Yes, Mummy,' I said.

'A real gentleman,' she went on. 'Wealthy, too, otherwise he wouldn't have had a silk umbrella. I shouldn't be surprised if he isn't a titled person. Sir Harry Goldsworthy or something like that.'

'Yes, Mummy.'

'This will be a good lesson to you,' she went on. 'Never rush things. Always take your time when you are summing someone up. Then you'll never make mistakes.'

'There he goes,' I said. 'Look.'

'Where?'

'Over there. He's crossing the street. Goodness, Mummy, what a hurry he's in.'

We watched the little man as he dodged nimbly in and out of the traffic. When he reached the other side of the street, he turned left, walking very fast.

'He doesn't look very tired to me, does he to you, Mummy?'

My mother didn't answer.

'He doesn't look as though he's trying to get a taxi, either,' I said.

My mother was standing very still and stiff, staring across the street at the little man. We could see him clearly. He was in a terrific hurry. He was bustling along the pavement, sidestepping the other pedestrians and swinging his arms like a soldier on the march.

'He's up to something,' my mother said, stony-faced.

'But what?'

'I don't know,' my mother snapped. 'But I'm going to find out. Come with me.' She took my arm and we crossed the street together. Then we turned left.

'Can you see him?' my mother asked.

'Yes. There he is. He's turning right down the next street.'

We came to the corner and turned right. The little man was about twenty yards ahead of us. He was scuttling along like a rabbit and we had to walk fast to keep up with him. The rain was pelting down harder than ever now and I could see it dripping from the brim of his hat on to his shoulders. But we were snug and dry under our lovely big silk umbrella.

'What is he up to?' my mother said.

'What if he turns round and sees us?' I asked.

'I don't care if he does,' my mother said. 'He lied to us. He said he was too tired to walk any further and he's practically running us off our feet! He's a barefaced liar! He's a crook!'

'You mean he's not a titled gentleman?' I asked.

'Be quiet,' she said.

At the next crossing, the little man turned right again.

Then he turned left.

Then right.

'I'm not giving up now,' my mother said.

'He's disappeared!' I cried. 'Where's he gone?'

'He went in that door!' my mother said. 'I saw him! Into that house! Great heavens, it's a pub!'

It was a pub. In big letters right across the front it said THE RED LION.

'You're not going in, are you, Mummy?'

'No,' she said. 'We'll watch from outside.'

There was a big plate-glass window along the front of the pub, and although it was a bit steamy on the inside, we could see through it very well if we went close.

We stood huddled together outside the pub window. I was clutching my mother's arm. The big raindrops were making a loud noise on our umbrella. 'There he is,' I said. 'Over there.'

The room we were looking into was full of people and cigarette smoke, and our little man was in the middle of it all. He was now without his hat or coat, and he was edging his way through the crowd towards the bar. When he reached it, he placed both hands on the bar itself and spoke to the barman. I saw his lips moving as he gave his order. The barman turned away from him for a second and came back with a smallish tumbler filled to the brim with a light brown liquid. The little man placed a pound note on the counter.

'That's my pound!' my mother hissed. 'By golly, he's got a nerve!'

'What's in the glass?' I asked.

'Whisky,' my mother said. 'Neat whisky.'

The barman didn't give him any change from the pound.

'That must be a treble whisky,' my mother said.

'What's a treble?' I asked.

'Three times the normal measure,' she answered.

The little man picked up the glass and put it to his lips. He tilted it gently. Then he tilted it higher...and higher...and higher...and very soon all the whisky had disappeared down his throat in one long pour.

'That was a jolly expensive drink,' I said.

'It's ridiculous!' my mother said. 'Fancy paying a pound for something you swallow in one go!'

'It cost him more than a pound,' I said. 'It cost him a twenty-pound silk umbrella.'

'So it did,' my mother said. 'He must be mad.'

The little man was standing by the bar with the empty glass in his hand. He was smiling now, and a sort of golden glow of pleasure was spreading over his round pink face. I saw his tongue come out to lick the white moustache, as though searching for the last drop of that precious whisky.

Slowly, he turned away from the bar and edged back through the crowd to where his hat and coat were hanging. He put on his hat. He put on his coat. Then, in a manner so superbly cool and casual that you hardly noticed anything at all, he lifted from the coat-rack one of the many wet umbrellas hanging there, and off he went.

'Did you see that!' my mother shrieked. 'Did you see what he did!'

'Ssshh!' I whispered. 'He's coming out!'

We lowered the umbrella to hide our faces, and peeped out from under it.

Out he came. But he never looked in our direction. He opened his new umbrella over his head and scurried off down the road the way he had come.

'So that's his little game!' my mother said.

'Neat,' I said. 'Super.'

We followed him back to the main street where we had first met him, and we watched him as he proceeded, with no trouble at all, to exchange his new umbrella for another pound note. This time it was with a tall thin fellow who didn't even have a coat or hat. And as soon as the transaction was completed, our little man trotted off down the street and was lost in the crowd. But this time he went in the opposite direction.

'You see how clever he is!' my mother said. 'He never goes to the same pub twice!'

'He could go on doing this all night,' I said.

'Yes,' my mother said. 'Of course. But I'll bet he prays like mad for rainy days.'

TRANSACTION
an agreement or exchange

When the reader or a character suddenly discovers or notices an important detail or fact, it is called a **realisation**.

🎬 OPENING ACT

1 Why were the narrator and her mother in London? EVIDENCE

2 What did they do after going to the dentist?

3 What two things was the narrator's mother suspicious of? EVIDENCE

4 Identify a simile used to describe a character. EVIDENCE

5 What does the mother think of the man immediately after she takes his umbrella? EVIDENCE

6 What does the mother think of the man after she follows him? EVIDENCE

7 What did the man really want the pound for? EVIDENCE

SPOTLIGHT

8 Were you suspicious of the man in this story? `OPINION` `REASON` `EVIDENCE`

9 Do you think there is humour in this story? `OPINION` `REASON` `EVIDENCE`

10 Which character do you think is more trusting, the narrator or her mother? `OPINION` `REASON` `EVIDENCE`

11 Describe the character of the mother in your own words. Try to identify at least two character traits and use a paragraph to discuss each one. `OPINION` `REASON` `EVIDENCE`

12 What is the revelation in this story and how is it revealed? `OPINION` `REASON` `EVIDENCE`

13 Why do you think readers enjoy unexpected twists and surprising revelations? `OPINION` `REASON`

CENTRE STAGE

Stop, Police!

Write a police report about another theft by the notorious umbrella thief of London. Imagine that you are the officer writing out the report.

You can include:
- two paragraphs for short witness statements explaining what happened, one from the mother and one from her daughter;
- a paragraph description of the thief to be circulated at other police stations;
- a plan to catch the thief.

Try to write at least four paragraphs.

IN YOUR OWN WORDS

TURNING POINT:

REALISATION:

closed Ending

The end.

In a short story the **setting** and **characterisation** have to be described and created with fewer words than a novel. **Characterisation** is the way that a character is created, by describing their personality, habits, traits and characteristics.

A short story must also **develop the plot** in less time than a novel. It takes skill to build up to a **climax** quickly and to end the story in a pleasing and interesting way. The following story has a **closed ending**. A closed ending is an ending where the plot is **resolved**, with no important details left untold.

The following short story is by Frank O'Connor, a renowned short story writer who came from Cork. The story has been split into two sections because it may take two classes to read it.

Pity

Frank O'Connor

PART I

Denis's school was in the heart of the country, miles from anywhere, and this gave the teachers an initial advantage, because before the boy even got to the railway station he had the prefects on his track. Two fellows Denis knew once got as far as Mellin, a town ten miles off, intending to join the British Army, but like fools the first thing they did in

INITIAL
first

14

Mellin was to go to a hotel, so they were caught in bed in the middle of the night by prefects and brought back. It was reported that they had been flogged on their knees in front of the picture of the Crucifixion in the hall, but no one was ever able to find out the truth about that. Denis thought they must have been inspired by the legend of two fellows who did once actually get on a boat for England and were never heard of afterwards, but that was before his time, and in those days escapes were probably easier. By the time he got there it was said there was a telescope mounted on the tower and that the prefects took turns at watching for fellows trying to get away.

You could understand that, of course, for the fellows were all rough, the sons of small farmers who smoked and gambled and took a drink whenever they got a chance of one. As his mother said, it wasn't a good school, but what could she do, and the small allowance she got from his father? By this time she and his father were living apart.

But one day a new boy came up and spoke to Denis. His name was Francis Cummins and he came from Dunmore where Denis's mother was now living. He wasn't in the least like the other fellows. He was a funny, solemn kid with a head that was too big for his body and a great flow of talk. It seemed that his people intended him for the priesthood, and you could see that he'd make a good sort of priest for he never wanted to do anything wrong, like breaking out, or smoking, or playing cards, and he was a marvel at music. You had only to whistle a tune to him and he could play it after on the piano.

Even the toughs in school let Francis alone. He was a fellow you couldn't get into a wax, no matter how you tried. He took every insult with a smile as if he couldn't believe you were serious, so that there was no satisfaction in trying to make him mad. And from the first day he almost pursued Denis. The other fellows in Denis's gang did not like it because if he saw them doing anything they shouldn't be doing he started at once to lecture them, exactly like a prefect, but somehow Denis found it almost impossible to quarrel with him. It was funny the way you felt to a fellow from your own place in a school like that, far from everywhere. And they did not know the feeling that came over Denis at times when he thought of Dunmore and his home and Martha, for all that he was ever fighting with her. Sometimes he would dream of it at night, and wake up thinking of it, and all that day it would haunt him in snatches till he felt like throwing himself on his bed and bawling. And that wasn't possible either, with forty kids to a room and the beds packed tight in four rows.

There was also another reason for his toleration of a cissy like Cummins. Every week of Cummins's life he got a parcel from home, and it was always an astonishment to Denis, for his parents sent him tinned meat, tinned fruit, sardines, and everything. Now, Denis was always hungry. The school food wasn't much at the best of times, and because his mother couldn't afford the extras, he never got rashers for breakfast as most of the others did. His father visited him regularly and kept on inquiring in a worried way if he was all right, but Denis had been warned not to complain to him, and the pound or two he gave Denis never lasted more than a couple of days. When he was not dreaming of home he dreamt of food. Cummins always shared his parcels with him, and when Denis grew ashamed of the way he cadged from Cummins, it was a sop to his conscience that Cummins seemed to enjoy it as much as he did. Cummins lectured him like an old schoolmistress, and measured it all out, down to the last candy.

WAX
angry fit

CISSY
a mammy's boy

CADGED
begged

SOP
a treat or bribe

'I'll give you one slice of cake now,' he would say in his cheerful argumentative way.

'Ah, come on!' Denis would growl, eyeing it hungrily. 'You won't take it with you.'

'But if I give it to you now you'll only eat it all,' Cummins would cry. 'Look, if I give you one slice now, and another slice tomorrow, and another on Sunday, you'll have cake three days instead of one.'

'But what good will that be if I'm still hungry?' Denis would shout.

'But you'll only be hungrier tomorrow night,' Cummins would say in desperation at his greed. 'You're a queer fellow, Denis,' he would chatter on. 'You're always the same. 'Tis always a feast or a famine with you. If you had your own way you'd never have anything at all. You see I'm only speaking for your good, don't you?'

Denis had no objection to Cummins speaking for his good so long as he got the cake, as he usually did. You could see from the way Cummins was always thinking of your good that he was bound to be a priest. Sometimes it went too far even for Denis, like the day the two of them were passing the priests' orchard and he suddenly saw that for once there wasn't a soul in sight. At the same moment he felt the hunger-pain sweep over him like a fever.

'Keep nix now, Cummins,' he said, beginning to shin up the wall.

'What are you going to do, Denis?' Cummins asked after him in a frenzy of anxiety.

'I only want a couple of apples,' Denis said, jumping from the top of the wall and running towards the trees. He heard a long, loud wail from the other side of the wall.

'Denis, you're not going to STEAL them. Don't steal them, Denis, please don't steal them!'

But by this time Denis was up in the fork of the tree where the biggest, reddest apples grew. He heard his name called again, and saw that Cummins had scrambled up on to the wall as well, and was sitting astride it with real tears in his eyes.

'Denis,' he bawled, 'what'll I say if I'm caught?'

'Shut up, you fool, or you will get us caught,' Denis snarled back at him.

'But Denis, Denis, it's a sin.'

'It's a what?'

'It's a sin, Denis. I know it's only a venial sin, but venial sins lead to mortal ones. Denis, I'll give you the rest of my cake if you come away. Honest, I will.'

Denis didn't bother to reply, but he was raging. He finished packing apples wherever he had room for them in his clothes and then climbed slowly back over the wall.

'Cummins,' he said fiercely, 'if you do that again I'm going to kill you.'

'But it's true, Denis,' Cummins said wringing his hands distractedly. ''Tis a sin, and you know 'tis a sin, and you'll have to tell it in Confession.'

'I will not tell it in Confession,' said Denis, 'and if I find out that you did, I'll kill you. I mean it.'

And he did, at the time. It upset him so much that he got almost no pleasure from the apples, but he and Cummins still continued to be friends and to share the parcels of food that Cummins got. These were a complete mystery to Denis. None of the other fellows he knew got a parcel oftener than once a month, and Denis himself hardly got one a term. Of course, Cummins's parents kept a little shop so that it wouldn't be so much trouble to them, making up a parcel, and anyway they would get the things at cost price, but even allowing for all this, it was still remarkable. If they cared all that much for Cummins, why didn't they keep him at home? It wasn't even as if he had another brother or sister. Himself, for instance, a wild kid who was always quarrelling with his sister and whose mother was so often away from home, he could see why he had to be sent away, but what had Cummins done to deserve it? There was a mystery here, and when he got home, Denis was determined to investigate it.

He had his first opportunity at the end of term when Cummins's father and mother came for him in a car and brought Denis back as well. Old Cummins was a small man with glasses and a little grey moustache, and his wife was a roly-poly of a woman with a great flow of talk. Denis noticed the way Cummins's father would wait for minutes on end to ask a question of his own. Cummins's manner to them was affectionate enough. He seemed to have no self-consciousness, and would turn round with one leg on the front seat to hold his mother's hand while he answered her questions about the priests.

*We know that the setting is the time and place where the story is set. The **social setting** is the society where the story is set and the era in which it is set. The **social setting** includes the **customs**, **rules** and **attitudes** of people and society at a particular time.*

🎭 OPENING ACT

1 What was the legend Denis had heard? **EVIDENCE**
2 Where was Francis from? **EVIDENCE**
3 How did the tough pupils treat Francis? **EVIDENCE**
4 What was Francis's reaction to Denis's orchard robbing? **EVIDENCE**
5 What job did Francis's parents have? **EVIDENCE**

📷 SPOTLIGHT

6 Would you like to live in this social setting? **OPINION** **REASON** **EVIDENCE**
7 If you went to this school, who would you rather be friends with, Denis or Francis? **OPINION** **REASON** **EVIDENCE**
8 Why do you think Denis stayed friends with Francis? **OPINION** **REASON** **EVIDENCE**
9 How do you think Denis felt about the packages Francis received? **OPINION** **REASON** **EVIDENCE**
10 'The social setting of the school gives the boys little privacy and personal space.' Would you agree or disagree with this statement? *Try to structure your answer into two paragraphs.* **OPINION** **REASON** **EVIDENCE**

PART II

A week later, Martha and Denis went up to the Cumminses' for tea. Mr Cummins was behind the counter of the shop with his hat on his head, and he called his wife from the foot of the stairs. She brought them upstairs in her excitable, chattering way to a big front room over the street. Denis and Cummins went out to the back garden with a pistol that Cummins had got at Christmas. It was a wonderful air-pistol that Denis knew must have cost pounds. All Cummins's things were like that. He had also been given a piano accordion. Denis did not envy him the accordion, but he did passionately want the pistol.

'Lend it to us anyway, for the holidays,' he begged.

'But, sure, when I want to practise with it myself!' Cummins protested in that babyish way of his.

'What do you want to practise with it for?' asked Denis. 'When you're a priest, you won't be able to shoot.'

'How do you know?' asked Cummins.

'Because priests aren't let shoot anybody,' said Denis.

'I'll tell you what I'll do with you,' Cummins said in his usual cheese-paring way, 'I'll keep it on weekdays and you can have it on Saturday and Sunday.'

Denis didn't want it for Saturday and Sunday; he wanted it for keeps; and it struck him as very queer in a cissy like Cummins, being so attached to a gun that he'd be scared to use.

Mrs Cummins and the three children had tea in the front room. Then Cummins and Martha played the piano while Mrs Cummins talked to Denis about school.

'Wisha, Denis,' she said, 'isn't it wonderful for ye to be going to a beautiful school like that?'

Denis thought she was joking and began to smile.

'And the grounds so lovely and the house so lovely inside. Don't you love the stained-glass window in the hall?'

Denis had never particularly noticed the stained glass, but he vaguely remembered it as she spoke and agreed.

'Ah, sure 'tis lovely, with the chapel there, to go to whenever you like. And Francis says ye have the grandest films.'

'Oh, yes,' said Denis, thinking he would prefer threepence-worth at the local cinema any day of the week.

'And 'tis so nice having priests for teachers in place of the rough, coarse country fellows you have around here. Oh, Denis, I'm crazy about Father Murphy. Do you know, I'm sure that man is a saint.'

'He's very holy,' said Denis, wondering whether Mrs Cummins would think Murphy such a saint if she saw him with a cane in his hand and his face the colour of blood, hissing and snarling as he chased some fellow round the classroom, flogging him on the bare legs.

'Oh, to be sure he is,' Mrs Cummins rattled on. 'And 'tisn't that at all, Denis boy, but the nice, gentlemanly friends you make there instead of the savages there are in this town. Look, 'tisn't wishing to me to have Francis out of my sight with those brutes around the streets.'

That finished Denis. A fellow would be a long time in Dunmore before he met savages like the two Corbetts from Cork or Barrett from Clare. But he saw that the woman was in earnest. When he returned home, he told his mother everything about their visit, and her amusement convinced him of what he had already suspected – that Mrs Cummins didn't know any better. She and her husband, small shopkeepers who were accustomed only to a little house in a terrace, nearly died with the grandeur when they saw the grounds and the lake and the tennis courts, just like the gentlemen's residences they had seen before but only from the roadway. Of course, they thought it was Heaven. And it explained the mystery about Francis, because, in place of wanting to get rid of him as his mother had to get rid of Denis, they were probably breaking their hearts at having

EARNEST
with keenness

GRANDEUR
splendour

★★★
14

to part with him at all, and doing it only because they felt they were giving him all the advantages that had been denied to themselves. Despite his mother's mockery he felt rather sorry for them, being taken in like that by appearances.

At the same time it left unexplained something about Francis himself. Denis knew that if he was an only child with a mother and father like that, he would not allow them to remain in ignorance for long. He would soon get away from the filthy dormitory and the brutal society. At first he thought that Francis probably thought it a fine place too, and in a frenzy of **altruism** decided that it was his duty to talk to Mrs Cummins and tell her the whole truth about it, but then he realized that Francis could not possibly have been taken in the same way as his parents. He was a weakling and a **prig**, but he had a sort of country **cuteness** which enabled him to see through fellows. No, Francis was probably putting up with it because he felt it was his duty, or for the sake of his vocation, because he thought that life was like that, a vale of tears, and whenever he was homesick or when fellows jeered at him, he probably went to the chapel and offered it up. It seemed very queer to Denis because when he was homesick or mad he waited till lights were out and then started to bawl in complete silence for fear his neighbours would hear.

He made a point of impressing on his mother the **lavishness** of the Cumminses, and told her all about the accordion and the pistol and the weekly parcels with a vague hope of creating larger standards of generosity in her, but she only said that Irish shopkeepers were rotten with money and didn't know how to spend it, and that if only Denis's father would give her what she was entitled to he might go to the best college in Ireland where he would meet only the children of professional people.

All the same when he went back to school, there was a change. A parcel arrived for him, and when he opened it there were all the things he had mentioned to her. For a while he felt a little ashamed. It was probably true that his father did not give her all the money she needed, and that she could only send him parcels by **stinting** herself; but still, it was a relief to be able to show off in front of the others whose parents were less generous.

That evening he ran into Cummins who smiled at him in his pudding-faced way.

'Do you want anything, Denis?' he asked. 'I have a parcel if you do.'

'I have a parcel of my own today,' Denis said cockily. 'Would you like peaches? I have peaches.'

'Don't be eating it all now,' Cummins said with a comic wail. 'You won't have anything left tomorrow if you do.'

'Ah, what difference does it make?' said Denis with a shrug, and with reckless abandonment he rewarded his friends and **conciliated** his **foes** with the contents of his parcel. Next evening he was almost as bad as ever.

'Jay, Denis,' Cummins said with amused resignation, 'you're a blooming fright. I told you what was going to happen. How are you going to live when you grow up if you can never keep anything?'

'Ah, boy,' Denis said, in his embarrassment doing the big shot, 'you wait till I am grown up and you'll see.'

ALTRUISM
kindness

PRIG
self-righteous

CUTENESS
smart

LAVISHNESS
luxury

STINTING
doing without

CONCILIATED
made peace with

FOES
enemies

THE SHORT STORY

'I know what I'll see all right,' Cummins said, shaking his head sadly. 'Better men than you went to the wall. 'Tis the habits we learn at this age that decide what we're going to be later on. And anyway, how are you going to get a job? Sure, you won't learn anything. If you'd even learn the piano I could teach you.'

Cummins was a born preacher, and Denis saw that there was something in what he said, but no amount of preaching could change him. That was the sort he was. Come day, go day, God send Sunday – and anyway it didn't really make much difference because Cummins with his thrifty habits usually had enough to keep him going till the next parcel came.

Then, about a month later as Denis was opening his weekly parcel under the eyes of his gang, Anthony Harty stood by, gaping with the rest. Harty was a mean, miserable creature from Clare who never got anything, and was consumed with jealousy of everyone who did.

'How well you didn't get any parcels last year, and now you're getting them all the time, Halligan,' he said suspiciously.

'That's only because my mother didn't know about the grub in this place,' Denis declared confidently.

'A wonder she wouldn't address them herself, so,' sneered Harty.

'What do you mean, Harty?' Denis asked, going up to him with his fists clenched. 'Are you looking for a puck in the gob?'

'I'm only saying that's not the writing on your letters,' replied Harty, pointing at the label.

'And why would it be?' shouted Denis. 'I suppose it could be the shopkeepers'.'

'That looks to me like the same writing as on Cummins's parcels,' said Harty.

'And what's wrong with that?' Denis asked, feeling a pang of terror. 'I suppose she could order them there, couldn't she?'

'I'm not saying she couldn't,' said Harty in his sulky, sneering tone. 'I'm only telling you what I think.'

Denis could not believe it, but at the same time he could get no further pleasure from the parcel. He put it back in his locker and went out by himself and skulked away among the trees. It was a dull, misty February day. He took out his wallet in which there was a picture of his mother and Martha, and two letters he had received from his mother. He read the letters through, but there was no reference to any parcel that she was sending. He still could not believe but there was some simple explanation, and that she had intended the parcels as a surprise, but the very thought of the alternative made his heart turn over. It was something he could talk to nobody about, and after lights out, he twisted and turned madly, groaning at the violence of his own restlessness, and the more he turned, the clearer he saw that the parcels had come from the Cumminses and not from his mother.

He had never before felt so humiliated. Though he had not realised it he had been buoyed up less by the parcels than by the thought that his mother cared so much for him; he had been filled with a new love of her, and now all the love was turning back on him and he realised that he hated her. But he hated the Cumminses worse. He saw that he

THRIFTY
not wasteful

PUCK
punch

PATRONISED
help or treat out of pity

had pitied and patronised Francis Cummins because he was weak and priggish and because his parents were only poor, ignorant country shopkeepers who did not know a good school from a bad one, while they all the time had been pitying him because he had no one to care for him as the Cumminses cared for Francis. He could clearly imagine the three Cumminses discussing him, his mother and his father exactly as his mother and he had discussed them. The only difference was that however ignorant they might be they had been right. It was he and not Francis who deserved pity.

'What ails you, Halligan?' the chap in the next bed asked – the beds were ranked so close together that one couldn't even sob in peace.

'Nothing ails me,' Denis said between his teeth.

Next day he bundled up what remained of the parcel and took it to Cummins's dormitory. He had intended just to leave it and walk out but Cummins was there himself, sitting on his bed with a book, and Denis had to say something.

'That's yours, Cummins,' he said. 'And if you ever do a thing like that again, I'll kill you.'

'What did I do, Denis?' Cummins wailed, getting up from his bed.

'You got your mother to send me that parcel.'

'I didn't. She did it herself.'

'But you told her to. Who asked you to interfere in my business, you dirty spy?'

'I'm not a spy,' Cummins said, growing agitated. 'You needed it and I didn't – what harm is there in that?'

'There is harm. Pretending my mother isn't as good as yours – a dirty old shopkeeper.'

'I wasn't, Denis,' Cummins said excitedly. 'Honest, I wasn't. I never said a word against your mother.'

'What did he do to you, Halligan?' one of the fellows asked, affecting to take Cummins's part.

'He got his people to send me parcels, as if I couldn't get them myself if I wanted them,' Denis shouted, losing control of himself. 'I don't want his old parcels.'

'Well, that's nothing to cry about.'

'Who's crying?' shouted Denis. 'I'm not crying. I'll fight him and you and the best man in the dormitory.'

He waited a moment for someone to take up his challenge, but they only looked at him curiously, and he rushed out because he knew that in spite of himself he was crying. He went straight to the lavatory and had his cry out there on the seat. It was the only place they had to cry, the only one where there was some sort of privacy. He cried because he had thought he was keeping his secret so well and that no one but himself knew how little toughness and insubordination there was in him till Cummins had come and pried it out.

After that he could never be friendly with Cummins again. It wasn't as Cummins thought that he bore a grudge. It was merely that for him it would have been like living naked.

THE SHORT STORY

INSUBORDINA-TION

to act against
authority

*An **open ending** is when the plot is not resolved at the end of the story. When we finish a story with an open ending the outcome of important events is not revealed to us. We aren't told what becomes of the characters in the story. We have to use our imagination to figure out what happens next and why. Have you ever read any stories or seen any films with open endings?*

🎬 OPENING ACT

1 What did Denis think of Francis's air-pistol? `EVIDENCE`

2 What impression of Father Murphy did Mrs Cummins have? `EVIDENCE`

3 What was Father Murphy actually like? `EVIDENCE`

4 Who was sending parcels to Denis? `EVIDENCE`

5 How did Denis find out who was really sending him parcels?

6 How does Denis describe Francis's mother when he is angry with him? `EVIDENCE`

🎥 SPOTLIGHT

7 What did Denis do with his own parcels? `OPINION` `REASON` `EVIDENCE`

8 Do you think the title of this story is suitable? *Try to structure your answer into two paragraphs.* `OPINION` `REASON` `EVIDENCE`

9 What do you think is the turning point of this plot? `OPINION` `REASON` `EVIDENCE`

10 How does Denis feel when the source of his parcels is revealed to him? `OPINION` `REASON` `EVIDENCE`

11 Can you sympathise with how Denis reacts to the revelation? *Try to structure your answer into two paragraphs.* `OPINION` `REASON` `EVIDENCE`

12 What narrative features most impressed you on reading this story? *Try to structure your answer into at least two paragraphs.* `OPINION` `REASON` `EVIDENCE`

13 Would you describe 'Pity' as a story with an open ending or a closed ending? Why? `OPINION` `REASON` `EVIDENCE`

14 Pick out your favourite character description in this story and explain why you like it. `OPINION` `REASON` `EVIDENCE`

15 Can you think of another story you have read that featured a turning point? *Name the text and author, and describe the turning point, explaining why it was an important moment in the plot. Try to structure your answer into two paragraphs.*

Make Notes

Making notes on a short story will help you during your exams. Make your own notes for this short story.

Structure your notes into sections:

- **plot summary;**
- **background;**
- **setting;**
- **characters;**
- **themes and issues;**
- **key moments;**
- **turning point;**
- **climax;**
- **resolution;**
- **quotation and reference;**
- **personal response.**

Put your notes in a safe place!

 ## IN YOUR OWN WORDS

CHARACTERISATION:

CLOSED ENDING:

OPEN ENDING:

SOCIAL SETTING: